MOON

ASHEVILLE
& THE GREAT
SMOKY MOUNTAINS

JASON FRYE

CONTENTS

1 colorful wall in Asheville

2 rose garden at the Biltmore Estate

3 craft beer sampler

4 deer in Cades Cove

5 musicians play on a street in Asheville

6 Pack Square Park

DISCOVER
ASHEVILLE & THE GREAT SMOKY MOUNTAINS

There's an energy in the mountain town of Asheville that you don't find in many other places in North Carolina. For more than a century, Asheville has been a hive of progressive thinking and a surprisingly cosmopolitan level of living. With all the writers, artists, musicians, dancers, and other eclectic personalities that have inhabited this town, it's easy to understand how it earned the nickname "Paris of the South."

Surrounding Asheville are the Great Smoky Mountains. Drawing more than 10 million visitors annually, the Smokies are laced with hiking trails, rivers, and waterfalls and populated with diverse wildlife—from rare salamanders to huge elk. The diversity is second only to the sublime mystery of the area. Throughout the 521,085-acre national park, you can find spots so remote they have stood undisturbed for untold lengths of time.

You'll also find people as varied as the landscape they inhabit and histories as wild as the mountains themselves. Come join them.

5 TOP EXPERIENCES

1 **Tour Historic Architecture:** Downtown Asheville is full of beautiful art deco and beaux arts masterpieces. Go check them out (page 19)!

2 **Hike in the Smokies:** The best way to explore the woods, peaks, and waterfalls in The Great Smoky Mountains is by foot (page 91).

3 **Taste Craft Brews:** Asheville's brewery scene is at the top of any beer geek's list (page 45).

4 **Seek Outdoor Adventure:** Zip line, paddleboard, or bellyak—there are tons of options for outdoor fun in Asheville (page 26 and page 27).

5 **Explore Indigenous Culture:** The Cherokee people have lived in the Smoky Mountains for thousands of years. Learn about their history and traditions (page 103 and page 104).

EXPLORE
ASHEVILLE & THE GREAT SMOKY MOUNTAINS

DAY 1: ASHEVILLE

Begin your journey in Asheville, where you'll find streets lined with galleries, one of the nation's largest collections of **art deco** architecture, and a growing array of **chefs, brewers, and mixologists.**

Head directly to the **Biltmore Estate.** Tour the **Biltmore Winery,** watch the **blacksmith** at Antler Hill Village make music with the anvil, and find lunch at **Cedric's Tavern.** Head downtown and check into **ASIA Bed and Breakfast Spa,** freshen up, and get ready to roam.

Dine downtown at **Cucina 24** or at **Wicked Weed Brewing,** then head to nearby **Orange Peel** for live music. Make one last stop at **The Imperial Life** for a nightcap.

DAY 2: ASHEVILLE CONTINUED

Start your day with breakfast at **Early Girl Eatery.** Window shop at **Malaprop's** bookstore and **Woolworth Walk art gallery,** and don't sweat lunch: a food tour with **Eating Asheville** will fill you up and point you in a direction for dinner. Walk off your food tour at the **Asheville Art Museum** while you debate whether to dine at **The Admiral, Cúrate,** or **Table.**

Known as a food city, Asheville's cocktail scene is just as strong.

fall color in Great Smoky Mountains National Park

DAY 3: ASHEVILLE TO CHEROKEE

The winding section of the **Blue Ridge Parkway** between Asheville and the southern terminus in Cherokee is quite beautiful. Before you hit the road, down a giant biscuit at **Biscuit Head**. Continue down the Parkway and take in the view of the **Pisgah Range**. Hike to **Devil's Courthouse** and stop at Richland Balsam Overlook, the highest point on the Blue Ridge Parkway.

Be sure to visit the Waterrock Knob Visitor Center for a four-state view and panorama of the **Great Smoky Mountains.** Head into Cherokee for the night where you can gamble, visit a spa, and grab a bite at **Harrah's Cherokee Casino.**

DAY 4: CHEROKEE TO GREAT SMOKY MOUNTAINS NATIONAL PARK

Before you start your short drive to **Great Smoky Mountains National Park**, visit the **Qualla Arts and Crafts Mutual** in Cherokee. Stop at the **Museum of the Cherokee Indian** across the street and the **Oconaluftee Indian Village** just up the hill. During the summer months, catch an evening performance of *Unto These Hills.* Head into the park, **reserve a campsite**, and prepare for exploring and hiking tomorrow.

At Biscuit Head, the biscuits are huge and the toppings freshly made.

Clingmans Dome

DAY 5: GREAT SMOKY MOUNTAINS NATIONAL PARK

Take the 30-mile Newfound Gap Road through the park into **Gatlinburg**, Tennessee, eat lunch, and head back to North Carolina. You're as likely to see a bear as a deer on this stunning scenic road, and you'll also pass a number of trailheads. Trails range from short jaunts to overnight hikes leading deep into the forest. The trails in **Cades Cove** and around **Clingmans Dome**—the highest point in the Smokies—are popular. The **Appalachian Trail** crosses Clingmans Dome, so take a stroll here if for no other reason than to say you've hiked on the AT. Fervent hikers may want to consider spending a few more days exploring the park.

ASHEVILLE AND THE SOUTHERN BLUE RIDGE

The "Paris of the South" was built on a series of hills around the confluence of the Swannanoa ("swan-uh-NO-uh") and French Broad Rivers. Commerce found its way here in the 18th and 19th centuries via water routes and a mountain stagecoach road. In the late 1800s the town experienced a boom as railroad lines began to bring vacationers by the tens of thousands. It was around that time that George Vanderbilt, scion of the massively wealthy Vanderbilt dynasty, began building his mountain home, the Biltmore, just south of downtown. From the 1880s to the

✪ **DOWNTOWN ARCHITECTURE:** In the early 20th century, wealthy visitors left their mark on Asheville's downtown, a district packed with art deco and beaux arts masterpieces (page 19).

✪ **BILTMORE ESTATE:** Asheville's most popular attraction is not only an awe-inspiring palace and symbol of the Gilded Age; it's also a collection of great little restaurants, shops, and a popular winery, all in a beautiful riverside setting (page 19).

✪ **NORTH CAROLINA ARBOTEUM:** One of the most beautiful garden spaces in the country, this enormous collection is worth a visit. Don't miss the special Bonsai Collection (page 23).

✪ **FOLK ART CENTER:** Learn about the master craftspeople of the southern Appalachians and purchase gorgeous handmade items such as traditional weaving, woodcarving, and fine-art furniture (page 26).

✪ **ZIP LINE WITH NAVITAT:** Get some adrenaline flowing on a monster ridge-to-ridge zip line (page 26).

✪ **WATER SPORTS:** Whether you decide to paddleboard at dawn, bellyak at noon, or float down the river in the afternoon, make time to get out on the water in Asheville (page 27).

✪ **LIVE MUSIC:** You'll hear great music everywhere here, from buskers on street corners to the nation's premier live music hall (page 30).

✪ **RIVER ARTS DISTRICT:** Asheville's repurposed warehouses have become a lively collection of art galleries and studios, restaurants and breweries (page 37).

1930s the mountain town underwent a long and rapid expansion, eventually becoming a small city in its own right.

Surrounding Asheville are mountains and hundreds of years of folk traditions, with folk art, music, dancing, and customs that survive today. Old-time Appalachian string-band music (not to be confused with bluegrass, although bluegrass is alive and well here, too) thrives in the hills and hollows among the descendants of the region's early settlers, whose songs, instruments, and techniques have been passed down over many generations. Four- and five-string banjo pickers,

guitarists, fiddlers, and other musicians have migrated here from all across the globe to be part of the music traditions and the thriving music scene. Asheville is one of the best places in the world to hear old-time and bluegrass music as well as a sidetrack genre known as mountain swing.

One of the epicenters for visual arts in the Southeast, Asheville draws from centuries-old Appalachian folkways and traditions like woodcarving, weaving, and other arts and merges them with elements of the modern craft and fine arts movement. The results from these seemingly disparate elements being put in Asheville's pressure cooker together is a vibrant set of studios and galleries where art and craft of all sorts have a home. Arts organizations such as the Southern Highland Craft Guild (www. southernhighlandguild.org) help preserve the traditional arts, while places like the River Arts District and a number of small guilds, groups, and galleries support contemporary artists.

All of this makes Asheville feel like a counterculture center. Elements of Haight-Ashbury circa-1968 mix with Woodstock, the Grand Ole Opry, Andy Warhol's Factory, and a beatnik vibe, but with better food, to create an electric atmosphere.

PLANNING YOUR TIME

Once the last leaf drops from autumn trees, many mountain towns close until spring. Asheville is vibrant year-round (although the pace does ease quite a bit when the snow falls). In winter, Asheville is less expensive; rooms at hotels, inns, and B&Bs are plentiful; and reservations at the hot-ticket restaurants are easier to score. Fortunately, the breweries and cocktail lounges don't slow down, and some of the best bands roll through town in winter months. The city will see snow several times throughout the season, but it's not generally a problem, despite that it does occasionally shut down the Blue Ridge Parkway, and some of those higher mountain roads can be dicey.

Once spring breaks and bunches of wildflowers start to show up in earnest, so do the warmer-weather visitors. This is a prime time for wildflower hikes and visits to waterfalls (which can be quite impressive with snowmelt and spring rains), plus there's an energy to the city as everyone and everything begins to wake up after the dark of winter. Spring at the Biltmore Estate is marvelous thanks to their outstanding gardens that are thick with tulips.

Summer, of course, is a great time to be in Asheville, as the elevation brings cooler air on the same day it will be sweltering across the Piedmont and Sandhills. Summer also brings a number of festivals and special events, and it's the time when the greens and blues of the Blue Ridge are most vivid. Fall colors arrive at slightly different times each year, so you'll want to keep an eye on leaf forecasts for ideal getaway times. Generally speaking, however, you can plan to see leaves start to turn in mid-September, peak in mid-October, and finish by the second week of November. Fall is prime season to visit Asheville, so make lodging reservations early and expect some delays on scenic routes like the Blue Ridge Parkway.

Asheville's proximity to Great Smoky Mountains National Park (GSMNP) makes it a natural launch point for trips into the park. Visiting the Smoky Mountains brings the same seasonal concerns as visiting Asheville. Fall is peak season and crowded with leaf-peeping visitors; things slow down in winter and pick up in spring as the wildflowers begin to bloom. Then summer brings the hikers and national park enthusiasts back in full force. The elevation of Newfound Gap Road, the only road across GSMNP, is such that it can have weather-related delays or closures, so keep this in mind when planning a visit.

The **Blue Ridge National Heritage Area** (www.blueridgeheritage.com) has a number of valuable trip-planning resources, but a preferred resource is **Explore Asheville** (www. exploreasheville.com), the Asheville

Asheville and the Southern Blue Ridge

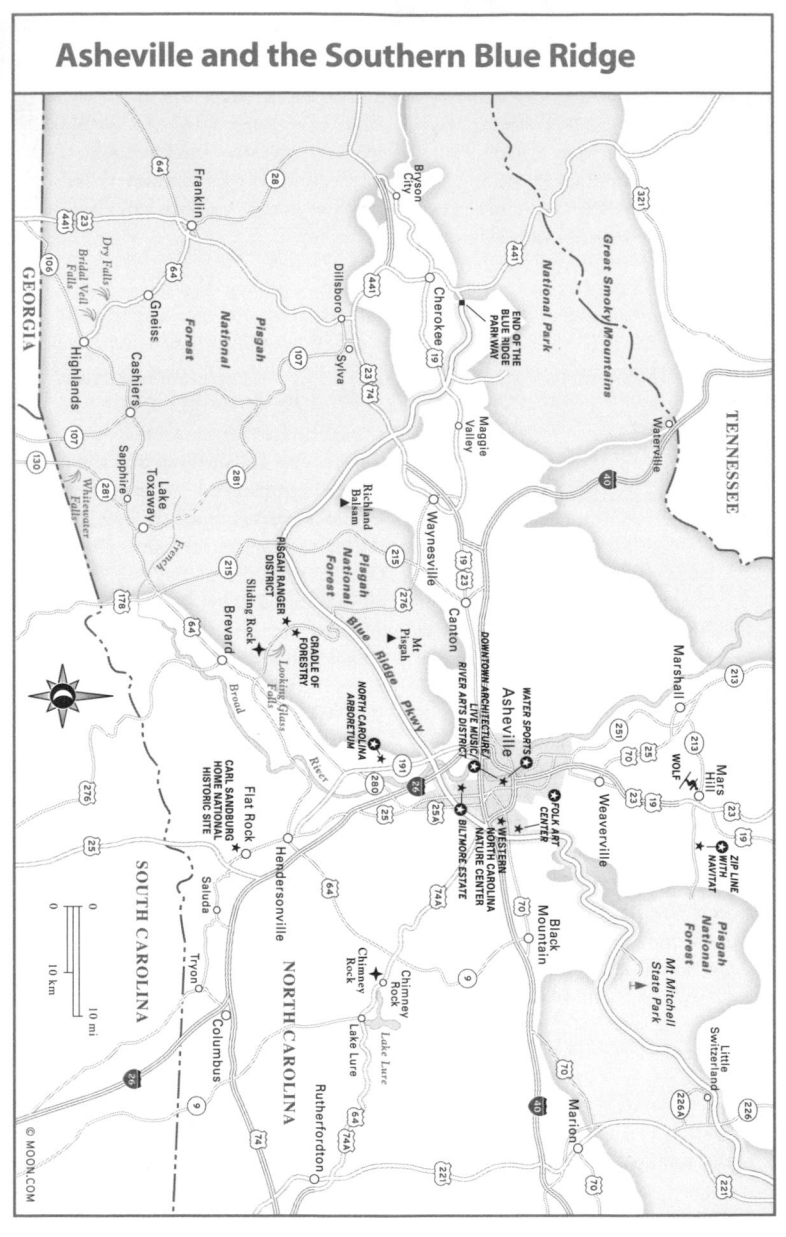

Convention and Visitors Bureau's website. The site's creators and the people at the **Asheville Visitors Center** (36 Montford Ave., 828/258-6129, www.exploreasheville.com, 8:30am-5:30pm Mon.-Fri., 9am-5pm Sat.-Sun.) take a lot of pride in their town and can help steer you toward new and old favorites in the area. For planning a trip to the Smoky Mountains, you'll find many resources through **Great Smoky Mountains National Park** (GSMNP, 865/436-1200, www.nps.gov/grsm); of course, you'll also find a number of resources through Asheville's local visitor services.

Asheville

SIGHTS

✪ DOWNTOWN ARCHITECTURE

As beautiful as Asheville's natural environment may be, the striking architecture is just as attractive. The Montford neighborhood, a contemporary of the Biltmore, is a mixture of ornate Queen Anne houses and craftsman-style bungalows. The Grove Park Inn, a huge luxury hotel, was built in 1913 and is decked out with rustic architectural devices intended to make vacationing New Yorkers and wealthy people feel like they were roughing it. In downtown Asheville is a large concentration of art deco buildings on the scale of Miami Beach. Significant structures dating to the boom before the Great Depression include the **Buncombe County Courthouse** (60 Court Plaza, built in 1927-1929), the **First Baptist Church** (Oak St. and Woodfin St., 1925), the **S&W Cafeteria** (56 Patton Ave., 1929), the **Public Service Building** (89-93 Patton Ave., 1929), and the **Grove Arcade** (1 Page Ave., 1926-1929).

The **Jackson Building** (22 S. Pack Square, built in 1923-1924) is a fine example of neo-Gothic architecture with a disturbing backstory. According to legend, on the day of the stock market crash in 1929 that started the Great Depression, one of the wealthiest men in Asheville lost it all and leaped to his death from the building. Three or four (depending on who's telling the story) more of Asheville's wealthiest followed suit. What is known to be true is that there's a bull's-eye built into the sidewalk in front of the building as a morbid monument to the story.

✪ BILTMORE ESTATE

Much of downtown Asheville dates to the 1920s, but the architectural crown jewel, the **Biltmore Estate** (1 Lodge St., 800/411-3812, www.biltmore.com, 9am-5pm daily, $55-85 adults, $28-43 ages 10-16, free under age 10, additional fees for activities), predates that by decades. It was built in the late 1800s for owner George Vanderbilt, grandson of Gilded Age robber baron Cornelius Vanderbilt. Like many of his wealthy Northern contemporaries, George Vanderbilt was first introduced to North Carolina when he traveled to Asheville for the mountain air and nearby hot springs. He found himself so awestruck by the land that

Asheville

To Asheville Log Cabin Motor Court
To ZIP LINE WITH NAVITAT
VINNIE'S
GROVE PARK INN RESORT & SPA
251
25
UNIVERSITY OF NORTH CAROLINA, ASHEVILLE
LUELLA'S BAR-B-QUE
Weaver
Weaver Park
MERRIMON AVE
TOWN MOUNTAIN RD
BOTANICAL GARDENS
BROADWAY ST
HILLSIDE ST
CHARLOTTE ST
ASHEVILLE ADVENTURE RENTALS
19
23
70
MONTFORD AVE
ASIA BED AND BREAKFAST SPA
GAN SHAN STATION
To Pisgah Brewing Company and Black Mountain
SEE "DOWNTOWN ASHEVILLE" MAP
240
WATER SPORTS
COLLEGE ST
70
TUNNEL RD
RIVERSIDE DR
DOWNTOWN ARCHITECTURE/ LIVE MUSIC
ASHEVILLE MUNICIPAL GOLF COURSE
PATTON AVE
HILLIARD AVE
THE GREY EAGLE TAVERN AND MUSIC HALL
Ashton Park
BUXTON HALL BBQ
MCCORMICK FIELD
PATTON AVE
19 23
RIVER ARTS DISTRICT
WEDGE BREWING COMPANY
CLINGMAN AV
FRENCH BROAD AVE
BILTMORE AVE
MCDOWELL ST
240
HAYWOOD RD
DEPOT ST
BON PAUL AND SHARKEY'S HOSTEL OF ASHEVILLE
SUNNY POINT CAFÉ
HAYWOOD RD
BISCUIT HEAD
THE ADMIRAL
BREVARD RD
LYMAN ST
LIVINGSTON ST
25
ASHEVILLE GREEN COTTAGE
ANTIQUE TOBACOO BARN
STATE ST
SWANNANOA RIVER RD
AMBOY RD
MEADOW RD
FIG
To NORTH CAROLINA ARBORETUM via Interstate 26
LODGE ST
BILTMORE VILLAGE
CORNER KITCHEN
40
HENDERSONVILLE RD
WINERY RD
INN ON BILTMORE ESTATE
40
ANTLER HILL VILLAGE
DEER PARK RD
3 MILE APPROACH RD
BILTMORE WINERY

0   0.5 mi
0   0.5 km

BILTMORE ESTATE

© MOON.COM

he amassed a 125,000-acre tract south of Asheville where he would build his "country home" and enjoy the area's restive and healthful benefits. He engaged celebrity architect Richard Morris Hunt to build the home, and because the land and the views reminded them of the Loire Valley, they planned to build the home in the style of a 16th-century French château. The Biltmore Estate was once the largest privately owned home in the country. Vanderbilt also hired the esteemed Frederick Law Olmsted, creator of New York City's Central Park, to design the landscape for the grounds, gardens, and surrounding forest, a project nine times the size of the New York park for which he is famous.

A three-mile-long approach road leads through manicured forests, revealing bits of the landscape and hiding the house until you are upon it, creating a sense of drama and wonder for arriving visitors. While the Biltmore Estate's original 125,000 acres are now greatly diminished—the estate comprises a little more than 8,000 acres today—it's easy to see just how big it was; standing on the South Terrace and looking south and west, everything in view was once part of the estate. A large tract of the land was sold to the federal government and has become part of the Pisgah National Forest; what remains is immaculately manicured.

Construction of the home was done primarily between 1888 and 1895, although there were a number of projects that continued up through World War II (when part of the home was turned into a bunker to store part of the National Gallery of Art's collection). Many are astounded at how long it took to complete the home, but think of the house this way: Approximately 5,000 tons of stone were used to build

it, there are 65 fireplaces and more than 250 rooms here, the square footage is nearly four acres, and they put up a 35-foot Christmas tree in the banquet hall. Most of the house is open to visitors on self-guided tours, and other parts—like the roof and some servants' areas—are accessible on behind-the-scenes tours. As astounding as this may be, it's nothing compared to the art collected here. There are paintings by Renoir, James Abbott Whistler, and John Singer Sargent; a collection of European antiques including Napoleon's chess set; and room upon room of masterwork in tiling, woodworking and carving, masonry, and stone carving. For its time, the Biltmore was a technological marvel, with electricity, elevators, central heat, and hot water. And we haven't even talked about the basement, where there's a heated pool, a gymnasium, and a bowling alley.

George Vanderbilt found the concept of a self-sustaining estate appealing, and he included a working farm with crops, herds of cattle, a dairy, and all the farmers and workers required for such an operation. The Asheville neighborhood known as **Biltmore Village** was part of this mountain empire.

If George Vanderbilt stepped onto his estate today, he'd be happy to find that one million people every year come to visit and that his vision of a self-sustaining estate endures. A vineyard (not open to the public) produces grapes that are processed at the estate's winery; a livestock breeding program produces fine stock; and a farm supplies more than 70 percent of seasonal and specialty vegetables to the estate's restaurants. Visitors can eat, shop, tour, explore, relax, and unwind without leaving the grounds, and there's easily enough here to fill a weekend.

ONE DAY IN ASHEVILLE

Only have one day to devote to Asheville? Here are the city's must-see, must-do, and must-eat attractions:

MORNING

Start the day with some great breakfast grub from **Sunny Point** in West Asheville. Spend the morning **exploring boutiques and galleries** like those in the **Grove Arcade** and **Woolworth Walk,** taking time to stroll by examples of Asheville's notable **downtown architecture,** including the First Baptist Church, the Jackson Building, and the **Buncombe County Courthouse.**

AFTERNOON

At lunchtime, linger downtown for the **Eating Asheville** food tour, which begins at the Grove Arcade. **Buxton Hall Barbecue,** a few blocks off downtown on the South Slope, is another good lunch option. After lunch, get a new perspective on the city by boarding the **LaZoom Comedy Tour** bus, floating down the French Broad River with **Zen Tubing,** or zip lining over the forests north of Asheville with **Navitat.**

You could spend the afternoon at the **Biltmore Estate,** a three-mile drive from downtown. Enjoy the first part of your afternoon at Antler Hill Village for a wine tasting at the **Winery,** and then lunch at the **Bistro,** making sure to leave at least three hours to tour the house and gardens before they close at 4:30pm (3:30pm in winter).

EVENING

Head back downtown for the evening, kicking the night off with beer flights at **Burial Beer Co.** or cocktails from **Sovereign Remedies.** When you're ready for dinner, try **Table** for inventive American cuisine or **Cucina 24** for Italian. Walk dinner off with a stroll—a number of buskers will entertain you. Grab a nightcap at **The Imperial Life** or a chocolate at **French Broad Chocolates.** If you're in town on a Friday, check out the drum circle at **Pritchard Park.**

The **Biltmore Winery** in **Antler Hill Village,** which is part of the estate, operates in what was formerly the estate's dairy; check out the industrial-farm rafters in the tasting room. Daily tours and tastings allow visitors to sample some award-winning wines and see how they're made. More than 500,000 people visit the tasting room annually, so expect a wait if you're here in high season.

Antler Hill Village is also home to **Cedric's,** a brewery named after a beloved family dog, as well as a small museum, a souvenir shop, and a green where you can relax. **River Bend Farm** is a beautiful compound that was once the hub of the estate's farming operation but now stands as a showpiece for traditional period crafts like woodworking and blacksmithing. Be sure

to stop by the blacksmith's shop and watch master blacksmith Doc Cudd speak with considerable eloquence about the art of smithing as he hammers out everything from common nails to decorative leaves, flowers, and other pieces. Ask him to make the anvil sing and he'll happily oblige; he's one of a handful of smiths who know how to play the anvil as a musical instrument in the 18th- and 19th-century fashion. It's a beautiful, almost haunting, sound you won't soon forget.

The **Equestrian Center** gives lessons and the opportunity to ride more than 80 miles of equestrian trails, many with sweeping views of the estate and glimpses of the main house that will take your breath away. Other ways to tour the estate include carriage rides, paved bike trails and mountain bike trails, canoes, kayaks, and rafts (the French Broad River bisects the estate), Segways, and, of course, on foot. You can even challenge your driving skills at the **Land Rover Experience Driving School.**

Admission cost for the Biltmore Estate varies by season and includes the house, gardens, and winery; activities such as horseback riding, rafting, and behind-the-scenes tours cost extra. Special events, like the Christmas Candlelight Tour (Nov.-Dec.) also have additional fees. Parking is free, and a complimentary shuttle runs to the house.

ASHEVILLE ART MUSEUM

In 2017 the **Asheville Art Museum** (2 S. Pack Square, 828/253-3227, www. ashevilleart.org, 10am-5pm Tues.-Sat., 1pm-5pm Sun., $8 adults, $7 students with ID, $7 over 60, free 5 and under) closed for major renovations and is slated to reopen in early 2019 with new exhibition space and a fresh approach to their collection. They've been around since 1948, and in the intervening decades have enriched the art community of Asheville by displaying works by some of the most important, influential, and up-and-coming artists of the 20th century. The permanent collection includes a wide array of media and styles, ranging from photo portraits to ceramics to statuary to beautiful modern pieces. A large collection from the nearby experimental school, Black Mountain College, shows the highlights of works created by faculty and students.

✪ NORTH CAROLINA ARBORETUM

The enormous **North Carolina Arboretum** (100 Frederick Law Olmsted Way, 828/665-2492, www. ncarboretum.org, 8am-9pm daily

the Quilt Garden at the North Carolina Arboretum

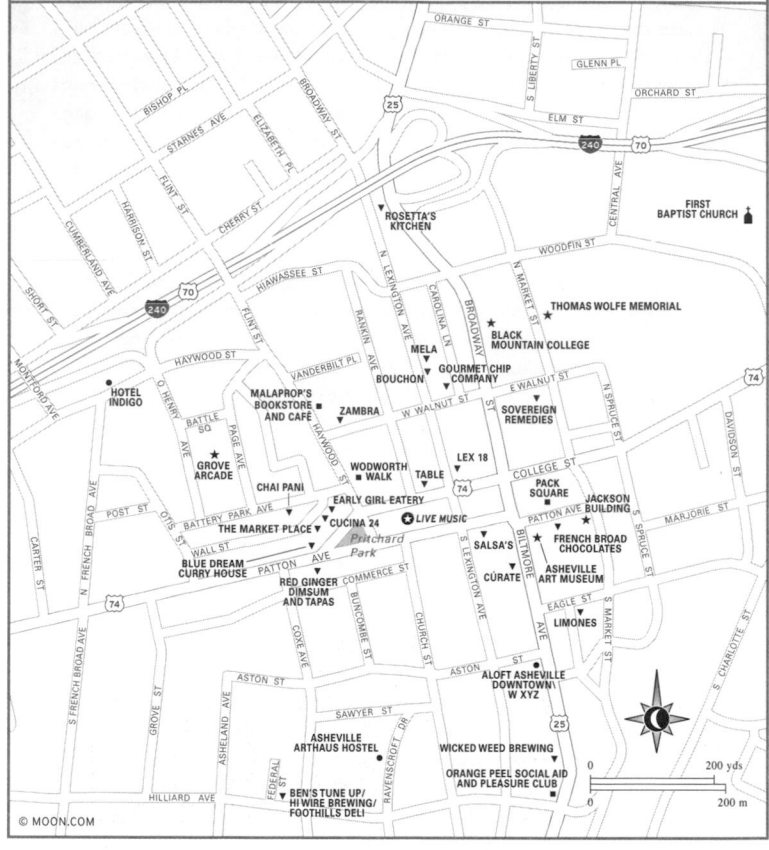

Downtown Asheville

© MOON.COM

Apr.-Oct., 8am-7pm daily Nov.-Mar., bonsai exhibition garden 9am-5pm daily, parking $14) is considered by many to be one of the most beautiful in the country. The 434 natural and landscaped acres back into the Pisgah National Forest, just off the Blue Ridge Parkway. Major collections include the National Native Azalea Repository, where you can see almost every species of azalea native to the United States as well as several hybrids, and the very special Bonsai Collection, where staff horticulturists care for more than

200 bonsai plants, many of their own creation.

Bicycles and leashed dogs are permitted on many of the trails. Walking areas range from easy to fairly rugged, but with 10 miles of hiking and biking trails, you will find one that suits your skill level. To learn a bit more about the history of the Arboretum, the plants themselves, and the natural history of the region, join one of the guided tours (1pm Tues. and Sat.). These two-mile walk-and-talk tours happen rain or shine, so dress for the weather. The Arboretum also has a very nice café, the **Bent Creek Bistro** (11am-4pm Tues.-Sun. Mar.-Nov., $4-9), and a gift shop, the **Connections Gallery** (9am-4pm daily Apr.-Oct., 11am-4pm daily Nov.-Mar.).

BOTANICAL GARDENS

The Botanical Gardens at Asheville (151 W. T. Weaver Blvd., adjacent to UNC-Asheville campus, 828/252-5190, www.ashevillebotanicalgardens.org, dawn-dusk daily year-round, donation) is a 10-acre preserve for the region's increasingly threatened native plant species. Laid out in 1960 by landscape architect Doan Ogden, the gardens are an ecological haven. The many "rooms" are planted to reflect different environments of the mountains, including the Wildflower Trail, the Heath Cove, and the Fern and Moss Trail. Spring blooms peak in mid-April, but the Gardens are an absolutely lovely and visually rich place to visit any time of year. Because of its serious mission of plant preservation, neither pets nor bicycles are allowed. Admission is free, but as the gardens are entirely supported by donations, your contribution will have a real impact. On the first Saturday in May, the **Day in the Gardens** brings food and music to this normally placid park, and garden and nature enthusiasts from all around come to tour and to buy native plants for their home gardens. There is also a visitors center and gift shop (11am-3pm Mar., 10am-4pm Mon.-Sat., noon-4pm Sun. Apr.-Oct., noon-4pm daily Nov.-Dec. 6, closed Dec.-late Feb.).

WESTERN NORTH CAROLINA NATURE CENTER

Asheville, and western North Carolina generally, tend to be very ecologically conscious, as reflected in the **Western North Carolina Nature Center** (75 Gashes Creek Rd., 828/259-8080, www.wildwnc.org, 10am-5pm daily, closed Thanksgiving Day, Dec. 24-25, and Jan. 1, $11 adults, $10 seniors age 65 and up, $7 ages 3-15, free ages 2 and under, discount for Asheville residents). On the grounds of an old zoo—don't worry, it's not depressing—wild animals that are unable to survive in the wild due to injury or having been raised as pets live in wooded habitats on public display. This is the place to see some of the mountains' rarest species—those that even most lifelong mountain residents have never seen: cougars, wolves, coyotes, bobcats, and even the elusive hellbender. What's a hellbender, you ask? Come to the Nature Center to find out.

BLACK MOUNTAIN COLLEGE

Considering the history of Black Mountain College from a purely numerical standpoint, one might get the false impression that this little institution's brief, odd life was a flash in the pan. In its 23 years of operation, Black Mountain College has had only 1,200 students, 55 of whom actually completed their degrees. But between 1933 and 1956, the unconventional school demonstrated an innovative model of education and community life.

The educational program was almost devoid of structure. Students had no set course schedule or requirements and lived and farmed with the faculty. Most distinguished as a school of the arts, Black Mountain College hired Josef Albers as its first art director when the Bauhaus icon fled Nazi Germany. Willem de Kooning taught here for a time, as did Buckminster Fuller, who began his design of the geodesic dome while he was in residence. Albert Einstein and William Carlos Williams were among the roster of guest lecturers. I had the honor of working with and befriending poet Robert Creeley, one of the few people to get a degree here and who taught here briefly before the school shut down in 1956, partly due to the prevailing anti-left climate of that decade.

The **Black Mountain College Museum and Arts Center** (56 Broadway, 828/350-8484, www.blackmountaincollege.org, 11am-5pm Mon.-Sat., free) is located in downtown Asheville rather than in the town of Black Mountain. It's both an exhibition space and a resource center dedicated to the history and spirit of the college.

✪ FOLK ART CENTER

Anyone with an interest in Appalachian handicrafts and folk or fine art should stop by the **Folk Art Center** (Blue Ridge Parkway milepost 382, 828/298-7928, 9am-5pm daily Jan.-Mar., 9am-6pm daily Apr.-Dec., free). Home to the Southern Highland Craft Guild, the Folk Art Center has around 30,000 square feet of space that includes three galleries, an auditorium, a research library, a tiny Blue Ridge Parkway info booth, and the Allanstand Craft Shop. Allanstand is the oldest continuously-operated craft shop in the United States. It was started in 1897 by a Presbyterian missionary and carries out the same vision it had the year it was born: to help preserve traditional art forms and raise the visibility of the arts and crafts of the Appalachian Mountains. Although the folk arts are well represented in beautiful pottery, baskets, weaving, and quilts, you'll also find the work of contemporary studio artists in an array of media, including gorgeous handcrafted furniture, clothing, jewelry, and toys. Bring your holiday shopping list even if it's April. Every day, one or more members of the Southern Highlands Craft Guild is on hand to demonstrate their craft at the entrance to the Folk Art Center. They may be whittling away at a chunk of wood with their pocket knife, spinning wool into yarn or weaving, or tying brooms. No matter what they're doing, they're happy to talk to you and explain their process and the history of their craft.

SPORTS AND RECREATION

Asheville is a "go out and do it" kind of town. It's not unusual to see mountain bikers, road riders, runners, hikers, flat-water kayakers, and their daredevil white water-loving cousins all on the streets in town. A number of gear shops call Asheville home, and trails, rivers, and mountain roads are all accessed right here.

✪ ZIP LINING

For a different perspective on the Asheville area, head north for 30 minutes along I-26 West and spend the day at **Navitat** (242 Poverty Branch Rd., Barnardsville, 855/628-4828 or 828/626-3700, www.navitat.com, 8am-5pm daily). You can streak through the forest canopy on a pair of zip line courses like an overgrown flying squirrel. The Blue Ridge Experience (from $99) has the tallest zip line here; it's an incredible 350 feet high—they say "don't look down," but do; it's amazing. The longest is more than 3,600 feet. Two rappels, a pair of sky bridges, and three short hikes provide interludes from all the zipping and flying, and there are plenty of opportunities for photos and action-camera videos. Their smaller course, the Moody Cove Adventure ($99) has 10 zip lines up to 2,000 feet long, a pair of bridges, and two rappels. Or you can combine the two courses ($169) into one giant day of adventure.

If you're tempted to zip line but want something a little less heart-pounding, think about **The Adventure Center of Asheville** (85 Expo Dr., 877/247-5539, www. ashevilletreetopsadventurepark. com, 9am-5pm daily). The Adventure Center has a number of high-flying adventures to try. **Their Treetops Adventure Park** ($47 adults, $44 ages 18 and under) has 60 challenges (read: rope swings, sky bridges, cargo nets, short zip lines, leaps from tall platforms) spread over five different adventure trails, allowing you to face the trail that presents you with the best challenges. Their **Zip Line Canopy Tours** ($59-86) has 11 zips, three sky bridges, and so many great views you'll forget about the zip lines. **Kid Zip** ($49 adults, $44 ages 18 and under) is a zip line course designed for kids aged 4-10. They also have the **KOLO Mountain Bike Park** ($19 adult full-day access, $14 youth full-day access, $9 late day youth access) where you can challenge yourself of build up your skills before you head out onto some of the singletrack trails south of town.

BICYCLING

In town, take a tour by bicycle. I know what you're thinking; "It's too hilly, I'll never be able to climb that." **The Flying Bike Electric Bike Tours** (meeting point 225 Coxe Ave., 828/450-8686, www.flyingbiketours. com. 9am, 1pm, 4pm daily Feb.15-Dec.15, $62 per rider, ages 12 and under ride free) provide you with pedal-assisted bikes that make the hills easier and the flats seem like nothing at all. To show off how well the pedal-assist system works, you start with the hill to the Grove Park Inn, the first stop on a two-hour tour around Asheville's historic and cultural sites. The bikes really are ingenious; rather than rely on a throttle like a moped or electric scooter, they use their power to make pedaling easier, meaning you still have to work, just not as hard, to get where you're going.

There are countless miles of **bicycle trails** on the Biltmore Estate, and you can bring your bike or rent one in Antler Hill Village from the **Bike Barn** (800/411-3812, single/speed beach cruiser $15/hour, mountain and hybrid bikes half-day and full day $30-60 adults, $20-40 children, $50 tandem bikes, estate admission not included). Riding on paved roads is not allowed (they're too narrow to share with cars), so stick to the marked paths, which will take you past prime photo spots and some of the most beautiful land on the estate.

TOP EXPERIENCE

✪ WATER SPORTS

Wai Mauna Asheville SUP Tours (159 Riverside Dr., 828/808-9038, www.waimaunaashevillesuptours. com, rentals $40, tours $65) is a natural fit for Asheville given "wai mauna" is Hawaiian for "mountain waters." Where most SUP outfitters ignore the two most beautiful parts of the day, dawn and dusk, these guys embrace it: Wai Mauna offers four tours daily at dawn, midmorning, midday, and sunset. And as much as people rave about sunsets, there's something to the Dawn Patrol tour. At that time, the river's often shrouded in fog, the birds are waking up, and the river is as still as it will ever be; it's a perfect time to paddle. All tours depart from the River Arts District, and paddlers are shuttled to Hominy Creek, a few miles away; then you paddle downstream back to where you started.

Tubing isn't a sport, inasmuch as you simply recline in an inner tube and float from point A to point B, but it's a lot of fun. If you want to go tubing in Asheville, do it with **Zen Tubing** (855/936-8823, www.zentubing.com, trips 10am-3pm daily, $20 $5 cooler carrier, same-day second trips $5). The French Broad is a calm river, especially on the sections where Zen sends their tubers (what else would you call one who rides a tube?). If you pick up a six-pack of your favorite canned (or plastic-bottled) beverage, you'll want the cooler carrier tube so you can keep any snacks and beverages close at hand. Tube trips take a while, but you'll have plenty of company, as the river is mobbed by tube enthusiasts. They have two locations, one in downtown Asheville (608 Riverside Dr.) and one in south Asheville (1648 Brevard Rd.), so check the website or call ahead to see which one will be the best to visit.

French Broad Outfitters (704 Riverside Dr., 828/505-7371, www.frenchbroadoutfitters.com, 10am-6pm daily, rentals from $30 per day) specializes in sports that get you wet, namely stand-up paddleboards, kayaks, and bellyaks—a cross between a kayak and an ergonomically designed surfboard. You lie down on a bellyak, paddle like you're swimming, and take the river's rapids head on. It's a fun ride on the small but exciting rapids of the French Broad River when it's at normal levels, and it's a thrilling ride

floating down the French Broad River with Zen Tubing

when the river is running a little high. If you've come to Asheville equipped with your own paddleboard or kayak, Adventure Rentals rents helmets, dry suits, PFDs, kayak skirts, and more.

The French Broad and Swannanoa Rivers offer a lot of opportunities to try your hand a stand-up paddleboarding on the river. It's much different than on a lake, marsh creek, or even the ocean, and you have to know how to read the river for underwater hazards and how to fall off correctly. **Asheville Outdoor Center** (521 Amboy Rd., 828/232-1970, www. ashevilleoutdoorcenter.com, tours $38-65) provides lessons to make sure you're safe on the river and rentals to make sure you keep having fun. They offer tours ranging from a few to many miles, but it's all scenic and mostly downstream.

HIKING

Ready for mountain air? Join **Blue Ridge Hiking Co.** (36 Montford Ave., 828/713-5451, http:// blueridgehikingco.com, $175-265) on private half-day or full-day hikes in the Pisgah National Forest; they even do private overnight trips (starting at $375 for two people). Founder Jennifer Pharr Davis has hiked more than 11,000 miles of long-distance trails and became the first woman to be the overall record holder for fastest through-hike of the Appalachian Trail: She hiked its 2,181 miles in 46.5 days. Don't worry, she and her guides don't go that fast on the trail; they like to slow down, enjoy the moment, and make sure everyone gets a look and feel for what they love about hiking.

Hiking on the Biltmore Estate can mean anything from walking the 2.5 miles of mulched paths in the manicured gardens to exploring the hills, meadows, streams, and riverbank on more than 22 miles of trails. None are rugged, so you don't need any special equipment, just water, your camera, and maybe a walking stick. The Outdoor Adventure Center in Antler Hill Village has maps and can help you identify the right hike.

GOLF

Golf in the mountains can be a challenge, with course layouts big on blind approaches and hard doglegs, but it pays off with beautiful views and long downhill shots that can make you feel like you hit it like a pro.

Play a round at the **Grove Park Inn Golf Club** (828/252-2711 or 800/438-5800, reserve tee times online at www. groveparkinn.com, 18 holes, par 70, greens fees $70-125 Mon.-Thurs. and $85-140 Fri.-Sun. Apr. 1-Nov. 30, $77-87 Dec. 1-Mar. 31, discounted rates for junior golfers, rental clubs are $40/nine holes and $70/18 holes), where President Obama played during his 2010 stay. *Golf Digest* named this course one of the top 10 courses that are at least 100 years old, and it plays beautifully. This is a must-play course for serious golfers, not just because the views are spectacular but also because the course contains so much history.

OTHER OUTDOOR ACTIVITIES

The Biltmore is an Orvis-endorsed **fly-fishing school,** and it's an excellent place to learn or hone your technique. Outings include two-hour introductory lessons ($125), half-day lessons ($225), kid's fishing outings ($125), full-day guided fishing float trips on the French Broad River, and wading trips on a private trout stream ($350-450 for 1-2 people), and no fishing license is required.

For a loud, blood-pumping good time, try **clay target shooting** ($100-750). If you've never handled a shotgun before or have never shot clay targets, the introductory sporting clays lesson will have you on target in no time. For more experienced shooters, two-hour advanced lessons, a sporting clay course, and even full-day shotgun sports clinics will challenge your skills and help you refine them. All equipment is provided for activities on the Biltmore Estate (except your hiking shoes). Stop in at the **Outdoor Adventure Center** (800/411-3812) in Antler Hill Village for the full scoop.

SPAS

After a day (or two) of playing hard in and around Asheville, you'll need to relax. The Grove Park Inn has a spa known the world over and there are several places around town where you can get a massage, but **Shoji Spa & Lodge** (96 Avondale Heights, 828/299-0999, www.shojiretreats.com, 10am-8pm Sun.-Thurs., 10am-10pm Fri.-Sat., Closed Tues. Mar.-Aug.) does things a little differently. This Japanese-inspired spa has private outdoor hot tubs as well as co-ed hot tubs, saunas, and cold-plunge pools open to spa guests ($45 one hour, $65 90 minutes, $90 two hours). The private hot tubs are big enough for groups up to six, and each is perched on the side of the mountain and open on one side, giving you a broad view of the mountain while keeping you out of sight from other guests. Shoji also offers massage treatments ($125-375). Their Hike-n-Soak package ($125/person for groups of five or more) includes a guided hike along the Mountains to Sea Trail and a 2-hour soak in one of their hot tubs; 25% of proceeds go to the conservation

and education efforts of the Southern Appalachian Highlands Conservancy.

ENTERTAINMENT AND EVENTS

NIGHTLIFE
✪ Live Music
Great live music is the rule rather than the exception in Asheville, in the form of national touring acts as well as regional and local bands that give them stiff competition for audiences on any given night. It seems that everywhere you turn in this town, you'll find live musicians—buskers playing on street corners, solo guitarists in cafés, or a bluegrass trio set up on a restaurant deck. Follow the sound of drums to **Pritchard Park** (Patton Ave. at Haywood St., and College St.), where a huge **drum circle** forms every Friday night. There are also formal music venues where you can hear rock, jam bands, bluegrass, funk, blues, country, rockabilly, alt-country, mountain swing, old-time music, and electronica.

My favorite spot for live music is the **Orange Peel Social Aid and Pleasure Club** (101 Biltmore Ave., 828/398-1837, www.theorangepeel. net, noon-midnight or later daily). They're billed as "the nation's premier live music hall and concert venue," and they can back that up with some powerful acts taking the stage. The Orange Peel is a cool concert hall with a great big dance floor, great sound, and great history.

One of the best venues in town for roots music and eclectic small bands is the **Grey Eagle Tavern and Music Hall** (185 Clingman Ave., 828/232-5800, www.thegreyeagle.com). It's a small space set up more like a listening-room than a bar or club, meaning folks come to listen to the music and interact with the performer rather than grab a beer and hop to the next bar.

Cocktails

Asheville is growing a reputation as a craft-cocktail destination to match its food renown, and one big contributor to that movement is **Sovereign Remedies** (29 N. Market St., 828/919-9518, www.soverignremedies.com, light bites 2pm-4pm and late night 4pm-2am Mon., light bites 2pm-4pm, dinner 4pm-10pm, and late night 10pm-2am Tues.-Fri., and brunch 10am-3pm, dinner 4pm-10pm, and late night 10pm-2am Sat.-Sun., $4-24) has quickly become a go-to for Asheville's cocktail lovers and those hankering a small, delicious plate of food. Between the bartenders and some local foragers, Sovereign Remedies stays stocked with wild herbs, berries, fruits, and roots they use to make cocktails, infuse or macerate various liquors, craft bitters, and create shrubs (drinking vinegars; don't make that face, they're delicious). As we've gotten to know the bartenders, we like to sit and chat (when it's not busy) and challenge them to create tasty drinks from odd ingredients like Montenegro, Aperol, and even more strange foreign spirits.

Nightbell (32 South Lexington Ave., 828/575-0375, www.thenightbell. com, 5pm-close Tues.-Sun., $4-34), from chef Katie Button, serves sophisticated, imaginative cocktails and some mighty fine nosh in a speakeasy-esque spot. Food ranges from oysters on the half shell to charcuterie boards to smoked duck breast with wild mushrooms.

Also of note is **The Imperial Life** (48 College St., 828/254-8980, http://imperialbarasheville.com, 4:30pm-late daily), specializes in pre-Prohibition

The Friday night drum circle has become a fixture in downtown Asheville.

cocktails, a wine list that showcases lesser-known varietals, and small batch spirits. They serve a limited menu of small plates made downstairs at Table (http://tableasheville.com), a much-lauded restaurant under the same ownership.

Downstairs from the tasty Indian restaurant Chai Pani is **MG Road** (19 Wall St., 828/254-4363, www.mgroadlounge.com, 5pm-midnight Mon.-Thurs., 5pm-2am Fri.-Sat.), the bar and lounge that prides itself on a selection of cocktails, local beers, and eclectic wines. The atmosphere is simultaneously neighborhood bar and haute hangout, and they're a sort of incubator space for pop-up restaurants. These pop-ups are always changing, so check in to see who's there and what they're cooking; it's bound to be interesting.

Breweries

Asheville earned the title Beer City USA for several years running and has been a contender for the title in subsequent years. It seems there's a brewery on every corner, or one planning to open there next month, and brewers are getting experimental, introducing new styles, funky ingredients, and any little twist they can to get people talking. And they do; loyal locals and pint hounds from all over frequent the bars, breweries, and pubs here.

Hi-Wire Brewing (828/738-2448, www.hiwirebrewing.com) came into Asheville with one location on the **South Slope** (197 Hilliard Ave., 4pm-11pm Mon.-Thurs., 2pm-1am Fri., noon-1am Sat., 1pm-10pm Sun.) and quickly expanded to a spot they call the **Big Top** (2 Huntsman Place, 4pm-10pm Mon.-Thurs., 3pm-midnight Fri., noon-midnight Sat., 1pm-10pm Sun., tours 1pm and 3pm Sat $5 21

and up, free under 21) near Biltmore Village. They focus on lagers, pale ales, and IPAs, but their winter brew, the Strongman Coffee Milk Stout, is one of my favorites.

Another good microbrewery is **Wedge Brewing Company** (37 Paynes Way, Suite 001, 828/505-2792, www.wedgebrewing.com, noon-10pm daily), located in an old warehouse in the River Arts District. Wedge has more than a dozen brews on tap, including pale ales, pilsners, and a Russian imperial stout flavored with raspberries. Their strong relationship with area food trucks makes this a great hangout for local beer and local grub with local beer enthusiasts any evening.

Burial Beer Co. (40 Collier Ave., 828/475-2739, www.burialbeer.com, 2pm-10pm Mon.-Thurs., noon-10pm Fri.-Sat., 10:30am-9pm Sun.) is one of my favorite biergarten spaces in Asheville, and they have an Instagram-worthy mural of Sloth from *The Goonies* and Magnum P.I. on one wall of the brewery. And then their beers. Start with the names— A Violent Voyage to Impermanence, When I Surfed The Sky, Ulfberht, This Golden Carriage to Oblivion, I Know For A Fact You Still Don't Party—they're improbably weird but perfectly fit the brews. Now, for what's in the glass; Burial isn't afraid of any style or flavor, so you'll find s'mores inspired, barrel aged imperial stouts; rich double IPAs infused with wine grapes or peaches and mangoes; IPAs with orange or pineapple sage; coffee saisons, and more.

Colorado's **New Belgium Brewing Company** (21 Craven St., 828/333-6900, www.newbelgium.com, 11am-8pm Mon.-Sat., 11:30am-8pm Sun. Tours 11:30am-4:30pm every hour on the half hour) found an East Coast home in Asheville and it sits across the French Broad from the River Arts District and has great views. It's bikable and very bike friendly and their brews on offer go beyond Fat Tire and the other cans you find in stores and they show off their top-notch barrel aging program with a slate of ever-changing and always-delicious brews like their Carnie Blood Golden Sour, Transalantique Kriek, and La Folie Sour Flanders Ale.

To sample a variety of Asheville's great microbreweries, join a tour from **Asheville Brews Cruise** (828/545-5181, www.ashevillebrewscruise.com, from $60). The enthusiastic beer experts will shuttle you from brewery to brewery in the Brews Cruise van to sample some beer, learn about the growth of Asheville's beer scene, and gain some insight in the art and craft of brewing. On the tour, you'll visit **Asheville Pizza and Brewing Company** (675 Merrimon Ave., 828/254-1281, http://ashevillebrewing.com, 11am-11pm Sun.-Wed., 11am-midnight Thurs.-Sat.), where you can start off the evening with one of this pizzeria, microbrewery, and movie house's tasty beers and fortify yourself for the evening by filling up on good pizza. The **French Broad Brewing Company** (828/277-0222, www.frenchbroadbrewery.com, 1pm-8pm daily) is another popular local nightspot that's grown up around a first-rate beer-making operation, where you can choose from a varied menu that includes signature pilsners, lagers, and ales while listening to some good live music. The third destination on the cruise is the **Highland Brewing Company** (12 Old Charlotte Hwy., Suite H, 828/299-3370, www.highlandbrewing.com, tasting room

3pm-9pm Mon.-Thurs., noon-10pm Fri.-Sat., noon-6pm Sun., tours 4:30pm and 5:45 pm Mon.-Thurs., 4:30pm, 5:45pm, and 6:30pm Fri., 2:30pm-6:30pm every hour on the half hour Sat., 2:30pm and 4:30pm Sun.), Asheville's first microbrewery. They've been making beer and raking in awards for well over a decade, and on first sip you'll understand why they're one of the Southeast's favorite breweries.

COMEDY

Around Asheville you may notice a giant purple bus zipping through the streets, laughter and bubbles (yes, bubbles) coming from the windows. That's the **LaZoom Comedy Tour** (14 Battery Park Ave., departing from 76 Biltmore Ave., 828/225-6932, www.lazoomtours.com, $29, must be at least 13 to join a tour), delivering tours big in history and hilarity. The tour guides are outrageous—they're some of Asheville's weirdest (in a good way) people—and I guarantee you'll learn a thing or two (some history, a joke you may or may not want to tell your mom). They also offer the Haunted Comedy Tour ($26), which adds in a supernatural note and tales of some of Asheville's spectral denizens. The Band & Beer Bus Tour ($34) visits a trio of area breweries for samples and some live music from local performers.

The **Altamont Theatre** (18 Church St., www.thealtamont.com) calls itself "Asheville's Best Listening Room," and they may be right. Hosting a variety of musical acts (country, soul, jazz, bluegrass, instrumental progressive space rock, you name it), spoken word (there's an erotic storytelling night as well as the occasional poet), and comedians. Comedian Cliff Cash, one of the funniest rising stars

GEORGE VANDERBILT'S GREAT OUTDOORS

The thing that drew George Vanderbilt to Asheville was the mountain air and glories of nature that surround this place. The **Biltmore Estate** was once a huge estate of some 125,000 acres, almost every bit of it untamed. Frederick Law Olmsted worked to groom the forest around the house, the same forest you see when you drive onto the estate, but the rest was left to be a sort of natural playground. Today visitors can play in the forests, fields, trails, and waters of the Biltmore Estate and try their hand at sports and activities from the familiar (bicycling) to the exotic (the Land Rover Experience Driving School). **The Adventure Center** (800/411-3812) in **Antler Hill Village** can make reservations and point you in the right direction for any number of outdoor activities.

The 22 miles of hiking and biking trails take you all across the estate, from Antler Hill Village to the house and gardens and back. Paved and wooded trails allow all experience levels to get out and ride, run, or hike. Rent a bike (from $10/hour) or bring your own. For something a little different, hop on one of the Segway Tours. They come in four flavors: the basic tour ($50) on a paved trail to the Lagoon below the house, an off-road tour ($75) to a vista of the house a little ways past the lagoon, the west-side tour ($100) which takes you to the seldom seen west side of the estate, and the advanced tour ($100) which follows the Deerpark Trail.

Equine enthusiasts can saddle up for an hour-long guided ride ($60), a two-hour private trail ride ($160), or a private trail ride and picnic lunch ($230). If you'd rather sit back and ride, there are carriage rides ($350 up to four guests) and wagon rides ($35), too.

If you'd rather spend the day on the water, you can. Guided raft trips ($35 adults, $25 ages 12 and under) and self-guided kayak trips ($25) on the French Broad give you a rare view of the estate, while a day on the water fly-fishing gives you a different experience altogether. Novice anglers may want a lesson (from $125, kids' lessons available), but experienced anglers will opt for a day-long wade trip or drift boat trip ($350 for two guests).

For something really adventurous, try learning to shoot sporting clays. If you've never handled a firearm, don't worry; they've got lessons ($175-225), and they'll have you knocking clay pigeons out of the sky in no time. There's also a Sporting Clay course ($100) and a full-day shotgun sports clinic ($450). Then there's the Land Rover Driving Experience. Get behind the wheel of a Land Rover and get a lesson ($250/one hour, $400/two hour) on off road driving. After your lessons, hit the trail ($400/two hours) or go out for a full day ($1,200) and master those off-road skills.

---

in the South, performs there regularly, and their comedy and improv shows are both smart and hilarious. Since Asheville doesn't have a dedicated comedy club, The Altamont gladly fills that role.

PERFORMING ARTS

As an artsy town, Asheville has a lively theatre and dance community. **Terpsicorps Theatre of Dance** (www.terpsicorps.org), a professional dance company and school, puts on a number of shows a year, as does **Asheville Ballet** (www.ashevilleballet.com), who puts on The Nutcracker every year.

NC Stage Company (828/239-0263, www.ncstage.org) performs many times throughout the year, staging contemporary, classic and holiday performances and **Asheville Community Theatre** (www.ashevilletheatre.org) draws on the deep well of talent in town to put on performances like Avenue Q, Footloose, Alice in Wonderland, and other surprising shows.

FESTIVALS

Twice yearly, in late July and late October, the Southern Highland Craft Guild hosts the **Craft Fair of the**

Southern Highlands (U.S. Cellular Center, 87 Haywood St., 828/298-7928, www.southernhighlandguild.org, 10am-6pm Fri.-Sat., 10am-5pm Sun., $8 adults, under age 12 free). Since 1948 this event has brought much-deserved attention to the Guild's more than 900 members, who live and work throughout the Appalachian Mountains. Hundreds of craftspeople participate in the event, selling all sorts of handmade items.

Probably the biggest of Asheville's festivals and fairs, or at least the most anticipated, is the annual Warren Haynes Christmas Jam (www.xmasjam.com). Warren Haynes, longtime guitarist for The Allman Brothers Band, founding member of Government Mule, and Asheville native, invites a who's-who of musical acts to come perform a benefit concert for Habitat for Humanity. The acts are generally biggies in the rock/jam world and bands on the rise.

Asheville's Restaurant Week (www.exploreasheville.com) generally takes place in late January. Given the city's food scene, it's a great opportunity to score some delicious meals at a bit of a discount; usually restaurants offer a prix fixe menu for anywhere from $15-30. Beer lovers should arrive in town in early June for the one-day Beer City Festival (www.beercityfestival.com). Here, more than 30 regional breweries and local musical acts entertain the crowds. And if you love beer and bluegrass (seems they go hand in hand today), September's Brewgrass Festival (www.brewgrassfestival.com) is a full day of outstanding craft beer and several bluegrass and newgrass bands like one of my favorites (and a band I've seen more than 100 times), Acoustic Syndicate.

The Mountain Dance and Folk Festival (www.folkheritage.org, 828/258-6101, ext. 345) is the nation's longest-running folk festival, an event founded in the 1920s by musician and folklorist Bascom Lamar Lunsford to celebrate the heritage of his native Carolina mountains. Musicians and dancers from western North Carolina perform at the downtown Diana Wortham Theater at Pack Place for three nights each summer. Also downtown, many of the same artists can be heard on Saturday evening at the city's Shindig on the Green concert series (Pack Square Park, 80 Court Plaza).

SHOPPING

ANTIQUES

For lovers of vintage, retro, and aged things, the Antique Tobacco Barn (75 Swannanoa River Rd., 828/252-7291, www.atbarn.com, 10am-6pm Mon.-Thurs., 9am-6pm Fri.-Sat., 1pm-6pm Sun. Mar.-Oct., 10am-5pm Mon.-Sat., 1pm-5pm Sun. Nov.-Feb.) has more than 77,000 square feet of goodies to plunder through. This perpetual winner of the *Mountain XPress* "Best Antiques Store in Western North Carolina" category has toys, art, tools, furniture, radios, sporting equipment, folk art, farm relics, oddball bric-a-brac, mid-century furniture, and all those great weird things you can only find in a collection this large. It takes a while to explore this humongous shop, so carve out some time.

Along Swannanoa River Rd., you'll find yourself in the Biltmore Antiques District (120 Swannanoa Rd.), a small shopping district that's packed with an intriguing group of antiques shops. Some specialize in imports, others in lamps, European furniture, or fine jewelry. Exploring here is always a good time because you never know what you'll find or where you'll find it.

GALLERIES

One of Asheville's shopping highlights is the 1929 **Grove Arcade** (1 Page Ave., 828/252-7799, www.grovearcade.com), a beautiful and storied piece of architecture that is now a chic shopping and dining destination in the heart of downtown. The expansive Tudor Revival building, ornately filigreed inside and out in ivory-glazed terracotta, was initially planned as the base of a 14-story building, a skyscraper by that day's standard. There are some fantastic galleries and boutiques, including **Mountain Made** (828/350-0307, www.mtnmade.com, 10am-6pm Mon.-Sat., noon-5pm Sun.), a gallery celebrating contemporary art created in and inspired by the mountains around Asheville. Another favorite is **Alexander & Lehnert** (828/254-2010, www.alexander-lehnert.com, 10am-6pm Mon.-Sat.), a gallery showcasing the work of two talented jewelers with different styles—Lehnert takes an architectural approach to designs, and Alexander chooses organic forms as inspiration. Not all stores in the Grove Arcade sell fine art and jewelry. **Battery Park Book Exchange & Champagne Bar** (828/252-0020, 11am-9pm Sun.-Thurs., 11am-late Fri.-Sat.) has two things that go great together: wine and books. And it's in a really relaxed atmosphere. Outside the Grove Arcade is a row of shaded stalls, and it's here that you'll find many of the best sell-it-on-the-street artisans selling everything from soap to miniature topiaries you can wear as a necklace to fine art prints.

There are a number of galleries in downtown Asheville, and while most exhibit works from multiple artists, none can match the size of the **Woolworth Walk** (25 Haywood St., 828/254-9234, www.woolworthwalk. com, 11am-6pm Mon.-Thurs., 11am-7pm Fri., 10am-7pm Sat., 11am-5pm Sun.), a two-story, 20,000-square-foot gallery featuring more than 160 local artists. Nearly every conceivable medium is represented, including digitally designed graphic prints, oil paintings, watercolors, jewelry, and woodworking. This gallery is a favorite not just because it has a soda fountain but because the work on display is affordable as well as stunning.

American Folk Art and Framing (64 Biltmore Ave., 828/281-2134, www. amerifolk.com, 10am-6pm Mon.-Sat., noon-5pm Sun.) does a wonderful job of displaying contemporary Southern folk artists, including potters, painters, and woodcarvers, as well as helping the art-appreciating public learn more about local folk-art traditions and styles. They host six openings a year in the gallery, so work changes frequently, keeping the place bubbling with energy.

BOOKS, TOYS, AND CRAFTS

One of the social hubs of this city is **Malaprop's Bookstore and Café** (55 Haywood St., 800/441-9829, www. malaprops.com, 9am-9pm Mon.-Sat., 9am-7pm Sun.). This fun and progressive bookstore carries a deep selection of books that includes tomes by North Carolina authors and a particularly fine collection of regional authors. You'll find the requisite coffee bar and café with wireless internet access, making it a particularly good spot to hang out. It's bright and comfortable, and the staff are well versed in all sorts of literature, so they can help you find a local author you'll enjoy reading. People in all walks of Asheville life come to Malaprop's, so expect to see creative dressers, the tattooed, business types, artists, students, and grannies.

There are a pair of great gem and crystal shops in Asheville, and these places always fascinate me. Not only do they have some breathtaking minerals for sale, but they also have fossils—of fish, starfish, plants, even claws and teeth and skulls—for sale. Our favorite is **Cornerstone Minerals** (52 N. Lexington Ave., 828/225-3888, www.cornerstoneminerals.com, 11am-7pm Sun.-Thurs., 10am-9pm Fri.-Sat.) because I like to stare at their sheets of fossil-imbued stone and my wife always finds some cool bauble there. A close second is **Enter the Earth** (1 Page Ave. #125, inside the Grove Arcade, 828/350-9222, www.entertheearth.com, 10am-6pm Mon.-Sat., 11am-5pm Sun.), where they have some very impressive fossils and a selection of jewelry using many of the stones and gems sold in the store.

The **Mast General Store** (15 Biltmore Ave., 828/232-1883, www.mastgeneralstore.com, 10am-6pm Mon.-Thurs., 10am-9pm Fri.-Sat., noon-6pm Sun.) is an institution in western North Carolina and beyond. They call themselves a general store, but they mean it in a very contemporary way. Cast-iron cookware, penny candies, and Mast logo shirts and jackets sit alongside baskets and handmade crafts. A good selection of outdoor clothing and equipment can get you outfitted for some time in the woods, or you can fill up a bag with candy and eat it while you drive the Blue Ridge Parkway—your call.

Dancing Bear Toys (518 Kenilworth Rd., 800/659-8697, www.dancingbeartoys.com, 10am-7pm Mon.-Sat., noon-5pm Sun.) is located among the motels and chain restaurants out on U.S. 70 (Tunnel Rd.), but inside it has the ambience of a cozy village toy shop. Dancing Bear has toys for everyone from babies to silly grown-ups: a fabulous selection of Playmobil figures and accessories, Lego, Brio, and other favorite lines of European toys; beautiful stuffed animals of all sizes; all sorts of educational kits and games; and comical doodads.

✪ RIVER ARTS DISTRICT

Along the Swannanoa River, many of Asheville's old warehouses and industrial buildings have been transformed into studio spaces, galleries, restaurants, and breweries in an area known as the **River Arts District** (www.riverartsdistrict.com). More than 160 artists have working studios here, and twice a year, during the first weekend of June and November, nearly every artist in the district opens their studios to the public for a two-day **Studio Stroll.** On the second Saturday of each month some of the studios (they rotate based on medium, so one month may be photography, the next clay, and so on) are open for **A Closer Look,** a day of artist demonstrations, classes, workshops, and creative activities.

Some studios are open daily, among them **Jonas Gerald Fine Art** (240 Clingman Ave., daily 10am-6pm), where the namesake artist specializes in abstract art that uses vivid colors and unusual composition to draw in viewers. He works across many media, so there's a lot to see. **Odyssey Center for Ceramic Arts** (236-238 Clingman Ave, www.odysseyclayworks.com, 9am-5pm Mon.-Sat., 1pm-5pm Sun.) is full of sculptors and teachers. Part of their mission is to promote artistic appreciation and advancement of ceramic arts; they hold regular classes, workshops, and talks led by master ceramic artists.

At the 1910 **Cotton Mill Studios** (122 Riverside Dr., at W. Haywood St., www.cottonmillasheville.com, hours vary), several painters work alongside potters and jewelers. **Riverview Station** (191 Lyman St., www.riverviewstation.com, hours vary) is a circa-1896 building that houses the studios of a wonderful array of jewelers, ceramicists, furniture designers, painters, and photographers. Another favorite gallery is **CURVE Studios & Garden** (6, 9, and 12 Riverside Dr., 828/388-3526, www.curvestudiosnc.com, most studios 11am-4pm Mon.-Sat.). A fun, funky studio that has been around since before the River Arts District was a thing, and once a punk rock club called Squashpile—you can't make up stuff like that—CURVE is home to encaustic painters, ceramic workers, jewelry designers, glass artists, fiber artists, and more. This is just a sampling of what's happening in the River Arts District; visit the website for detailed listings of the artists and their studios.

FOOD

No matter what you're craving, from Mediterranean to vegetarian, four-star to down-home, Asheville has eateries that both embrace the Southern traditions of its mountain home and explore well beyond its borders. This is a town that clearly loves its food, with more than 17 local tailgate farmers markets, more than 250 independent restaurants, and more breweries per capita than any other city in the United States (26 in town, 60 in the region as of this writing). Farmers work with restaurants to provide the highest-quality produce and meats, and artisanal bakers and cheese makers supply their tasty foodstuffs to restaurants high and low.

With such a robust food scene, it can be hard to pick out where you want to go. For a sampling of the best of what Asheville has to offer the gastronome, take a walking tour with **Eating Asheville** (828/489-3266, http://eatingasheville.com, classic tour $56, high-roller tour $69). Tours stop in at six of Asheville's best farm-to-table restaurants for a taste of what they're cooking. Restaurants provide two drink pairings as well as a talk about their food philosophy and sometimes a chance to meet the chef. The deluxe high-roller (2pm Thurs.-Sat.) tour visits seven of the top restaurants, one of which is a James Beard Award nominated, and includes four beverage pairings (wine, beer, and craft cocktails); for just a few bucks more, it's the way to go. Their Dinner and Drinks Tour (4pm-6pm Fri.-Sat., $74) visits three of the top mixologists, breweries, and eateries in town and features larger portions and drinks everywhere you go.

ECLECTIC AMERICAN

One of the most amazing restaurants in Asheville—and that's quite the qualification given the food scene here—is ✪ **Rhubarb** (7 N. Pack Square, 828/785-1503, rhubarbasheville.com, hours: 3pm-9:30pm Mon., 11:30am-9:30pm Wed.-Thurs., 11:30am-10:30pm Fri., 10:30am-10:30pm Sat., 10:30am-9:30pm Sun., $11-48). Chef John Fleer is a culinary magician and he's got a kitchen full of eager and talented cooks helping create dish after masterful dish. Using the best of farmed, foraged, and pasture-raised ingredients, dishes like the Mongolian barbecued lamb ribs with collard green kimchi, or the pork meatballs, or the summer squash cassoulet with smoked shiitake mushrooms, or the seared duck breast with seasonal berries are dishes you'll have dreams about.

In West Asheville, **Biscuit Head** (733 Haywood Rd., 828/333-5145, www.biscuitheads.com, 7am-2pm Mon.-Fri., 8am-3pm Sat.-Sun., around $8) serves up an Appalachian specialty, cat-head biscuits, so named because they're huge—the size of a cat's head. These biscuits are dynamite. Order the fried green tomato biscuit and you'll get more than you can eat: a cat-head biscuit, split and topped with a fried green tomato, brie, a sliced tomato, poached eggs, and smoked tomato hollandaise. Or just get the "Biscuit And," which comes with a biscuit and your choice of crazy butters, jams, hot sauces, infused honeys, and toppings from the biscuit bar, featuring all house-made spreadables.

✪ **The Admiral** (400 Haywood Rd., 828/252-2541, www.theadmiralasheville.com, 5pm-9:30pm nightly, $23-39) in West Asheville has been a food destination since it opened in a humble cinderblock building in what they call "the wage-earning side of town." Blue-collar roots or not, they serve some distinguished, and much-lauded, New Southern food that keeps the kitchen on its toes with interesting techniques and seasonal ingredients. It's small, but cozy and chic while somehow retaining a sort of dive-bar vibe. The cocktails aren't half bad either.

Early Girl Eatery (8 Wall St., 828/259-9292, www.earlygirleatery.com, 7:30am-3pm Mon.-Wed., 7:30am-9pm Thurs.-Fri., 8am-9pm Sat.-Sun., $10-15) has caused a stir among area localvores and is gaining a following among visitors. More than half of the vegetables, meat, and fish used at Early Girl were raised or caught within 20 miles of the restaurant. The menu accommodates Asheville's large vegetarian and vegan contingent, but non-veg diners can feast on pan-fried trout with pecan butter, free-range chicken, or cheeseburgers made from hormone-free beef and topped with farmstead cheese, basil mayo, and all the fixings. Their breakfast, served all day, is among the best in Asheville. Their multigrain pancakes are out of this world.

If you're in the mood for a killer hotdog, burger like no other, or a Cuban sandwich that will make you think about proposing marriage to the guy or gal operating the grill, or even a bologna sandwich (seriously), head to ✪ **Foothills Food Truck** (2 Huntsman Place at Hi-Wire's Big Top, 828/606-9372, www.foothillslocalmeats.com, 4pm-10pm Mon.-Thurs., 4pm-11pm Fri., noon-11pm Sat., 1pm-10pm Sun., $8-14). I love this place and it's become one of my go-tos in Asheville. We meet friends at Hi-Wire's Big Top, grab a couple of orders of poutine and a sandwich, then enjoy the beer and food and company.

In the River Arts District, **The Bull and Beggar** (37 Paynes Way #007, 828/575-9443, www.thebullandbeggar.com, 5pm-10pm Mon.-Sat., $10-80) has become the dinner spot of choice for those in the know. With a menu that runs from the raw bar to the $80 bone-in rib eye for two, they serve rich, filling, French-inspired entrées along with a killer charcuterie platter and a list of sides ($4-8) that are meal-worthy in and of themselves. On Monday nights they offer a $9.99 burger. When I once asked a friend if we should go, she was rendered temporarily speechless by her memory of the previous week's burger.

When you've been at the Grey Eagle or the Orange Peel, the show has just let out, it's the middle of the night, and you need to refuel with some good food, the lights are on at **Rosetta's Kitchen** (116 N. Lexington Ave., 828/232-0738, www.rosettaskitchen. com, 11am-11pm Mon.-Sat., $10). There's so much to recommend about this place: The food is very good, it's all vegetarian and mostly vegan, and it's made with local produce in season. Best of all, it's open late on weekends. They compost everything that makes its way back to the kitchen, recycle all their trash, and make sure their used vegetable oil goes to power biodiesel cars—it's Asheville's signature countercultural reinterpretation of the South, and it's one of the best vegetarian places in town.

Since opening in 2005, **Table** (48 College St., 828/254-8980, http:// tableasheville.com, 11:30am-2:30pm Wed.-Fri., 5:30pm-close dinner daily, 11:30am-2:30pm Sat. brunch, 10:30am-2:30pm Sun. brunch, lunch $8-14, brunch $6-14, dinner $19-34) has been on the receiving end of much critical acclaim, including becoming a James Beard Award semifinalist. This restaurant is upscale, interesting, innovative, and above all, good. They use ingredients like locally caught bass and mountain-raised pork and lamb, creating a menu that takes full advantage of the culinary riches of western North Carolina. You can find some unusual ingredients on their menu, like sweetbreads and quail, and they're known for their charcuterie, much of which is made in house. The chef takes a minimalist approach to food, choosing to do as little as possible to

coax out the maximum flavor, which is why this tiny restaurant is always packed. Call for reservations, and if you're feeling bold, go with the chef's tasting menu, a selection of dishes that showcase the best this minuscule kitchen (you'll see it on your way in) has to offer.

West Asheville's **Sunny Point Café** (626 Haywood Rd., 828/252-0055, www.sunnypointcafe.com, 8am-2:30pm Sun.-Mon., 8am-9:30pm Tues.-Sat., $10-17) serves three meals most days but is so famous for its brunch that a line sometimes forms out the door. The breakfast menu is popular and served any time of day, although the lunch and dinner menus are also well worth a trip. This is a great bet for vegetarians—the meatless options are imaginative and beautifully created. Whatever you get, you must order one of their angel biscuits; those things are tall, airy, and so good.

White Duck Taco Shop (12 Biltmore Ave., 828/232-9191, www. whiteducktacoshop.com, 11:30am-9pm daily, $4-6) serves tacos that intrigue and delight. I know that sounds trite or overhyped, but White Duck lives up to every word. You can get jerk chicken, fried chicken, Korean beef bulgogi with kimchi, duck confit with mole and cranberry salsa, even a banh mi tofu taco that tastes like the awesome Vietnamese sandwich. Priced so you can scarf down two or three without breaking the bank, they're just about perfect, but if you're a taco fan (who isn't?) and someone who likes to try things that are a little left of center, this is your place.

Barbecue

What's a trip to North Carolina without barbecue? ✪ **Buxton Hall Barbeque** (32 Banks Ave.,

828/232-7216, www.buxtonhall.com, 11:30am-3pm and 5:30pm-10pm daily, $5-16) Buxton is a blend of old-school barbecue at its best with new-school spins and sides courtesy of chef Elliot Moss. Moss and company crisscrossed the Carolinas, dining in dozens of barbecue joints to create his menu. Chicken Bog (rice, chicken and sausage) from the low country of South Carolina is right there beside Eastern North Carolina whole-hog barbecue; South Carolina Barbecue Hash; and smoked sausages, fried catfish, smoked chicken, all accompanied by an excellent selection of classic barbecue sides. A personal favorite here isn't barbecue (I know, a favorite dish at a barbecue restaurant that isn't barbecue? Crazy!), it's a fried chicken sandwich that's an homage to one you'll find at a popular southern chain restaurant known for being closed on Sundays; and it's way better.

At **Luella's Bar-B-Que** (501 Merrimon Ave., 828/505-7427, www.luellasbbq.com, 11am-9pm Sun.-Thurs., 11am-10pm Fri.-Sat., $7-15) you can try the range of styles and sauces that make North Carolina 'cue distinct. Ribs, chopped pork, brisket, smoked wings, and sides like mac-and-cheese, fried okra, collard greens, and hush puppies are staples here, but there's a surprising item on the menu: barbecued tempeh. (Tempeh is a cousin of tofu.) I'm a barbecue judge (really, I'm certified), so trust me when I say it's good. As is everything here, from the grub to the vibe to the impressive array of local beer on draft.

Biltmore Village

In one of the historic cottages of Biltmore Village is the **Corner Kitchen** (3 Boston Way, 828/274-2439, www.thecornerkitchen.com, 7:30am-10:30am and 11:30am-3pm Mon.-Fri.,

Luella's Bar-B-Que has excellent food and a great selection of beer on tap.

5pm-close daily, 9am-3pm Sat.-Sun. brunch, breakfast $6-13, brunch $6-14, lunch $9-14, dinner $21-37). Head chef Joe Scully, first in his class at the Culinary Institute of America, counts among his illustrious former gigs New York's Waldorf Astoria and the United Nations, where he served as executive chef. He is joined in the Corner Kitchen by Josh Chapman, a young Carolina-born chef with an impressive résumé and a hunger (no pun intended) to grow his culinary career. They've put together an elegant menu that combines home-style and haute cuisines quite harmoniously, and they have a long, outstanding wine list. Prices range $20-275 by the bottle, and a number of wines are available by the glass ($6-12).

Also in Biltmore Village is the excellent **Red Stag Grill** (11 Boston Way, 828/398-5600, www.kesslercollection. com/red-stag-grill, 6:30am-11am daily, 11:30am-2:30pm Mon.-Sat., 5pm-10pm daily, 11:30am-2:30pm Sun. brunch, lounge open 11am-11pm, breakfast $9-15, lunch $8-29, dinner $11-54, brunch $8-23) in the Grand Bohemian Hotel. Breakfast is great, but at lunch, the $29 Nueske's Bacon Burger is a little pricey, although the combo of this peppery bacon and blue brie from Germany makes it worth every penny and every calorie. Dinner is high-end: elk loin, duck breast with fresh mushrooms, local rib eye beef, even a bison hanger steak. This place looks phenomenal, too. Lots of leather, amber lighting, red accent walls, and plenty of antlers and game trophies hang throughout.

Biltmore Estate

There are no fewer than nine places to eat (plus snacks, ice cream, and coffee) on the Biltmore Estate (800/411-3812, www.biltmore.com, estate admission required to visit restaurants). The **Dining Room** (7am-10:30am daily for breakfast, 7am-11am daily for breakfast buffet, 5:30pm-9:30pm Sun.-Thurs., and 5:30pm-10pm Fri.-Sat., reservations required, breakfast $56-20, buffet $13-22, 3-course tasting menu $65, 5-course tasting menu $95) is an elegant restaurant featuring estate-raised Angus beef, mountain trout, Biltmore wines, and vegetables grown on estate gardens. The food is spectacular, and tables with a mountain view make the meal all that much better. Evening dress and reservations are recommended.

The **Biltmore Bistro** (noon-9pm Sun.-Fri., 11:30am-9pm Sat., lunch $8-21, prix fixe lunch $29, dinner $19-44, prix fixe dinner $52) in Antler Hill Village, adjacent to the winery, has a well-rounded gourmet menu sourced from the Biltmore's own kitchen garden, locally raised heirloom crops, meat and seafood delicacies, and artisanal cheeses and breads. Lunch and dinner are dramatically different (pizza at lunch, braised veal cheeks at dinner), but each menu features something from the wood-fired oven.

The dining room of the **Deerpark Restaurant** (11am-2pm Fri.-Sat., 10am-2pm Sun., Fri.-Sat. buffet $20, free kids ages 9 and under, Sun. buffet $35, free ages 9 and under) is a former barn designed by architect Richard Morris Hunt, now renovated to airy splendor with walls of windows. Expect hearty and homey meals based on Appalachian cuisine. Like the Deerpark, the **Stable Café** (lunch 11am-4pm daily, $14-35) was once livestock housing, and guests can sit in booths that were once horse stalls. This is a meat eater's paradise, where you can order estate-raised

Angus beef and pork barbecue with the house special sauce, among others.

In the stable area near the house, both the **Bake Shop** (8:30am-6pm daily) and the **Ice Cream Parlor** (11am-6pm Mon.-Wed., 11am-10pm Thurs.-Sun.) serve fresh treats, and **The Courtyard Market** (11am-4pm daily) has hot dogs, salads, and snacks. The **Creamery** (11am-8pm Mon.-Wed., 11am-9pm Thurs.-Fri., 10am-9pm Sat.-Sun.) is the place for sandwiches and hand-dipped ice cream in Antler Hill Village, and **The Conservatory Café** (from 11:30am daily), adjacent to the gardens, will keep you fed after a day admiring the roses. If you have a hankering for barbecue, a quick sandwich, some snacks, or a cold drink, the **Smokehouse** (11:30am-3:30pm Fri.-Sun.) in Antler Hill Village serves just what you need.

While you're in Antler Hill Village, check out **Cedric's Tavern** (11am-10pm Mon.-Fri., 11am-10pm Sat.-Sun., lunch $11-23, dinner $18-44). Named for George Vanderbilt's beloved Saint Bernard (you can see his huge collar on display at the entrance), Cedric's pays homage to pubs and taverns found in Britain, with a Southern twist. The fish and chips and scotch egg are both delicious. You can also grab a pint of Cedric's Pale or Brown Ale, both brewed by the Biltmore Brewing Company. Also in Antler Hill Village is the new Village Hotel on the Biltmore Estate and its restaurant, **Village Social** (828/257-5968, 7am-midnight daily, $6-36). With a menu focused on small plates and tasting menus—all of which will be seafood-centric—is a place to make a meal as light or as filling as you'd like.

INDIAN

Mela (70 Lexington Ave., 828/225-8880, www.melaasheville.com, 11:30am-2:30pm daily, 5:30pm-9:30pm Sun.-Thurs., 5:30pm-10pm Fri.-Sat., $10-19) is one of the best Indian restaurants in North Carolina. The elaborate menu offers dozens of choices, combining cuisines of both northern and southern India with great meat, seafood, and vegetable dishes. The restaurant is dark and elegant, but the prices are surprisingly low; you can put together a great patchwork meal of appetizers, which start at $3, along with soup and roti. Don't miss the samosas.

Local favorite ✪ **Chai Pani** (22 Battery Park Ave., 828/254-4003, www.chaipaniasheville.com, lunch 11:30am-3:30pm Mon.-Sat, noon-3:30pm Sun., 5pm-9:30pm Sun.-Thurs., 5:30pm-10pm Fri.-Sat., under $14) continues to win fans because of its cool atmosphere and great food. The restaurant's name means "tea and water," a phrase that refers to a snack or a small gift. This restaurant is inspired by Indian street-food vendors and serves casual and affordable specialties from all over India.

ASIAN

✪ **Gan Shan Station** (143 Charlotte St., 828/774-5280, www.ganshanstation.com, 11:30am-10pm Mon.-Sat., lunch $4-15, dinner $10-24) offers up a refreshing bit of fine dining to Asheville's world of Asian food. Their menu is loaded with dishes spanning nations and cuisines, from ramen (Japan) to bulgogi (Korea) to mapo doyfu (China) to citrus shrimp (Thailand), but the real treat is the Chef's Table ($45, 48 hours' advance reservation required), where from your kitchen-side table, you'll interact with the chefs as they serve up dishes for the curious and adventurous eater. **Blue Dream Curry House** (81 Patton Ave., 828/258-2500, www. bluedreamcurry.com, 11:30am-3pm and 5pm-9pm Mon.-Thurs., 11:30am-3pm and 5pm-10pm Fri., noon-10pm Sat., $7-12) is one I hope becomes an Asheville staple. They have a taco served on naan; they serve pickled peanuts in a spicy, curried, briny sauce; their curries are Japanese, Indian, Thai, and Peruvian; and they aren't afraid to offer up a couple of meat options on a veggie- and vegan-centered menu.

Just across the way from Blue Dream is **Red Ginger Dimsum & Tapas** (82 Patton Ave., 828/505-8688, www.redgingerasheville.com, 11:30am-3pm and 5pm-10pm Mon.-Thurs., 11:30am-3pm and 5pm-11pm Fri., 11:30am-11pm Sat., 11:30am-9:30pm Sun., $6-15), and if you're a fan of dumplings, it's a must-dine. The crystal shrimp dumplings, *gua bao* (Chinese pancake with pork belly), scallion pancake, and pan-fried vegetable dumplings are spectacular dishes to share.

LATIN AMERICAN

Ask an Asheville resident for restaurant recommendations, and chances are **Limones** (13 Eagle St., 828/252-2327, http://limonesrestaurant.com, 5pm-10pm daily, 10:30am-2:30pm Sun., $12-22) is one of the first places mentioned. Chef Hugo Ramírez, a native of Mexico City, combines his backgrounds in Mexican and French-inspired Californian food to create some dishes that are as flavorful as they are memorable. If you're trying to work your way through the menu of margaritas, tequilas, and mescals, though, your recollection of

what you ate may grow a little fuzzy. Next door you'll find ✪ **En La Calle** (15 Eagle St., 828/232-7012, www. enlacalleasheville.com, 5pm-11pm Mon.-Thurs., 5pm-midnight Fri.-Sat., 5pm-10pm Sun., $5-13) a Mexican/Latin tapas joint where they say their "sole purpose is to put a smile on that beautiful face of yours." Well, they do. Every. Time. It doesn't matter if you get the *sopa del día* (soup of the day), scallops with kimchi and chermoula, any of the ceviches, the lobster nachos, or the grilled street corn, you are in for an exceptional meal. And when you consider the atmosphere—loud, fun, vibrant—and the menu of awesome cocktails, it's an exceptional evening.

EUROPEAN

✪ **Cúrate** (13 Biltmore Ave., 828/239-2946, www.curatetapasbar. com, 11:30am-10:30pm Tues.-Thurs., 11:30am-11pm Fri., 10am-11pm Sat., 10:30am-10:30pm Sun., small plates $5-20) features the food of chef Katie Button, a James Beard Award semifinalist who cooked at legendary restaurant elBulli in Spain. She serves a Spanish tapas-style menu, so you'll get to try a variety of flavors and textures. The *table de jamón* (a selection of three delicious and very different Spanish hams) and the *pulpo a'la gallega* (octopus and paprika with potatoes) are good dishes to share. There are also a number of vegan and gluten-free selections on the menu. The can't-miss street dish that people rave about is the *berenjenas la taberna*—fried eggplant drizzled in wild mountain honey and garnished with rosemary. This dish is incredible and can even serve as a component to a dessert course if you like a savory-sweet combination. There's a lot of energy in this restaurant, partially because a long bar faces

CRAFT BREWS IN BEER CITY

Asheville is regarded as the epicenter of North Carolina's beer and culinary scenes, and it's well deserved. Asheville is packed with award winning restaurants and breweries. Winner of the title "Beer City USA" and perpetually at the top of any beer geek's list of cities to visit, Asheville's brewery scene is exemplary in terms of variety, innovation, and sheer volume.

- **Burial Beer Co.** (40 Collier Ave., 828/475-2739, www.burialbeer.com) makes intriguing brews with intriguing names. Their taproom, with it's indoor and outdoor spaces, excellent food truck, and funky mural, make it a great place to stop and enjoy one of their double IPAs.

- **Hi-Wire Brewing** (828/738-2448, www.hiwirebrewing.com) has a pair of locations, on the South Slope (197 Hilliard Ave.) and the Big Top (2 Huntsman Pl.). At the Big Top you'll find their flagship brews and a killer food truck, and on the South Slope you'll find experimental quaffs to try.

- **Zillicoah Beer Company** (870 Riverside Dr., Woodfin, 828/424-7929, www.zillicoahbeer.com) is new to the scene but coming strong with beer aged in French oak, collaboration brews with local breweries, and an exceptional kölsch.

- **One World Brewing** (10 Patton Ave., 828/785-5580, www.oneworldbrewing.com) sits tucked down an alley just off the main square in downtown Asheville, but don't miss their New World IPA, Queen of the Forest, or their Mosaic S.M.A.S.H., a dry-hopped gose.

- **Green Man Brewery** (23 Buxton Ave., 828.252-5502, www.greenmanbrewery.com) has lagers, fruity IPAs, even tart berlinerweisses, but their monster Rainmaker Double IPA is a hit, as are their barrel aged and sour beers like Bootsy and Snozzberry.

- **Catawba Brewing Co.** (32 Banks Ave., 828/552-3934, www.catawbabrewing.com) has a relaxing tap room with a bevvy of crushable beers on tap. Their White Zombie white ale, Drum Circle Haze double IPA, and Festbier lager are favorites.

- **New Belgium Brewing Company** (21 Craven St., 828/333-6900, www.newbelgium.com) is one of the biggest in the area, and their tour is exceptional. Most craft beer fans know Fat Tire and their other brews, but the taproom here carries specialties and barrel-aged beers not available elsewhere.

- **Sierra Nevada Brewery** (100 Sierra Nevada Way, Mills River, 828/681-5300, www.sierranevada.com) was described to me as "the Taj Mahal of Beer" and "like Willy Wonka's factory, but with beer," and it's mighty impressive. There's a good restaurant on site, a great tour, an impressive facility, and looooong tap list that goes beyond what you expect from Sierra Nevada.

- **Oskar Blues Brewery** (342 Mountain Industrial Dr., Brevard, 828/883-2337, www.oskarblues.com) is the East Coast outpost for this Colorado staple. Old Chub Scotch Ale, Mama's Little Yella Pils, and their Pinner IPA are made fresh here.

- **Highland Brewing Company** (12 Old Charlotte Hwy., Suite H, 828/299-3370, www.highlandbrewing.com) has the honor of being the first microbrewery in Asheville, and it's a fine one. They continue to keep their flagship brews relevant by tweaking the recipes, but they also continue to innovate, releasing an impressive set of single-hop brews.

the kitchen, putting everyone from chef Button to her expert kitchen brigade on display.

✪ Cucina 24 (24 Wall St., 828/254-6170, http://cucina24restaurant.com, 5:30pm-close Tues.-Fri., 5pm-close Sat.-Sun., $11-31) is, as executive chef Brian Canipelli says, "not a fettuccine alfredo and lasagna kind of place; we do cooking like it's done in Italy, but with North Carolina ingredients." I visit Cucina 24 on every trip to Asheville, and every time I'm smitten with what Canipelli does in his kitchen. The pizzas are creative, accessible, and just a bit decadent (I mean, who microplanes black truffles over pizza?); the pasta is always fresh and always elevated by an interesting ingredient like sunchokes, trumpet mushrooms, pork cheeks, or smoked mackerel broth; and the charcuterie is made in house.

In the River Arts District—a neighborhood that's cooler every time I swing through—Josiah and Shannon McGaughey found the perfect space to transition from their window-service kitchen at Burial Beer and open Vivian (348 Depot St., Ste. 190, 828/225-3497, www.vivianavl.com, 5pm-11pm Tues.-Sat., 10:30am-3pm Sun., dinner $12-45, brunch $6-16), a restaurant that blends European flavors and techniques with chef Josiah's Southern roots. Named for his grandmother, a woman who threw some fantastic, "Julia Child-like" dinner parties, the menu features tasty treats like sweet 'n' sour okra, ham and peaches, quenelles, smoked oysters, a phenomenal steak, duck, and a brunch that's, for me, just about perfect: French toast, duck confit salad, coddled egg, *poffertjes* (miniature pancakes) and a killer cocktail menu. Restaurants like this keep Asheville's food scene injected with excitement and a sense of culinary adventure, and I'm excited to see how far they can go here.

Vinnie's Neighborhood Italian (641 Merrimon Ave., 828/253-1077, www.vinniesitalian.com, 5pm-9:30pm Sun.-Thurs., 5pm-10:30pm Fri.-Sat., $11-26), is an Italian eatery they say is "reminiscent of Brooklyn, the Bronx and the North End of Boston." That means pasta, pizza, heroes, and calzones are offered in abundance, along with heartier veal and chicken dishes, lasagna, and eggplant parmigiana. It also means big portions that could feed a family, which is exactly what this style of Italian is all about.

SNACKS

French Broad Chocolates (10 S. Pack Square, 828/252-4181, http://frenchbroadchocolates.com, 11am-11pm Sun.-Thurs., 11am-midnight Fri.-Sat.) describes itself as "a sacred space for chocophiles," and with its prominent location in Pack Square, hordes of chocophiles are getting in line to find out why this particular chocolatier has been the talk of the town for a decade. French Broad offers chocolate truffles, brownies, pastries, sipping chocolates, floats, bars, beans, and a laundry list of chocolate products near as long as the line here on a Friday night (and trust me, it's long). This is a true "bean-to-bar" chocolatier, as they roast their own cacao in a rooftop solar roaster at their nearby factory (21 Buxton Ave., 828/504-4996, tours 11am Sat. by reservation only), and it's getting closer to being a "farm-to-bar" chocolatier, as the owners also happen to own a cacao farm in Costa Rica which they hope to harvest any season now.

The Gourmet Chip Company (43 1/2 Broadway St., 828/254-3335, www.

gourmetchipcompany.com, 11am-8pm Mon.-Sat., 11am-6pm Sun.) has made me love potato chips again. They make chips fresh all day (and have a huge stack of potato sacks to prove it) and top them with some lovely and intriguing ingredients: goat cheese and sea salt, dehydrated apple cider vinegar and a balsamic reduction, dark chocolate and applewood smoked bacon, buffalo sauce and bleu cheese, honey and lavender. Served up in a paper cone, they're attractive dishes that are fun to eat. The only downside is this: They're so good you'll want to eat them fast, and that means using both hands, which means you can't walk down the street gobbling these delicious chips. But you should sit over them for a while and savor them anyway.

ACCOMMODATIONS

HOTELS

For the longest time downtown Asheville had only a couple of hotels, with **Aloft Asheville Downtown** (51 Biltmore Ave., 828/232-2838 or 866/716-8143, www.aloftashevilledowntown.com, $188-534) being the hippest spot to rest your head. There is a trendy bar serving rock-star cocktails, plush modern guest rooms, and fantastic city and mountain views from most rooms (others are poolside). Some of the best restaurants in Asheville are a few minutes' walk away, and the best live music in town is just a couple of blocks south. As of 2018, that's changed and there are several hotels open or under construction downtown. **AC Hotel by Marriott Downtown Asheville** (10 Broadway St., 828/258-2522, www. marriott.com, from $340) is one of my favorites for the spacious rooms, generally excellent views, and a great

rooftop bar, **Capella on 9** (828/771-5156, 4pm-11pm Sun.-Mon., 4pm-midnight Tues.-Thurs., 2pm-1am Fri.-Sat., $6-16) On the roof you can get cocktails, wine and beer, and order from a tasty tapas menu—olives, charcuterie and cheese boards, *patatas bravas*, even pan-fried trout—while you take in the views.

If you've spent the day touring Biltmore House, viewing the incredible splendor in which a robber baron of the Gilded Age basked, it may be jarring to return to real life, unless you're Richard Branson or European royalty. You can soften the transition with a stay at the luxurious **Inn on Biltmore Estate** (866/336-1245, www.biltmore.com, from $629 peak season, from $269 off-season, suites up to $2,000). It's everything you'd wish for from a hotel in this location. The suites are beautifully furnished and luxurious, the views are magnificent, and the lobby, dining room, and library have the deluxe coziness of a turn-of-the-20th-century lodge. **Village Hotel on Biltmore Estate** (rooms from $400, packages from $550) in Antler Hill Village has 209 rooms and is a testament to the ongoing and growing popularity of the Biltmore.

RESORTS

The **Grove Park Inn Resort & Spa** (290 Macon Ave., 828/252-2711 or 800/438-5800, www.groveparkinn. com, $349-942 peak season, $177-755 off-season, spa and golf packages available) is the sort of place Asheville residents bring their out-of-town houseguests when giving them a grand tour of the city, simply to walk into the lobby to ooh and aah. The massive stone building—constructed by a crew of 400 who had only mule teams and a single steam shovel to aid them—was erected in 1912 and 1913, the project of St. Louis millionaire E. W. Grove, the name behind Grove's Tasteless Chill Tonic, a medicinal syrup that outsold Coca-Cola in the 1890s.

The opening of the Grove Park Inn was cause for such fanfare that William Jennings Bryan addressed the celebratory dinner party. In the coming years, at least eight U.S. presidents would stay here, as would a glittering parade of early-20th-century big shots, among them Henry Ford, Thomas Edison, Eleanor Roosevelt, Harry Houdini, F. Scott Fitzgerald, Will Rogers, and George Gershwin. Even if you don't stay at the Grove Park while you are visiting Asheville, swing by just to see it. You can drive right up to the front door, and if you tell the valets that you just want to go in and see the lobby, they'll probably be willing to watch your car for five minutes (a tip helps). The lobby is amazing, a cross between a Gilded Age hunting lodge and the great hall of a medieval castle. There are 14-foot fireplaces at each end, and the elevators, believe it or not, are inside the chimneys. It's easy to imagine flappers, foreign dignitaries, mobsters, and literati milling about the lobby with their martinis when this hotel was young. You can also park your car and head inside for a cocktail or dinner at one of their many on-site establishments. Each of their venues—**Vue 1913** (5:30pm-9:30pm nightly, $25-85) has French and American dishes that are well done but not particularly creative; **Edison Craft Ales + Kitchen** (4pm-11pm Mon.-Thurs., 4pm-midnight Fri., 11am-midnight Sat., 11am-11pm Sun., $8-28) serves some high-quality bar food and craft beer; **Blue Ridge** (6:30am-10:30am daily,

breakfast $17-25, brunch $40, dinner $44) is a farm-to-table artisanal buffet (yes, I too am confused as to how artisanal and buffet work together); and the **Sunset Terrace** (11am-3pm and 5pm-10pm daily, $15-24 lunch, $22-59 dinner) and **Sunset Cocktail Terrace** (11am-3pm and 5pm-10pm daily, lunch $15-32, dinner $24-85)—has phenomenal views. Whether it's dinner or a glass of wine you have while watching the sun set, it'll be a memorable experience.

Being a guest at the Grove Park is quite an experience. In addition to the spectacle of the lodge and its multiple restaurants, cafés, bars, and shops, for an additional charge guests have access to its world-famous spa ($90 daily). The pass gives access to the lounges, pools, waterfall, steam room, inhalation room, and outdoor whirlpool tub. The indoor pool is a fantastic place, a subterranean stone room with vaulted skylights and tropical plants. For extra fees ($120-540, most $200-300), guests can choose from a long menu of spa treatments: massages, facials, manicures, aromatherapy, and body wraps. For $70 you can have your aura photographed before and after the treatment to gauge the depth of your relaxation.

There's also an exceptional Donald Ross-designed **golf course** (828/252-2711 or 800/438-5800, reserve tee times online at www.groveparkinn.com, 18 holes, par 70, greens fees $70-125 Mon.-Thurs. and $85-140 Fri.-Sun. Apr. 1-Nov. 30, $77-87 Dec. 1-Mar. 31, rental clubs are $40/nine holes and $70/18 holes) here. The 6,400-yard course is where President Obama played when he stayed at the Grove Park Inn; one look around at the mountains and views from the elevated tee boxes and you know he was impressed.

BED-AND-BREAKFASTS

Just off the Blue Ridge Parkway north of Asheville is an inn that's a true retreat. The ✪ Sourwood Inn (810 Elk Mountain Scenic Hwy., Asheville, 828/255-0690, www.sourwoodinn. com, $155-195 for rooms in the inn, $190 for a separate cabin) charmed me so much the first time I saw it, I made reservations for an anniversary weekend. Situated on the end of a ridgeline, the inn offers a view of nearly 270 degrees from every bedroom window and balcony. Your cell phone won't work here, and there's no Wi-Fi (by design), so you can truly unplug. There are a couple of miles of easy hiking trails, a pond, a bamboo grove, and some sculptures tucked in the woods nearby, but if you're feeling adventurous, they have a couple of options. The innkeeper's son-in-law happens to be a fly-fishing guide and an active hawker—that means he hunts with a hawk named Rocket Girl; packages are available that will put you on the fish or put Rocket Girl on your arm. Other specials include a Blue Ridge Parkway package that includes fly-fishing, a massage, horseback riding, Biltmore Estate passes, and wild food foraging. Call for directions—it's tricky to find.

✪ ASIA Bed and Breakfast Spa (128 Hillside St., 828/255-0051, www. ashevillespa.com, $189-419) is one of my favorite places in town to stay. Every room has a big, comfortable bed and a two-person hot tub; there's a sauna and cold shower for guests to use, and a European steam shower, too; breakfast is a healthy, filling affair; and, most importantly, the rooms are private and quiet. ASIA keeps a group of massage therapists and estheticians on call, so you can arrange for treatments of almost any kind on

From the rocking chairs on the porch of the Sourwood Inn, you can watch the leaves change or just soak up the mountain air.

site. Throughout the house, comfortable seating areas make it easy to find a spot for breakfast or tea or just to read or talk; my favorite spot is the tatami porch overlooking the Japanese garden at the front of the house.

A truly lovely bed and breakfast here is **Sweet Biscuit Inn** (77 Kenilworth Rd., 828/250-0170, www.sweetbiscuitinn.com, $160-250). I have to admit, I was drawn here by the name, but the place, the host, the breakfast, all of it conspired to make me like it even more. The seven bedrooms and carriage house are accented by tiger oak wood floors and high ceilings. Beds are comfy (and all queens or kings) and breakfast is excellent, especially the biscuits.

The **Asheville Bed & Breakfast Association** (www.ashevillebba.com) has a constantly-growing membership of inns and B&Bs in the area, and they band together to promote getaways, tours, and seasonal packages, so check with them for any specials members may be running.

HOSTELS

With so many neo-hippie types, college kids, dirt bags (it's not an insult, it's what rock climbers often call themselves), kayakers, hikers, and bikers coming through, it's no surprise to find a nice hostel nestled in among the hotels and bed-and-breakfasts. At the **Asheville Hostel & Guest House** (16 Ravenscroft Dr., 828/423-0256, www.avlhostel.com, $65, bungalow with private bath $95) you'll find only private guest rooms and even a private bungalow. Reservations are available up to five months in advance, so it's easy to get a room if you know when you're traveling. At the hostel you'll find free waffles, coffee, and tea at make-your-own stations; free Wi-Fi;

free parking; and downtown within walking distance.

Bon Paul and Sharky's Hostel of Asheville (816 Haywood Rd., 828/775-3283, www.bonpaulandsharkys.com, cash only) is a pleasant old white house with a porch and a porch swing, high-speed internet access, and dorm-style bunks in women-only or coed shared rooms ($30-33) as well as camping ($21) in the yard. If you want a little more of a retreat, a private room with a TV and a queen bed ($72) and a cottage ($100) are available. Dogs ($12) must stay in the outdoor kennels. And Bon Paul and Sharky, because I know you were wondering, were goldfish.

MOTOR COURTS

In the days of yore, before budget hotels became the norm, the motor court or cottage court was the stay-over of choice for middle-class travelers. Today, these motor courts and cottage courts are relics of the past and few remain, but the mountains of North Carolina still contain a handful of fine examples; in the Asheville area at least two are still operating today, providing travelers with retro accommodations. **Asheville Log Cabin Motor Court** (330 Weaverville Hwy., 828/645-6546, www.cabinlodging.com, 2-night minimum stay weekends, $94-305, two pets allowed, $15/night one pet, $25/night 2 pets) was constructed around 1930 and appears in the fantastic 1958 Robert Mitchum movie *Thunder Road*. The cabins have cable TV and wireless internet access but no phones. Some are air-conditioned, but that's not usually a necessity at this elevation. Another great cabin court is the **Pines Cottages** (346 Weaverville Hwy., 828/645-9661, http://ashevillepines.

com, $103-204, $15 per pet, up to 2 pets allowed). Billed as "A nice place for nice people," how could you resist staying here?

INFORMATION AND SERVICES

The **Asheville Visitors Center** (36 Montford Ave., near I-240 exit 4C, 828/258-6129), can set you up with all the maps, brochures, and recommendations you could need. Other sources are **Explore Asheville** (www.exploreasheville.com) and the **Asheville Area Chamber of Commerce** (www.ashevillechamber.org). **Mission Hospital** (509 Biltmore Ave. 428 Biltmore Ave., 828/213-1111, www.missionhospitals.org) in Asheville has two campuses and two emergency departments.

Listen to public radio at **WCQS** (88.1 FM) and **WNCW** (88.7 FM); **WTMT** (105.9 FM) and **WOXL** (96.5 FM) are music stations.

As Asheville is the best gateway city when venturing into the Smoky Mountains, know you'll find some information on planning a trip to the Smokies at www.exploreasheville.com. Great Smoky Mountain National Park's website (www.nps.gov/gsmnp) has trip planning tools useful for day trips or overnight excursions into the park.

GETTING THERE AND AROUND

Asheville is spread around the junction of I-40, North Carolina's primary east-west highway, and I-26, a roughly north-south artery through the Southern highlands. U.S. 19 runs at a diagonal, deep into the Smokies in one direction and into the northern Blue Ridge in the other. Asheville has an extensive public bus system called **ART** (www.ashevillenc.gov, 6am-11:30pm Mon.-Sat., $1, $0.50 seniors), connecting most major points in the metropolitan area, including the airport, with downtown. See the website for routes and schedules. **Asheville Regional Airport** (AVL, 61 Terminal Dr., 828/684-2226, www.flyavl.com) is a 20-minute drive on I-26 south of the city in Fletcher. Several airlines have flights to Atlanta, Charlotte, and other U.S. cities.

From Asheville it's easy to get to Great Smoky Mountains National Park (GSMNP). In just over an hour you can be in Cataloochee, at the north end of the park, to camp, hike, and watch for elk in a serene mountain cove; to get there, take I-40 west to exit 20 and follow the signs. You can also take I-40 west into Tennessee, follow the Foothills Parkway to U.S. 321, and skirt the edge of GSMNP to Gatlinburg, Tennessee, and the entrance to the park (a trip of about 90 minutes). From Gatlinburg, you can make a loop back to Asheville by taking Newfound Gap Road across GSMNP to Cherokee, North Carolina (about 2.5 hours), and then back to Asheville via U.S. 441 to U.S. 19 to I-40, a total loop of about 3.5 hours and some 175 miles.

You can also head straight to Cherokee from Asheville and enter GSMNP via Newfound Gap Road there. It's an hour drive following I-40 west to exit 27, then taking U.S. 19 south to U.S. 441, which carries you right into Cherokee. Alternately you can take the more scenic, but much longer, route and get to Cherokee via the Blue Ridge Parkway. This route is only 83 miles, but it takes 2-2.5 hours. If you want to go this way, head south out of Asheville along U.S. 25 and pick up the Blue Ridge Parkway about

5.5 miles out of town; turn south on the Parkway and drive until you reach Cherokee and GSMNP. And, of course, you can reverse the course if you're making that grand loop and return to Asheville via the Blue Ridge Parkway by picking it up in Cherokee and driving north.

Around Asheville

Throughout the mountains around Asheville you'll come across towns official and unincorporated, some collections of houses at a wide spot on a mountain road, others established towns with deep histories and more than a little creative juice flowing in their collective blood. Whatever the reason for visiting, these towns have personalities, histories, cultures, and environments distinct enough to allow the truly curious to discover a small town (or two) full of surprises.

BLACK MOUNTAIN

Named for a onetime train depot, the town of Black Mountain sits 15 miles west of Asheville and is one of several bedroom communities serving the city. At one time, Black Mountain's claim to fame was the experimental Black Mountain College and its intellectual and artistic legacy. The school is long gone, and the Black Mountain College Museum and Arts Center is located in Asheville, but some of the artistic residue is still around in the form of the Lake Eden Arts Festival, or LEAF, which takes place on the former college campus.

SIGHTS

Step into the **Swannanoa Valley Museum** (223 W. State St., 828/669-9566, www.swannanoavalleymuseum. org, 10am-5pm Tues.-Sat. Apr.-Oct., $5) to learn about the history of this area, including settlement by the Cherokee people, early industrialization, and the shutdown of the Beacon Blanket Factory. The museum offers something a little different: hikes, and not just short ones. The **Swannanoa Rim Explorer Series** (hikes $30/members, $50/nonmembers, series of 11 hikes $280/members, $500/nonmembers) and **Valley History Explorer Hiking Series** (hikes $20/members, $30/nonmembers, or purchase the seven-hike package from $175) take museum members and guests on a series of hikes that reveal the history, geography, and rugged beauty of the Swannanoa Valley. Some of these hikes are difficult—steep, long, exposed in places—and others are geared toward beginners; check with the museum to register and for questions on difficulty and schedules.

The **Black Mountain Center for the Arts** (225 W. State St., 828/669-0930, http://blackmountainarts.org, 10am-5pm Mon.-Fri.) is a gallery and performance space in the heart of town. Once the town hall, the Center for the Arts now houses art classes and summer camps for kids and adults, workshops and talks, performances (of all sorts: concerts, dance, poetry, storytelling, live theater), and gallery openings.

SHOPPING

Black Mountain Books (103 Cherry St., 828/669-8149, 11am-5pm Tues.-Sat., 1pm-4pm Sun.) specializes in rare and out-of-print titles and is a great place to find unusual volumes on North Carolina, Black Mountain College, the Southern Appalachians, and even 18th- and 19th-century England and Scotland.

There are several galleries in Black Mountain, so you'll have your choice of where to browse and where to buy. Stop in at **Mountain Nest** (133 Cherry St., 828/669-0314, www.mtnnest.com, 10am-6pm Mon.-Sat., 11am-5pm Sun.), a galler of art and handcrafted pieces; you'll find work from many North Carolinians for sale here, as well as pieces from fine artists from around the world. Styles and skill levels vary from artist to artist, but there's solid and reasonably priced work. **Seven Sisters Craft Gallery** (117 Cherry St., 828/669-5107, www.sevensistersgallery.com, 10am-6pm Mon.-Sat., noon-5pm Sun.) has been around for more than 30 years and carries large-scale photos, oil paintings by local and regional artists, and other art in a host of styles, media, and price points.

ENTERTAINMENT AND EVENTS

In May and October, Black Mountain is the scene of the **Lake Eden Arts Festival** (377 Lake Eden Rd., 828/686-8742, www.theleaf.org), better known as LEAF. Based around roots music, LEAF is also a festival of visual arts, poetry, food, and even the healing arts. It's an amazing scene, and it takes place, appropriately, at Camp Rockmont, once the campus of Black Mountain College, the short-lived but historically important avant-garde institution that was home to a number of influential American artists and writers.

Nightlife

Pisgah Brewing Company (150 Eastside Dr., 828/669-0190, www.pisgahbrewing.com, 4pm-9pm Mon.-Wed., 2pm-11pm Thurs.-Fri., noon-11pm Sat, 1pm-10pm Sun., open late for concerts, cash only) is both a brewpub and a music venue, featuring an eclectic mix of bands from roots music to rock. Pisgah was the Southeast's first certified organic brewery, and several beers are on tap all year, including their pale ale, porter, and stout; a long list of seasonal brews rotates through the year, and a growing list of specialty brews, like their sour brown ale, is gaining a loyal following. Tour the brewery at 2pm or 3pm on Saturday, but stop in a try a beer anytime they're open.

Black Mountain Ciderworks (104 Eastside Dr. #307, 828/419-0089, www.blackmountainciderworks.com, 2pm-8pm Mon. and Wed.-Thurs., 1pm-9pm Fri.-Sat., 1pm-8pm Sun.) is one of several spots across the state making cider and one of only a select few to make mead (that's a fermented honey beverage that should make you think of Vikings and Beowulf). Their ciders aren't cloyingly sweet or closer to carbonated apple juice than an alcoholic beverage; rather, they're on the dry side and tend to be complex in flavor. At any time they're pouring a half-dozen of their ciders and meads, and many are blended to make some interesting concoctions. In summer, they'll throw basil into a mix of mead and cider, or blend apple cider and cherry mead, or try something completely different by adding blueberry and cardamom, fresh ginger, lavender, quince, or rose.

Golf

Black Mountain Golf Club (17 Ross Dr., 828/669-2710, www.blackmountaingolf.org, 18 holes, par 71, greens fees $20-24 walking, $27-40 with cart) is something of a legend. Not because Donald Ross designed the front nine or because the Black Mountains surrounding the course make for a breathtaking round, but because it's the home of one of the longest holes in the world. In fact, that hole was once the longest in the world. The par-6 (yes, par-6) 17th hole measures in at an unbelievable 747 yards; a friend of mine said of the hole, "don't bother bringing your short game."

FOOD

Berliner Kindl German Restaurant (121 Broadway Ave., 828/669-5255, http://berlinerkindl.homestead.com, 11am-8pm Mon.-Sat., 11:30am-3pm Sun., $9-28) serves traditional German food like schnitzel, a variety of sausages, and the sides you'd expect: fried potatoes, German potato salad, sauerkraut, and red cabbage. They make their own sauerkraut in house.

Stop in at Dripolator Coffeehouse (221 W. State St., 828/699-0999, 7am-9pm daily, $2-6) for coffee, pastries and the like. This cute little shop keeps winning "Best of WNC" (Western North Carolina) from *Mountain Xpress* (a free magazine found nearby), and folks keep coming, not because of the awards, but for the best coffee in the North Carolina mountains.

When you're ready for dinner, try Black Mountain Bistro (203 E. State Rd., 828/669-5041, www.blackmountainbistro.com, 11am-9pm Mon.-Thurs., 11am-9:30pm Fri.-Sat., $9-27). This spot has a great couple of steaks on the menu, but the pork chop with blackberry barbecue sauce is quite tempting. The fish-and-chips is made with grouper, making for a hearty bite.

ACCOMMODATIONS

The Inn around the Corner (109 Church St., 828/669-6005, www.innaroundthecorner.com, $155-245) is a classic bed-and-breakfast in a lovely 1915 home with a huge front porch. Just about every room has a great view, but the best is from the porch bed, where you'll fall asleep under the gaze of the mountains and wake when the birds start their day.

Arbor House of Black Mountain (207 Rhododendron Ave., 828/357-8525, www.arborhousenc.com, $120-230), a four-room bed-and-breakfast, hosts travelers year-round, but like at most places in the area, peak season coincides with the turning of the leaves every fall. Views from the inn are wide and beautiful, especially when the leaves are out, but book early for leaf season.

INFORMATION AND SERVICES

The Black Mountain and Swannanoa Chamber of Commerce (www.blackmountain.org) maintains a list of member businesses and has a small bit of visitor information on its site, but the best visitor information for Black Mountain is going to be at www.ExploreAsheville.com.

GETTING THERE AND AROUND

On I-40, take exit 70 or exit 64 to get to Black Mountain. From Asheville, Black Mountain is about 15 minutes east.

WEAVERVILLE

Weaverville, just 10 minutes north of Asheville, served as a vacation town for wealthy city and Piedmont dwellers in the late 1800s, though it had been settled by a handful of families since the 1780s. At one time, a pair of grand hotels—the Dula Springs Hotel and Blackberry Lodge—welcomed well-heeled and notable visitors like author O. Henry when they escaped to the mountains. The town never grew to be much more than a bucolic getaway, and today, with a population hovering around 2,500, Weaverville holds onto its former identity even as it grows into a bedroom community for Asheville. The Weaverville Business Association maintains www.visitweaverville.com, which lists all of the town's amenities.

SIGHTS

At the **Dry Ridge Museum** (41 N. Main St., 828/250-6482, 10am-2pm Sat., free) you'll find a collection of artifacts, letters, and photos telling the history of Weaverville. It's small and has odd hours but may be of interest to local history buffs.

A few miles down the road is the birthplace of North Carolina's Civil War governor, Zebulon T. Vance (if ever there was a Civil War governor's name, that's it). The **Vance Birthplace** (911 Reems Creek Rd., 828/645-6706, www.nchistoricsites.org, 9am-5pm Tues.-Sat.) has a reconstructed log house as well as a tool house, smokehouse, spring house, slave cabin, and a few more recreated structures. Tours of the home are available at the bottom of the hour.

RECREATION

Curtis Wright Outfitters (24 N. Main St., 828/645-8700, www.curtiswrightoutfitters.com, 9am-6pm Mon.-Sat.) keeps a store stocked with fly-fishing gear, clothing, tackle, and supplies. They offer a range of guided fishing trips ($200/half day wading, $300/full day wading, $350/half day float trip) on area streams and rivers. You can also grouse hunt (grouse are similar to pheasant) for a half day ($295) or full day ($395), or take part in one of their fly fishing schools ($175) or classes ($75) to hone your technique or learn to tie flies.

SHOPPING

There are a lot of great potters in western North Carolina, but Rob and Beth Mangum of **Mangum Pottery** (16 N. Main St., 828/645-4929, www.mangumpottery.com, 9am-5pm Mon.-Fri., 10am-4pm Sat.) are two of the most innovative. They make beautiful earthy-colored dinnerware and mugs to satisfy the practical side of life, and they also build the most unexpected things out of pottery—ceramic clocks, ceramic furniture, ceramic musical instruments that really play—all in Seussian shapes and colors.

Maggie B's Wine & Specialty Store (10-C S. Main St., 828/645-1111, www.maggiebswine.com, 10am-6:30pm Mon.-Wed., 10am-8pm Thurs.-Sat.) is Weaverville's first wine and specialty food shop opened by a husband and wife who know what tastes good. Maggie B's has an excellent selection of wine and beer and an assortment of meats, cheeses, and snacks to make for a perfect picnic. If you're here and you're hungry, they do have a menu of sandwiches and salads ($5-11) and they sell wine and beer by the glass.

The artwork at **MIYA Gallery** (20 N. Main St., 828/658-9655, www.miyagallery.com, 10am-5pm Mon.-Sat.) includes fine art, jewelry, furniture, and sculpture. More than 90 area artists and craftspeople have their work on display here. Pick something up, or just admire the leather books, exquisite and experimental wooden vessels, and fine photo prints of mountain scenes.

FOOD

A few doors down from Mangum Pottery you'll find **Well-Bred Bakery & Café** (26 N. Main St., 828/645-9300, www.wellbredbakery.com, 7:30am-7pm Mon.-Thurs., 7:30am-9pm Fri., 8am-9pm Sat., 8am-7pm Sun.), which sells soups, sandwiches, quiche, and salads, as well as a dazzling array of artisanal breads and elaborate desserts. They promise "karma-free coffee" (I think that means fair-trade), and even sell the *New York Times,* so you don't have to go into crossword-puzzle withdrawal on your trip.

If you're in Weaverville and you have a hankering for pizza, **Blue Mountain Pizza and Brew Pub** (55 N. Main St., 828/658-8778, www.bluemountainpizza.com, 11am-9pm Tues.-Thurs. and Sun., 11am-10pm Fri.-Sat., $7-25) is your spot. The building dates to the 1820s and now houses a two-barrel brewing system, meaning the brewmasters get to experiment a lot; they've had a positive reception. Blue Mountain Pizza serves specialty pizzas, calzones, stromboli, subs, and salads. Their Henny Penny Pizza is a barbecued chicken pizza with red onion and bacon, and the Marge is simply olive oil, Roma tomatoes, fresh mozzarella, and basil.

Also in Weaverville, **Glass Onion** (18 N. Main St., 828/645-8866, www.glassonionasheville.com, 11:30am-3pm and 5pm-9pm daily, brunch 11:30am-3pm Sun., lunch $6-15,

dinner $8-27, brunch $11-14) is a strong dining option. For lunch, the eggplant stack is delicious, but the sesame Scottish salmon burger is a killer. At dinner, do yourself a favor and go for the wild boar Bolognese, where the sauce is a great use for this rich pork. Brunch is all about eggs (unless you want French toast), and I think the smoked trout Benedict is remarkable.

ACCOMMODATIONS

Dry Ridge Inn Bed and Breakfast (26 Brown St., 828/658-3899, www.dryridgeinn.com, $149-189) has eight guest rooms in a former parsonage built in 1849. Rooms feature king or queen beds, a gas fireplace, and reliable Wi-Fi. And there's a fridge stocked with complimentary beverages on the main floor. Breakfast is served either in the dining room or on the patio. Weather permitting, have breakfast outside and feel that fresh mountain air that made this town a vacation spot for generations.

The **Inn on Main Street Bed and Breakfast** (88 S. Main St., 828/645-4935 or 877/873-6074, www.innonmain.com, $119-219) offers an eco-friendly place to rest your head. They use no cleaning chemicals or deodorizers in the Inn, all bath products are natural, and they cook their vegetarian meals using as many organic ingredients as possible. There are five rooms in the main house and a pair in a separate cottage; the rooms are comfortable and homey without being too saccharine (as many B&Bs are wont to do).

INFORMATION AND SERVICES

The Weaverville Business Association provides visitor information at www.

VisitWeaverville.com. You can also find visitor information at www. ExploreAsheville.com.

GETTING THERE
Weaverville is just 10 minutes north of Asheville along a very easy drive. Simply follow U.S. 70W/U.S. 19 N/U.S. 23 N, then turn right on Weaver Blvd.

MADISON COUNTY
North of Asheville, Madison County is a world unto itself. Just 30 minutes north of Asheville, the wild mountain terrain is spotted with hot springs and towns no bigger than ink blots on a map, but still this county, which shares a border with an equally wild corner of Tennessee, draws visitors. Some come for the solitude, others the hot springs, others the rafting and to explore the great outdoors; still others come for the music. As is true all along the Appalachian Range and especially in the Blue Ridge Mountains, music plays an important role in the identity of the place. In most towns you'll find a stage, porch, coffee shop, or gas station where bluegrass musicians will gather to play, carrying on the long-held traditions of the people here.

SPORTS AND RECREATION
On a 4,700-foot mountaintop above Mars Hill, the **Wolf Ridge Ski Resort** (578 Valley View Circle, 800/817-4111, www.skiwolfridgenc. com, 9am-10pm Mon.-Sat., slopes closed 4:30pm-6pm daily, Dec.-Mar., $26-78 adults, $21-62 students and ages 5-18, free under age 4, rentals $24-34) has more than 80 acres of prime skiing and snowboarding slopes. It is also the home of the Snow Sports School, which offers private and group lessons for all ages of beginning and intermediate winter

sports enthusiasts. There are multiple lifts, two lodges to relax in, and multiple hearty dining options. The attached **Scenic Wolf Resort** offers year-round cabin accommodations ($300-550 in season), a huge indoor heated pool, and numerous recreational activities.

Sandy Bottom Trail Rides (1459 Caney Fork Rd., Marshall, 828/649-3464 or 800/959-3513, www. sandybottomtrailrides.net, 8am-5pm daily, 1 hour $39, 2 hours $69, 3 hours $89), based at a 100-year-old family farm, leads horseback treks deep into the forest to an early-19th-century garnet mine. They'll also carry you in style in a horse-drawn buggy, if you prefer.

There are plenty of white-water rafting opportunities in the area, with several guide companies to choose from. **Hot Springs Rafting Co.** (181 Bridge St., 843/319-4586, www.hotspringsraftingco.com, rafting $40-65, funyak $30-35/day, river tubing float trips $20) keeps you on the river right around Hot Springs. Their guided rafting trips are quite the thrill, but the unguided trips and funyaks (think white-water raft meets inflatable kayak) can give you a satisfying day on the water. **French Broad Rafting and Ziplines** (U.S. 25/70, Marshall, 800/570-7238, www. frenchbroadrafting.com, white-water rafting $53-80, flat-water rafting $32-48, zip lining $89, canyoneering $199) can get you equipped and ready for a guided or unguided rafting trip on the French Broad River, which has both white-water and calm sections. Or get your adrenaline rush in the trees on a course that mixes zip lines, rappels, and short hikes to make a unique mountain experience.

ENTERTAINMENT AND EVENTS

Mars Hill, a tiny college town, is a center of mountain culture thanks to Mars Hill College. The Bascom Lamar Lunsford "Minstrel of the Appalachians" Festival (early fall, 828/689-1115, www.blueridgemusicnc.com.com, free) is a nearly 50-year-old annual gathering of some of the best mountain musicians, dancers, and craftspeople from this hotbed of folk traditions. Mars Hill College is also the home of the Southern Appalachian Repertory Theatre (Owen Theater, 44 College St., 828/689-1239, http://sartplays.org), a highly regarded ensemble presenting a range of contemporary drama, musicals, and family productions. SART's stage is in the Owen Theater, a great-looking old Baptist Church on the Mars Hill College campus.

Many other venues in Madison County towns feature live bluegrass and old time music. Zuma Coffee (7 N. Main St., Marshall, 828/649-1617, www.zumascoffee.com, 7am-6pm Mon.-Tues. and Fri., 7am-9pm Wed.-Thurs., 9am-4pm Sat., under $10) has a free bluegrass jam session every Thursday starting at 7pm and serves up a good cup of coffee. The Depot (282 S. Main St., Marshall, 828/206-2332), a former railroad depot building, has free concerts every Friday starting at 6:30pm. And the Madison County Arts Council (152 N. Main St., Marshall, 828/649-1301, www.madisoncountyarts.com) wouldn't be worth their salt if they didn't host a few concerts, but lucky for you, they have plenty. The Arts Council puts on shows at their headquarters on Main Street and at the Ebbs Chapel Performing Arts Center (271 Laurel Valley Rd., Mars Hill, 828/689-3465, www.ebbschapelauditorium.com); check the schedule for shows, times, and prices.

FOOD

The Smoky Mountain Diner (70 Lance Ave., Hot Springs, 828/622-7571, www.hotspringsnc.org, 6am-8pm Mon.-Wed., 6am-9pm Thurs.-Sat., closed Sun., breakfast $1-15, lunch and dinner $5-17) is one part diner, one part your granny's kitchen table. Country staples like cornbread, pinto beans, chicken livers, and pork chops are on the menu, as are biscuits, pancakes, French toast, omelets, and even pizza. If you're so inclined, they have all-you-can-eat pinto beans for $5.

There's bar food available at Iron Horse Station (24 S. Andrew Ave., Hot Springs, 828/622-0022, www.theironhorsestation.com, 11:30am-9pm Sun.-Thurs., 11:30am-10pm Fri.-Sat., lunch under $12, dinner $7-23), but it's not exactly the bar food you'd expect. Sure, there are onion rings and fried green tomatoes, but also a tofu napoleon, penne pasta (which you can get with blackened tofu), and fresh rainbow trout. You can stay here, too ($75-160), in one of four rooms, each named after a different type of Pullman car from the heyday of railroads.

When you head over to Dave's 209 (13075 Hwy. 209, Hot Springs, 828/622-0001, www.daves209.com, 11:30am-7:30pm Tues.-Fri., 7am-7pm Sat., 11:30am-5pm Sun., $2-11.50), be ready for a cravable burger and a milkshake you'll adore. This motorcycle-friendly spot is frequented by visitors on two wheels, four wheels and more, and it's because of those burgers and the secret seasoning—Mountain Dust—they put on their fries. One taste and you'll get it.

ACCOMMODATIONS

Defying that worn-out stereotype of mountain isolation, Madison County has for centuries been a destination for vacationers because of its natural hot springs. Going back at least to the mid-18th century—and, according to tradition, long before the first European settlers arrived—the springs have had a reputation for curative powers. A succession of grand hotels operated at Hot Springs, all long since burned down. In one of the area's odder historical moments, the resort served as an internment camp for German prisoners during World War I, mainly commercial sailors and members of an orchestra who had the misfortune of being in the United States when the war broke out.

Modern visitors can still take a dip in the mineral springs. Hot Springs Resort and Spa (U.S. 25/70, at the entrance to the town of Hot Springs, 828/622-7676, www.nchotsprings. com, suites $109-225, cabins $60-180, camping $30-65) is a much simpler affair than the old hotels; it's not a luxury destination but a place where you can lodge or camp for the night and soak in the famous 100°F water. Spa services run $50-130, and there's a series of outdoor mineral baths. Baths are open Mon.-Thurs. from noon-10pm and Fri.-Sun. 10am-midnight and range in price from $20/person to $60 for The Bath House; come early as rates increase after 6pm.

The Mountain Magnolia Inn (204 Lawson St., Hot Springs, 828/622-3543 or 800/914-9306, www.mountainmagnoliainn.com, $100-275) provides lodging in an ornate 1868 home and in nearby creek-side cabins. The inn's dining room is a nice gourmet restaurant (breakfast for guests daily, dinner for guests and non-guests 5:30pm-9pm Thurs.-Mon., $8-34) that features locally raised organic produce, meats, cheeses, and wines.

Appalachian Trail hikers, and those who like to play hard and live cheap, should take notice of Laughing Heart Lodge (289 NW Hwy. 25/70, Hot Springs, 828/622-0165, www. laughingheartlodge.com). Here you'll find several types of accommodations. First, the hostel ($15 bunk room, $30 single private room, $45 double private room), which was built in 1974 but still offers a modicum of comfort and privacy; then, the lodge ($100-140), which has seven rooms, each with a private bath, and the cabin ($125-150).

INFORMATION AND SERVICES

You'll find visitor information through the Madison County Tourism Administration at www. visitmadisoncounty.com. This site covers all the towns in the county and is therefore comprehensive. If you'd like to get more specific, try www.hotspringsnc.org from the Hot Springs Tourism Association for details on the town of Hot Springs and www.townofmarshall.org, for information that's more municipal than touristy on the town of Marshall. Mars Hill's website—www.townof-marshill.org—is also geared more toward municipal information than tourist interests, but there is some that visitors may find of interest.

GETTING THERE

To get to Madison County and the towns of Marshall and Hot Springs, you'll want to head north out of Asheville along U.S. 25/U.S. 70. Take exit 19A for Weaverville/Woodfin, but continue on U.S. 25/U.S. 70. You'll reach Marshall first, a 20-mile drive from Asheville; Hot Springs is another 16 miles north. Mars Hill is a 20-minute drive north from Asheville via U.S. 23/U.S. 19. Simply follow U.S. 25/U.S. 70 out of Asheville and stay on this route past Weaverville, where it will turn into U.S. 23/U.S. 19; take exit 11 onto N.C. 213 to get to Mars Hill.

Southern Blue Ridge and Foothills

The mountains of Polk, Rutherford, and Henderson Counties, south of Asheville, have an air of enchantment to them—meaning that the area gives the impalpable sense of having had a spell cast on it. No doubt a parapsychologist could assign a name to this atmosphere; it has a weird energy where it seems as likely that you'll encounter a fairy or an alien as a postal worker. There are some quantifiable symptoms of this peculiarity. For one, Polk County has its own climate; called the Thermal Belt, the meteorological pocket formed on this sheltered slope of the Blue Ridge has distinctly milder summers and winters than the surrounding areas. In the 19th century it became a favorite summering spot for the Southern elite. Some old houses and inns remain as vestiges of this genteel past.

In early 1874, Bald Mountain, north of Chimney Rock, began to rumble; it grew louder until, by the spring of that year, the mountain shook with such force that windows and crockery in valley homes shattered. A smoking, hissing crack opened in the side of the mountain, causing residents to fear a volcanic eruption. Many moved away or found religion. The shaking and rumbling eventually settled down. A crew of spelunkers a generation later concluded that the mountain was hollow and that enormous boulders sometimes became dislodged inside, showering into the caves below and causing the enormous booms. At least that's one theory.

Chimney Rock itself was the scene of bizarre phenomena in the first decade of the 1800s. Locals and visitors began to report witnessing spectral gatherings, crowds of people gathered on top of the rock and rising together into the sky. In the fall of 1811 multiple witnesses saw, on different occasions, two armed cavalries mounted on winged horses battling in the air over Chimney Rock, their gleaming swords clashing audibly. Whichever phantom cavalry triumphed in that battle, the rock is now maintained by the state of North Carolina and climbed daily by hundreds of visitors, none of whom have reported sightings of any spectral cavalry, horse droppings, or flashing sabers.

BREVARD

Brevard is the pleasant seat of the improbably named Transylvania County (unlike in vampire stories, it's not creepy, but beautiful in a Gothic forest way) only 48 minutes southwest of Asheville. As you might expect, Halloween is a big deal in this town.

Brevard is also known for sheltering a population of rather startling and odd-looking white squirrels. The local legend about their origins is that their ancestors escaped from an overturned circus truck in Florida in 1940 and made their way to Brevard as pets. More likely, say researchers, they came from an exotic pet breeder in Florida and were acquired by a Brevard area family. In any case, the white squirrels escaped into the wild of Transylvania County, and you'll probably see their descendants in the area when you visit.

SPORTS AND RECREATION

About 10 miles south of Brevard, **Dupont State Forest** (U.S. 276, 828/877-6527, www.dupontforest. com) has more than 90 miles of hiking trails covering 10,000 acres. Some of Transylvania County's beautiful waterfalls are located within the forest and accessible on foot via moderate or strenuous forest trails or, with special permits and advance reservation for people with disabilities only, by vehicle. Visitors should use caution, wear brightly colored clothing, and leave that bearskin cape at home from September through December, when hikers share the woods with hunters.

Many of the hiking and mountain biking trails are true rugged forest paths; others, like those that lead to a trio of waterfalls—Hooker, Triple, and High Falls—are wide, maintained avenues through the woods. I do recommend hiking to Triple and High Falls; in spring and summer it can be a hot, sweaty affair, so bring water, but the views are more than worth it. After you make this longer hike, make the shorter one to the lower Hooker Falls and go for a swim in the crisp mountain water. Already

one of Brevard's famous white squirrels

cool, it will feel downright cold—and quite refreshing—on a hot day.

ENTERTAINMENT AND EVENTS

The Brevard Music Center (349 Andante Lane, 828/862-2100, www.brevardmusic.org) has attracted the highest-caliber young musicians for more than 70 years for intensive summer-long classical music instruction. Throughout the summer, Brevard Music Center students, as well as visiting soloists of international fame, put on world-class concerts, performing works from Tchaikovsky to Gilbert and Sullivan.

SHOPPING

A center for a very different sort of music is Southern Comfort Records (16 W. Main St., 828/884-3575, www.celestialmtnmusic.com, 10am-5:30pm Mon.-Fri., 10am-4pm Sat.). Among more usual musical items, this nice little shop carries two lines of locally made instruments. Cedar Mountain Banjos, of the open-backed, old-time variety, are beautifully crafted and ring clear and pretty. The work of local fiddle builder Lyle Reedy is also sold at Celestial Mountain Music. His fiddles are handmade of a variety of fine woods and have a deep, biting sound. Musicians and woodworkers alike will enjoy a stop at this Main Street shop.

The White Squirrel Shoppe (2 W. Main St, 828/877-3530, www.whitesquirrelshoppe.com, 10:30am-5:30pm Mon.-Thurs., 10am-6pm Fri.-Sat., 11:30am-5pm Sun.) is one of those quaint souvenir emporiums that has a bit of everything. Need a candle that smells like cookies? They got it. Want some hand towels embroidered with Brevard's legendary white squirrel? Got those, too. The shop is charming,

and the owners are nice; it's the kind of place where I buy a little something for my mom or mother-in-law when I'm in town.

At O.P. Taylor's (16 S. Broad St., 828/883-2309, www.optaylors.com, 10am-6pm Mon.-Thurs., 10am-9pm Fri.-Sat., noon-5pm Sun.) you'll find a toy shop loaded with Lego and Playmobil toys, board and card games for the family, gags and gifts, and playthings old fashioned and newfangled. This is a fun shop, especially if you're traveling with or bringing back a gift for kids.

Brevard is also home to a number of artists. If you're here for a quick bite and then it's back to the Parkway, take the time to stick your head in Number 7 Fine Arts and Crafts Cooperative (2 W. Main St., 828/883-2294, www.number7arts.org, 10am-6pm daily). This gallery has featured works by a diverse group of around 25 Transylvania County artists for more than 15 years. Many of the works are inspired by and created in the midst of the phenomenal nature here.

FOOD

One of the top restaurants in Brevard is ✪ The Square Root (33 Times Arcade Alley, 828/884-6171, www.squarerootrestaurant.com, 11am-9pm Sun.-Mon. and Wed.-Thurs., 11am-10pm Fri.-Sat., $6-25). Inside, the exposed brick walls create a warm room where the food is more like delicious art. Something as simple as a burger and onion rings comes out as a tower of food, and fine dinner entrées, like the five-spice tuna or the filet mignon, are almost too pretty to eat. Almost.

The Falls Landing Eatery (18 E. Main St., 828/884-2835, www.thefallslanding.com, 11:30am-3pm Mon.-Sat., 5pm-9pn Tues.-Sat., lunch

$7-14, dinner $9-29) is a spot popular among locals. They specialize in seafood (foreshadowed by the rainbow trout on their sign), and their North Carolina trout sautéed in lemon butter and bourbon is particularly good. Don't discount their burgers, steaks, or lamb chops, though, because they deliver on flavor and value.

There's something soothing about getting a burger at a spot like **Cardinal Drive-In** (344 S. Broad St., 828/884-7085, 10:00am-10pm Sun.-Thurs., 10:30am-11pm Fri.-Sat., $3-10). Maybe it's the quaintness of the drive-in, from ordering through the little speakers to someone bringing a tray of food to your car, but it's special. As are the burgers here. And the onion rings. Yeah, it looks a little rough, but that's part of the charm—well, that and the milkshakes.

For a quick bite or a shake, malt, or ice cream soda, check out **Rocky's Grill & Soda Shop** (50 S. Broad St., 828/877-5375, www.ddbullwinkels. com, 10am-6pm Mon.- Sat., 11am-6pm Sun.). This place has been around since 1942, and the nostalgic counter with its line of chrome stools takes you back to the heyday of this soda fountain. You can grab lunch for around $8, and for $5 or less you can get a malt, milkshake, ice cream soda, root beer float, or even egg cream (try one if you've never had one). It's a must stop, especially as a reward after a morning hike or bike ride. Attached is D. D. Bullwinkel's, a shop specializing in outdoor gear and cool touristy T-shirts.

There are four breweries in Brevard as of the writing of this book. One of the most popular is **Oskar Blues Brewery** (342 Mountain Industrial Dr., 828/883-2337, www.oskarblues. com, noon-9pm Mon.-Thurs.,

noon-10pm Fri.-Sat., noon-8pm Sun.), a brewery born in Colorado that chose Brevard as the home of their East Coast brewery because of the small-town vibe, proximity to awesome mountain biking, and ease of distribution from here. Tour the brewery any day of the week (4pm Mon.-Thurs., hourly 2pm-5pm Fri.-Sun.) and grab a taste of one of their brews; my friends are partial to their Pinner Throwback IPA and Mama's Little Yella Pils (a pilsner), but I prefer the Old Chub Scotch Ale.

Brevard Brewing Company (63 E. Main St., 828/885-2101, www.brevard-brewing.com, 2pm-11pm Mon.-Thurs., noon-midnight Fri.-Sat., 2pm-10-pm Sun.) specializes in German-style lagers and pilsners, though they also brew IPAs, dunkels, and some seasonal specialties. The tap room is wide open and friendly; they don't serve food, but you're welcome to bring some in from elsewhere.

PISGAH RANGER DISTRICT

Just north of Brevard in the town of Pisgah Forest is the main entrance to the **Pisgah Ranger District** (U.S. 276, Pisgah Forest, 828/877-3265, www. fs.usda.gov, 8am-5pm daily mid-Apr.-mid-Nov., 8am-4:30pm daily mid-Nov.-mid-Apr.) of the Pisgah National Forest. The forest covers 500,000 acres, which is a large swath of western North Carolina, but this 157,000-acre ranger district has many of the forest's favorite attractions. A good topographic map is available from National Geographic (www.natgeomaps.com). In the ranger district are more than 275 miles of hiking trails and several campgrounds; the most easily accessible is **Davidson River Campground** (828/877-3265, reservations at www.

recreation.gov, year-round, $22-44), which is 1.5 miles from the Brevard entrance. It has showers and toilets.

The **Shining Rock Wilderness** and the **Middle Prong Wilderness,** which adjoins Shining Rock to the southwest, are a rugged terrain that rises from 3,200 feet at its lowest point, along the West Pigeon River, to a towering 6,400 feet at Richmond Balsam. **Cold Mountain,** made famous by the book and movie of the same name, is a real peak located within the Shining Rock Wilderness, and seeing it helps make the struggles of the fictional characters more real. These mountains are steep and the forests dense, and what trails there are have no signage. This is a popular area among experienced backwoods trekkers, but it is not recommended for casual visitors because it is exceedingly easy to get lost. At a minimum, hikers should be adept at using both a compass and a topographic map before venturing into these wilderness areas.

Not to be confused with Shining Rock, **Sliding Rock** is an easily accessible waterfall and swimming spot with a parking lot ($2), bathhouse, and lifeguards (10am-6pm daily late May-early Sept.). You can actually ride down the 60-foot waterfall, a smooth rock face (not so smooth that you shouldn't wear sturdy britches), over which 11,000 gallons of water rush every minute into the chilly swimming hole below.

If you have kids with you, make sure you stop at the **Cradle of Forestry** (U.S. 276, Pisgah Forest, 828/877-3130, www.cradleofforestry.com, 9am-5pm daily mid-Apr.-early Nov., $6 adults, $3 ages 4-12). This museum and activity complex commemorates the rise of the forestry profession in the United States, which originated here at a turn-of-the-20th-century training school

Sliding Rock waterfall

in the forests once owned by George Washington Vanderbilt, master of Biltmore. Plow days and living history days throughout the year give an interesting glimpse into this region's old-time methods of farming and frontier living. Self-guided trails lead through the woods to many interesting locations of this campus of America's first school of forestry. Most of what's here is geared toward little ones.

ACCOMMODATIONS

Slip back in time at the ✪ **Sunset Motel** (523 S. Broad St., 828/884-9106, www.thesunsetmotel.com, $89-129). This kitschy motel is a throwback to the days of the classic roadside motel experience: It's cheap, comfortable, and has chairs right outside your door so you can visit with your neighbors (and they have the best modern convenience—free Wi-Fi). The staff is super friendly and ready to help with suggestions for places to eat and things to do. You can add on tickets to the Brevard Music Center, waterfall tours, and more when you book your room. And for film buffs, Robert Mitchum stayed here when he was filming *Thunder Road*.

The **Campbell House Bed and Breakfast** (243 W. Main St., 800/553-2853, www.campbellhousebrevard.com, from $159) was renovated in 2014 after a few years of neglect. The new owners didn't just return it to its former beauty; they surpassed it. The five rooms feature queen beds and private baths—none are suites, but all are spacious. Though other accommodations in town are bicycle-friendly, Campbell House is the home of bicycle enthusiasts.

The **Inn at Brevard** (315 E. Main St., 828/884-2105, www.theinnatbrevard.com, $165-235) is spacious, beautiful, and kid-friendly. Their 14 rooms are well appointed, and they serve a full breakfast.

Camping

Davidson River Campground (Davidson River Circle, reservations 800/444-6777, local information 828/862-5960, www.recreation.gov, open year-round, sites $22-44) is just outside of Brevard in the Shining Rock Wilderness Area. There are around 160 sites here, some with river access, but all have access to hot showers and flush toilets; each site comes equipped with a picnic table, fire ring, and grill. It's the most convenient campground for exploring the hiking and fishing in the area as well as checking out the waterfalls here.

Just 10 minutes outside of Brevard, on 14 mountaintop acres, is **Ash Grove Mountain Cabins and Camping** (749 East Fork Rd., Brevard, 828/885-7216, www.ash-grove.com, tents and RVs $27-44, cabins $118-168). This retreat is open year-round, unlike others in the area, so you can experience all four seasons in this lovely spot. The cabins are quaint and cozy, and the tent and RV sites are well maintained. Common areas include a bonfire pit, a few lawn games, and a tiny waterfall.

Just 12.5 miles south of downtown Brevard, **Black Forest Family Camping Resort** (280 Summer Rd., Cedar Mountain, 828/884-2267, www.blackforestcampground.com, Mar. 15-Nov. 15, limited facilities in winter, tent sites $32, RV sites $32, RV with full hookup $38-44, cabin $56) has 100 campsites that are level and, more importantly, shaded. Nearby you'll find hiking, fishing, rock climbing, and mountain biking; but on site, you'll find a playground complete with horseshoe pits, a large heated swimming pool, and a video arcade. There's also free Wi-Fi (a must these days, even if you're car camping).

HENDERSONVILLE

An easy drive of 30 minutes south from Asheville, Hendersonville is a comfortable small city with a walkable downtown filled with boutiques and cafés. It's also the heart of North Carolina's apple industry. Hundreds of orchards cover the hillsides of Henderson County, and all along the highway, long packinghouses bustle in late summer as they process more than three million tons of apples. There are also many shops and produce stands run by members of old orchard-owning families, where you can buy apples singly or by the bushel, along with cider, preserves, and many other apple products.

SIGHTS

One of North Carolina's cool small transportation museums is located at the Hendersonville Airport. The **Western North Carolina Air Museum** (1340 Gilbert St., 828/698-2482, www.wncairmuseum.com, 10am-5pm Sat., noon-5pm Wed. and Sun. Apr.-Oct., noon-5pm Sat.-Sun. and Wed. Nov.-Mar., free) houses a collection of more than a dozen historic small aircraft, both originals and reproductions. Most are from the 1930s and 1940s, though some are even older; all are wonderfully fun contraptions to visit.

Sierra Nevada Brewery (100 Sierra Nevada Way, Mills River, 828/681-5300, www.sierranevada. com, 11am-9pm Sun.-Thurs., 11am-10pm Fri.-Sat.) is about 20 minutes from Hendersonville, midway between here and Asheville, and it's a beer lover's playground. They have tours of the

brewery (on the hour from 11am-3pm Mon.-Thurs., 11am-4pm Fri.-Sat., and noon-4pm Sun., free), tours showing off their sustainable practices (2:30pm Fri.-Sat., free), and a three-hour Beer Geek Tour (their name, not mine; $30, 2:30pm Thurs.), as well as plenty of beer to sample. There's a fantastic little restaurant ($9-28) on site and an indoor and outdoor space for concerts and special events.

SHOPPING

Hendersonville's downtown **Curb Market** (221 N. Church St. at 2nd Ave., 828/692-8012, www.curbmarket.com, 8am-2pm Tues., Thurs., and Sat.) has been in operation since 1924. Here you can buy fresh, locally grown fruits, vegetables, and flowers; fresh-baked cakes, pies, and breads; jams, jellies, and pickles made in local home kitchens; and the work of local woodcarvers, weavers, and other craftspeople.

Along the curved main street cutting through downtown there are plenty of shops (and some adorable man-sized bear statues that shop owners and community members have painted, bedazzled, and displayed), but one that stands out is **Dancing Bear Toys** (418 N. Main St., 828/693-4500, www.dancingbeartoys.com, 10am-6pm Mon.-Sat., noon-5pm Sun.). This place is lousy with games, toys, kits, models, gadgets, and accessories for kids and lighthearted adults.

FOOD

✪ **Umi Japanese Fine Dining** (633 N. Main St., 828/698-8048, www. umisushinc.com, 11am-3pm and 4:30pm-9:30pm Mon.-Thurs., 11am-3pm and 4:30pm-10:30pm Fri., noon-10:30pm Sat., noon-9:30pm Sun., $8-28) surprised me. For starters, I didn't expect to find good sushi anywhere in the mountains except maybe Asheville, but this is some of the best I've eaten in the state. Every roll is as close to perfect as you'll get because their sushi chef and his crew of maki rollers take fish deliveries three to four times a week. Sure, you can get beef teriyaki or miso salmon, but why would you when the rolls are so good? They also have a nice sake menu, and they serve their own wine here.

You can dine on some tasty grub and benefit a program devoted to aiding the survivors of violence at **Dandelion, a local eatery** (127 5th Ave., 828/595-9365, www.safelightfamily.org, 9:30am-2:30pm Mon.-Thurs., 9:30am-3pm Fri., breakfast under $6, lunch $8-10). Here they keep it simple as they work with their constituents, so expect to find biscuits, bowls of grits heaped with toppings, and omelets at breakfast, and chicken pot pie, grilled pimento cheese sandwiches, as well as tuna salad, chicken salad, and egg salad sandwiches.

ACCOMMODATIONS

Pinebrook Manor (2701 Kanuga Rd., 828/698-2707, www.pinebrookmanor. com, $165-245) has four rooms named for literary figures, and I think their pricing reveals something about the owners' literary tastes. The hosts are top notch, the whole place is lovely, and the breakfast is much better than the typical B&B quiche.

At **Melange Bed & Breakfast Inn and Gardens** (1230 Fifth Ave. W., 828/697-5253, www.melangebb.com, $189-245) is just a short walk from downtown and is the sort of place you don't want to leave. The six rooms are comfy and tastefully decorated (not overdone with thematic decorations or antiques like too many B&Bs),

and you just feel at home here. If you have special dietary needs—vegan, paleo, gluten-free—they're happy to accommodate.

There are some chain hotels in Hendersonville, but a good alternative is **Cedarwood Inn** (1510 Greenville Hwy., 828/692-8284 or 800/832-2072, www.cedarwood-inn.com, $114-210). To some it may not look like much from the outside, but it is, in many ways beyond its appearance, a throwback to those family motels of the 1950s and 60s, and they hit that experience (minus the kitsch) right on the head. It's clean, comfortable, and cheap; why look elsewhere?

FLAT ROCK
SIGHTS

Just south of Hendersonville is the historic village of Flat Rock. Founded in the early 19th century as a vacation spot for the Charleston plantation gentry, Flat Rock retains a delicate, cultured ambience created many years ago. Many artists and writers have lived in this area, most famously Carl Sandburg, whose house, Connemara, is preserved as the **Carl Sandburg Home National Historic Site** (81 Carl Sandburg Lane, Flat Rock, 828/693-4178, www.nps. gov/carl, 9am-5pm daily, house tour $5 adults, $3 over age 61, free under age 16). Sandburg and his family lived here for more than 20 years, and during that time he wrote and won the Pulitzer Prize for *Complete Poems*, no doubt observed bemusedly as his wife and daughters raised champion dairy goats (a herd of goats lives on the grounds today). Half-hour tours take visitors through the house to see many of the Sandburgs' belongings. There is a bookstore in the house and more than five miles of trails through the property. As a poet whose first steps were in the mountain clay, I have a soft spot for this place, and it's easy for me to see what Sandburg found so inspiring and appealing about the quiet, the air, and the space; take a moment to sit and reflect while you're here, and try writing a couple of lines of your own.

Throughout the mountains you're in apple country. **Sky Top Orchards** (1193 Pinnacle Mountain Rd., 828/692-7930, www.skytoporchard.com, 9am-6pm Aug. 1-Dec. 1) is a pick-your-own orchard with 22 varieties of apples as well as fresh cider, jams and jellies, and awesome apple cider donuts. Be sure to bring cash when you visit, as their card reader doesn't always work.

ENTERTAINMENT AND EVENTS

Another literary landmark in the village is the **Flat Rock Playhouse** (2661 Greenville Hwy., Flat Rock, 828/693-0731, www.flatrockplayhouse.org). Now the state theater of North Carolina, the Flat Rock Playhouse's history dates to 1940, when a roving theater company called the Vagabonds wandered down from New York and converted an old gristmill in the village into a stage. They returned every summer for the next few years, entertaining the locals with plays held in a succession of locations, from the old mill to a circus tent, eventually constructing a permanent theater. They now have a 10-month season, drawing more than 90,000 patrons each year.

SHOPPING

You'll find quite a few nice galleries and studios in Flat Rock along a strip called Little Rainbow Row. One place that jumps out is the anchor of Little

Rainbow Row, **The Wrinkled Egg** (2710 Greenville Hwy., 828/696-3998, www.thewrinkledegg.com, 10am-5pm Mon.-Sat., 12:30pm-5pm Sun.). This weird little store sells custom care packages for kids heading off to scout camp, equestrian camp, religious camp, and whatever other summer camps kids go to these days. It's a fun place to stop to get a little something for the kids in your life.

Sweet Magnolia Gallery (2720 Greenville Hwy., 828/697-2212, www.sweetmagnoliagallery.com, 11am-5pm Tues.-Sat., 12:30pm-5pm Sun.) carries some stunning jewelry and is the flagship store for Melinda Lawton Jewelry. In addition to Lawton's designs, you'll find vintage pieces for an intriguing mix of styles, stones, and prices.

FOOD

Flat Rock's a pretty small town, but there are a couple of eateries of note. For barbecue, grab a table at **Hubba Hubba Smokehouse** (2724 Greenville Hwy., 828/694-3551, hubbahubbasmokehouse.com, 11am-3pm Mon. and Wed., 11am-7pm Thurs.-Sun., $4-24). They serve a range of sauces that encompass North and South Carolina styles, and they throw in a little Texas for good measure. Many claim the 'cue here is so good you can eat it naked (meaning without sauce, not without pants), but I'm a sauce lover, so you'll have to decide for yourself. **Flat Rock Village Bakery** (2710 Greenville Hwy., 828/693-1313, www.flatrockwoodfired.com, 7am-5pm Mon.-Wed., 7am-7pm Thurs.-Sun., $4-14) is the parent of Hendersonville's West First Wood-Fired, and they serve pizzas, sandwiches, salads, and baked goods. Stop in for a snack or a full meal; they've got you covered on both fronts.

SALUDA AND VICINITY

Just 10 minutes east and south of Hendersonville, bordering South Carolina, Polk County is home to several interesting little towns, most notably Tryon and Saluda, along with a lot of beautiful mountain countryside. In Saluda you'll find a tiny downtown laid out along the old Norfolk Southern Railway tracks. The tracks at Saluda are the top of the steepest standard-gauge mainline railroad grade in the United States. This county's history abounds with exciting stories of runaway trains that derailed at spots like "Slaughterhouse Curve," and more than two-dozen railroad workers have been killed on this grade. Visitors information on Polk County is available through **First Peak of the Blue Ridge** (www.firstpeaknc.com).

SPORTS AND RECREATION

Equestrian life plays a growing role in Polk and the surrounding counties of North Carolina's southern mountains. The **Foothills Equestrian Nature Center** (3381 Hunting Country Rd., Tryon, 828/859-9021, www.fence.org), known as FENCE, occupies 380 beautiful acres along the border with South Carolina. The equestrian center has stables for 200 horses and two lighted show rings. FENCE hosts cross-country, three-day, A-rated hunter and jumper, dressage, and many other equestrian events throughout the year, along with offering regular hikes and bird-watching excursions on its beautiful property.

The Gorge (166 Honey Bee Dr., Saluda, 828/749-2500, www.thegorgezipline.com, $97) gives you a treetop view of the mountains and Green River Gorge as you zip line from tree to tree. There are 11 zips, three rappels, and a heart-pounding sky bridge on this course that descends 1,100 feet in total. The zips total well over a mile, and it is one of the best zip lines in the state; if adrenaline is your thing, you have to check it out.

ENTERTAINMENT AND EVENTS

For one weekend every July, Saluda busts at the seams with visitors to the **Coon Dog Day Festival** (800/440-7848, www.saluda.com). Hundreds of beautifully trained dogs from all over the region come to town to show off in a parade and trials, while the humans have a street fair and a 5K race. The town's **Top of the Grade Concert Series** runs from June to September and brings in artists for one free concert every month. Genres range from rock to country to Americana; check the website (www.saluda.com) for the current schedule. Like any good North Carolina town, Saluda holds a **Town BBQ**—called the Pig Out—in September; if you're the type to want to mingle with the locals, this is the perfect chance.

FOOD

For such a tiny town, there are an awful lot of eating places in Saluda. Just stand in the middle of Main Street and look around; there are several choices, and you won't go wrong at any of them. The menu at **The Purple Onion** (16 Main St., 828/749-1179, www.purpleonionsaluda.com, 11am-3pm Sun., 11am-9pm Mon.-Sat., dinner $7-49, lunch $5-13, brunch $5-13) draws inspiration from across the Mediterranean and you'll find tabbouleh, pizza and Spanish flavors landing on nearby tables, making it easy to select a dish.

The fresh mountain trout BLT, pimento-cheese stuffed half-chicken, and *puttanesca alla linguini* are crowd favorites.

Wildflour Bakery (173 E. Main St., 828/749-3356, http://wildflourbakerync.com, 5pm-8pm Tues., 8am-8pm Wed. and Fri., 9am-3pm Thurs. and Sat., 10am-3pm Sun., breakfast and lunch $2-9, pizza night $6-23) stone-grinds wheat every morning to make absolutely delicious breads. Breakfast and lunch are served, making this a great place to fill up before a day of kayaking or hiking. Don't miss Pizza Night (Wed. and Fri.), where they serve up regular or thin-crust (and even gluten-free) pies with your choice of toppings, along with 10 specialty pizzas. You can bring your own wine or beer on pizza night, so order a pie or two, crack open a local brew, and settle in for a little while.

CHIMNEY ROCK AND LAKE LURE

Chimney Rock State Park (U.S. 64/74A, Chimney Rock, MP 384.7 via U.S. Alt. 74 East, 800/277-9611, www.chimneyrockpark.com, 10am-4:40pm Fri.-Tues. Jan.-early Mar., 8:30am-5:30pm daily mid-Mar.-early Nov., 8:30am-4:30pm early Nov.-late Nov., 10am-4:30pm late Nov.-Dec 31, park open for 90 minutes after ticket plaza, $15 adults, $7 ages 5-15, 4 and under free) is just one of the many geological beauties you'll find along the Blue Ridge Parkway corridor. The 315-foot tower of stone that is Chimney Rock stands on the side of the mountain. To get to the top of the chimney, you can take a 26-story elevator ride, or hike the **Outcroppings Trail,** a 0.25-mile trail nicknamed "The Ultimate Stairmaster." No matter how you get there, the view is spectacular.

There are number of additional

Chimney Rock State Park

dizzying views to take in and mountain-hugging trails to hike in Chimney Rock State Park. The **Needle's Eye** and **Opera Box** are two such formations. The **Hickory Nut Falls Trail** takes you to the top of the 400-foot Hickory Nut Falls via a moderately difficult 0.75-mile trail. One of the most recognizable views is on the **Skyline-Cliff Trail** loop, a strenuous two-hour hike that will take you to some places you may recognize from the 1992 film *The Last of the Mohicans*. There are also kid-friendly trails. Bring your little ones along on the 0.6-mile **Woodland Walk,** where animal sculptures and "journal entries" from Grady the Groundhog wait to be discovered. A trail map covering the entire park is available at the park's website (www.chimneyrockpark.com).

Chimney Rock is more than just hiking trails. In November, Santa rappels down the tower in a pre-Christmas display of his chimney-navigating prowess, but year-round you'll find rock climbers in the park for bouldering, top-rope, and multi-pitch climbs. Want to try but don't know the terms? **Fox Mountain Guides** (888/284-8433, www.foxmountainguides.com, lessons from $45 for two hours, $225-255 for half- and full-day novice climbs, discounts for groups) will gear you up and show you the ropes.

Nearby **Rumbling Bald Mountain** (Boys Camp Rd., Lake Lure) was recently made part of Chimney Rock State Park, and climbers couldn't be happier. Here you'll find more than 1,500 bouldering "problems" (a form of low-altitude, ropeless climb that often traverses a rock face) to "solve" (traverse successfully). Currently, only the south face is open to climb, and no commercial climbing guides are allowed to operate there.

SPORTS AND RECREATION

Lake Lure, a 720-acre artificial highland lake, was created in the 1920s. Several local outfitters will set you up for a day on the lake or on area rivers. Try **Lake Lure Adventure Company** (470 Memorial Hwy., 828/625-8066, www.lakelureadventurecompany.com, 9am-8pm daily) for ski trips ($185 per hour), fishing (half-day $275), to ride around (from $75 per hour), or kayaking and stand-up paddleboarding (rentals from $20/hour). For a relaxed sightseeing tour on the lake, **Lake Lure Tours** (next to Lake Lure Town Marina, 877/386-4255, www.lakeluretours.com, 10am-5pm daily Apr.-May and Sept.-Oct., 10am-6pm daily Jun.-Aug., call for hours in Nov., closed Dec.-Mar., tours depart hourly from 11am, $16 adults, $14 seniors, $7 under age 12) offers dinner and sunset cruises as well as daytime jaunts.

In nearby Mill Springs, about 15 minutes south on N.C. 9, is a huge equestrian center hosting competitions, horse shows, lessons, and rides year-round. **Tryon International Equestrian Center** (25 International Blvd., Mill Spring, 828/863-1000, www.tryon.coth.com)—or TIEC—puts on free hunter-jumper shows and competitions, hosts concerts and events, and has everything riders, spectators and equine enthusiasts could want. Choose from eight on-site restaurants including **Legends Grille** (828/863-1122, 4pm-9pm Wed., 5pm-9pm Mon., 11am-9pm Tues.-Thurs., 11am-10pm Fri.-Sat., 11am-9pm Sun., $14-47), an upscale eatery serving steaks and seafood; **Roger's Diner** (828/863-1113, 7am-9pm Sun.-Fri., 7am-10pm Sat., $7-14), serving breakfast and traditional diner fare; and **Blue Ginger Sushi & Noodles** (828/863-1121, 11am-9pm Wed.-Sun., $9). There's also a coffee shop, snack bar, pizza oven, and sandwich-centric café.

Since riders and show enthusiasts travel from far and wide, TIEC has lodging for horse and rider. The **Stable House Inn** (828/863-1015, $125) has 50 rooms, each with two queen beds; the **Tryon River Cabins** have one- ($185), three- ($750), and five-bedroom cabins ($1,000) available, each with weekly rental discounts; as well as several RV pads ($43).

There are two golf courses at **Rumbling Bald Resort** (112 Mountains Blvd., Lake Lure, www.rumblingbald.com). **Bald Mountain Golf Course** (828/694-3042, 18 holes, par 72, greens fees $50 weekdays, $55 weekends) makes the most of the bald rock faces that gave the course its name and gives you some beautiful views of them as they tower overhead. You may recognize the 16th hole, a picturesque par 3 where a couple of scenes from *Dirty Dancing* were shot. At **Apple Valley Golf Course** (828/694-3042, 18 holes, par 72, greens fees $60 weekdays, $65 weekends) you'll find a set of links that's been called one of the most beautiful mountain courses. This is especially true in fall when the hillsides surrounding the course are in full blaze.

FOOD

In addition to the dining options at Rumbling Bald, the Lodge on Lake Lure, and TIEC, there are a few other spots worth checking out.

Medina's Village Bistro (430 Main St., Chimney Rock, 828/989-4529, www.medinasvillagebistro.com, 7:30am-2pm Mon., 7:30am-9pm Wed.-Sat., 7:30am-3pm Sun., breakfast $3-8, lunch $4-11, dinner $8-22) is a great spot for breakfast with the locals. They pack the place, read the paper,

talk politics a little too loudly, and generally inhabit the place as only locals can; they're a friendly bunch, though. The cinnamon rolls here are out-of-this-world good.

Dining at **La Strada at Lake Lure** (2693 Memorial Hwy., Lake Lure, 828/625-1118, www.lastradaatlakelure.com, 11:30am-late daily, $6-29) is Italian American through and through, and you're bound to see plenty of rock climbers in there carbing up as they prepare for a day on the rock face. The menu is packed with pizza and pasta, with many of the classics—chicken parm, lasagna, chicken alfredo—appearing alongside daily specials that use ingredients that are a little more close to home.

I am a fool for French toast and at **Victory Kitchen & Restaurant** (959 Buffalo Creek Rd., Lake Lure, 828/436-5023, 8am-2pm Mon.-Sat., breakfast $3-11, lunch $3-11) I've found a version I look forward to getting, if I don't order the shrimp and grits, that is. This place has great breakfast—sleepyheads take note: it's served until 11am—and a great lunch, including a killer cheeseburger topped with a fried egg, just in case you like a little breakfast with lunch.

ACCOMMODATIONS

The 1927 **Lake Lure Inn and Spa** (2771 Memorial Hwy., 888/434-4970, www.lakelure.com, from $129) is a grand old hotel that was one of the fashionable Southern resorts of its day. Franklin Roosevelt and Calvin Coolidge stayed here, as did F. Scott Fitzgerald. The lobby is full of strange antiques that are the picture of obsolete opulence—a Baccarat chandelier much older than the hotel and a collection of upright disc music boxes, up to eight feet tall, that were all the rage before the invention of the phonograph. The Lake Lure Inn has been restored beautifully and equipped with two restaurants, a bar, and a spa.

In 1937 the **Lodge on Lake Lure** (361 Charlotte Dr., Lake Lure, 828/625-2789 or 800/733-2785, www.lodgeonlakelure.com, $180-310) was born as a retreat for North Carolina Highway Patrolmen and their families; in 1990, it opened to the public. There are 17 guest rooms here and an excellent restaurant. **Tree Tops Restaurant** (8am-9:30am daily, 6pm-9pm Thurs.-Sat., reservations required, breakfast $6-12) serves a prix-fixe menu ($65/two diners) of three to five appetizers, entrées, and desserts. The menu has a strong focus on seasonal ingredients and sources much of their product from local and regional farms. Try the rainbow trout (caught daily) and anything with mushrooms.

Rumbling Bald Resort on Lake Lure (112 Mountains Blvd., Lake Lure, 828/694-3000 or 800/260-1040, www.rumblingbald.com) has studios ($90-125), condos ($120-295), motor coach facilities ($65-80), and vacation homes ($175-590) in a quiet mountain cove. On the resort's property there a few miles of hiking and biking trails as well as a variety of water activities: pontoon boats (from $80/hour); kayaks, canoes, paddleboats, and stand-up paddleboards (from $20/hour); and scenic cruises ($18 adults, $17 for seniors, military and ages 4-12, $8 under 4). There's also a fitness center, golf, and tennis.

At Rumbling Bald there are several restaurants to choose from, the best being **Legends on the Lake** (828/694-3032, 11am-9pm daily, bar 11am-10pm Sun.-Thurs., 11am-11pm Fri.-Sat, $9-24); there's also a pizza place and seasonal lunch cruises ($25

and wine cruises ($34, call or visit www.rumblingbald.com for schedule).

HIGHLANDS AND VICINITY
WATERFALLS

This part of the country is blessed with some beautiful waterfalls, some of which are easily visited. **Whitewater Falls** (Hwy. 281, at the state line, south of Highlands, $2 per vehicle), at over 400 feet, is reported to be the highest waterfall east of the Rockies. An upper-level viewing spot is located at the end of a wheelchair-accessible paved trail, while a flight of more than 150 steps leads to the base of the falls. The falls are a fabulous sight, but remember to stay on the trails; several visitors have fallen to their deaths when they left the trail to get a different perspective. A much smaller but still very beautiful waterfall is **Silver Run Falls** (Hwy. 107, 4 miles south of Cashiers), reached by a short trail from a roadside pullout. **Bridal Veil Falls** (U.S. 64, 2.5 miles west of Highlands) flows over a little track of road right off U.S. 64. You'll see a sign from the main road where you can turn off and actually drive behind the waterfall, or park and walk behind it. Another waterfall that you can walk through is **Dry Falls** (U.S. 64, between Highlands and Franklin, $2 per vehicle), reached by a small trail off the highway, curving right into and behind the 75-foot waterfall.

SPORTS AND RECREATION

North Carolina's newest state park, **Gorges State Park** (Hwy. 281 S., Sapphire, 828/966-9099, http://ncparks.gov, park 7am-9pm daily, picnic areas 8am-8:30pm daily, visitor center 9am-5pm Mon.-Thurs. and 9am-5:30pm Fri.-Sun.) is a lush mountain rainforest that receives 80 inches of precipitation annually. The steep terrain rises 2,000 vertical feet in four miles, creating a series of rocky waterfalls and challenging trails. This 7,500-acre park is the only state park west of Asheville, and it's a sight, with a collection of waterfalls and a fantastic concentration of rare and unique plant and animal species; explore on a number of rugged trails for hiking, mountain biking, and horseback riding, or fish for rainbow and brown trout as well as smallmouth bass. Primitive camping (free) is permitted in designated areas.

FOOD AND ACCOMMODATIONS

The 3,500-foot-high town of Cashiers ("CASH-ers") is home to the **High Hampton Resort** (1525 Hwy. 107 S., 828/743-0263 or 800/334-2551, www.highhamptoninn.com, 2-night minimum, from $199), a popular resort for generations of North Carolinians. This was originally the home of Confederate General Wade Hampton, the dashing Charlestonian cavalryman. The lodge, a big old 1930s wooden chalet with huge cozy fireplaces in the lobby, is surrounded by 1,400 acres of lakeside woodlands, with an 18-hole golf course, a good buffet-style restaurant (dinner jacket requested in the evening), clay tennis courts, and a fitness center that features a climbing tower.

INFORMATION AND SERVICES

In addition to Asheville's **Mission Hospital** (509 Biltmore Ave., 428 Biltmore Ave., Asheville, 828/213-1111, www.missionhealth.org), there are several regional hospitals with emergency or urgent care departments. In Hendersonville, the primary hospital is **Pardee Hospital** (800 N. Justice St., Hendersonville, 828/696-1000, www.pardeehospital. org). In Brevard, the main hospital is **Transylvania Regional Hospital** (90 Hospital Dr., Brevard, 828/884-9111, www.missionhealth. org), and in Rutherfordton it is **Rutherford Regional Medical Center** (288 S. Ridgecrest Ave., Rutherfordton, 828/286-5000, www. myrutherfordregional.com).

Maps and guides are available at the **Hendersonville and Flat Rock Visitors Information Center** (201 S. Main St., Hendersonville, 800/828-4244, www.visithendersonvillenc. org) and at the **Transylvania County Tourism Development Authority** (175 W. Main St., Brevard, 800/648-4523, www.visitwaterfalls.com).

GETTING THERE AND AROUND

The Brevard-Hendersonville area is an easy drive from Asheville, with Hendersonville less than 30 minutes down I-26 and Brevard a short jog west from it on U.S. 64. To reach Tryon and Rutherfordton, follow U.S. 74 south and east from Hendersonville. **Asheville Regional Airport** (AVL, 61 Terminal Dr., 828/684-2226, www. flyavl.com), south of Asheville, is very convenient to this region; several airlines have flights to Atlanta, Charlotte, and other U.S. cities.

THE GREAT SMOKY MOUNTAINS

The Smokies draw more than 10

million visitors annually. It's easy to see why: These mountains are laced with hiking trails, rivers, and waterfalls and populated with diverse wildlife—from rare salamanders to huge elk.

The diversity is second only to the sublime mystery of the area. The wild forests of the The Great Smoky Mountains have historically been home to outlaws and rebels hoping to hide from the world under the cover of the fertile land-scape. In fact, in 1996, the Atlanta Olympic Park bomber fled to the Smokies to evade capture.

✪ **CADES COVE:** The most visited spot in Great Smoky Mountains National Park is a formerly bustling mountain village that is witness to the depth of history in the Southern highlands (page 84).

✪ **CLINGMANS DOME:** From this third-highest peak in the eastern United States, set in a dramatic alpine environment, you'll find an astounding view of up to 100 miles on a clear day (page 88).

✪ **NEWFOUND GAP ROAD:** Bisecting the park, the 33-mile route offers plenty of long views, short hikes, and streamside driving (page 89).

✪ **MUSEUM OF THE CHEROKEE INDIAN:** The Cherokee people have lived in the Smoky Mountains for thousands of years. This excellent museum tells unforgettable tales of their history (page 103).

✪ **QUALLA ARTS AND CRAFTS MUTUAL:** Ancient craft traditions still thrive among Cherokee artists in western North Carolina. At the Qualla Mutual, visitors can learn about and purchase the work of today's masters (page 104).

✪ **OCONALUFTEE INDIAN VILLAGE:** Demonstrations in traditional cooking, flint knapping for arrowheads and spear points, and ritual dance give visitors a glimpse into 18th-century tribal life at this recreated Cherokee Indian Village (page 104).

✪ **NANTAHALA RIVER GORGE:** So steep that in some places the water is only brushed by sunlight at high noon, this gorge is an unbeatable place for white-water rafting (page 108).

✪ **JOHN C. CAMPBELL FOLK SCHOOL:** For nearly a century the Folk School has been a leading light in promoting American craft heritage, nurturing new generations of artists, and securing the future of Appalachian artistic traditions (page 123).

While people watching the news were scratching their heads, wondering how one man could vanish in such a relatively small geographical area, folks in these parts had their doubts he'd ever be found. After driving a little ways in the high country southwest of Asheville, among the rugged terrain and the lush vegetation, it isn't difficult to imagine how anyone could hide here unnoticed.

The 521,085-acre Great Smoky National Park straddles the North Carolina/Tennessee state line, and is just about equally split between the states. The slightly larger North Carolina side of the park is wilder and less developed than the Tennessee side, and in both places you can find spots so remote they have stood undisturbed by humans for untold lengths of time. You'll also find places like Cades Cove, a wide, secluded valley that welcomed some of the first pioneers to push west into Tennessee.

In addition to pioneers traveling

Great Smoky Mountains

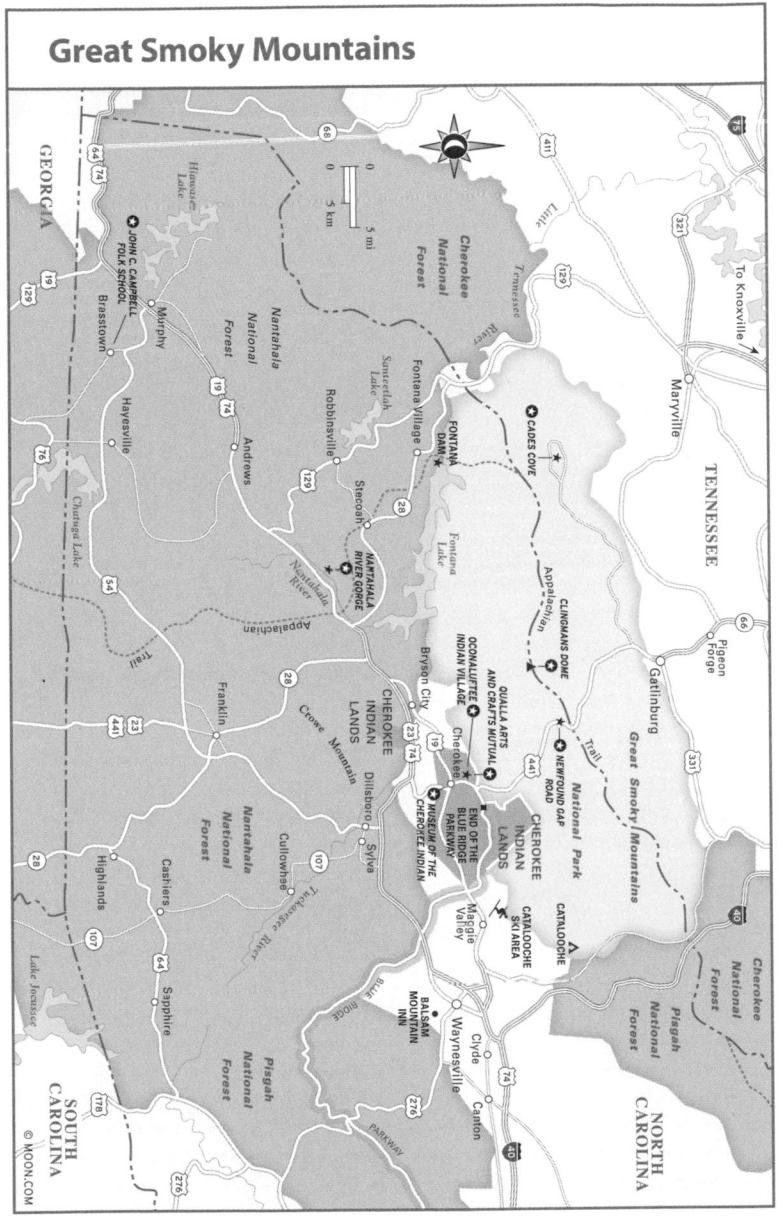

westward, the Smokies were also home to the Cherokee people, who have roots here going back centuries, from the early days described in their mythology, when the Ani-gituhwa-gi shared these mountains with witches, fairies, and birds the size of bears. The early 19th century and the Trail of Tears were the darkest hour for them, when they were split into two groups—those forced into exile and those forced into hiding and resistance. Today, the Cherokee Nation is still split, but the Eastern Band's seat of government is here in the land known as the Qualla Boundary.

PLANNING YOUR TIME

Many people plan visits to the Smokies around what's blooming or turning color on the mountainsides, but it's a wonderful area to visit any time of year. Spring wildflowers begin to appear in late March, peaking in late April. Azaleas, mountain laurels, and rhododendrons put on the best show during summer, blooming first at lower elevations and then creeping up the mountains. Flame azalea is a funny plant, peaking in different areas as the microclimates dictate; they're ablaze with color April to July. Mountain laurel overlaps with blooms in May-June, and rhododendron shows its color in June-July. Fall colors appear in the opposite order, with the mountaintops the first to show autumn's arrival in early October. Colors then bleed down until late October and early November, when trees from the foot to the crest of the mountains are aflame with color. Summer heat can throw off the schedule for blooms and fall colors, as can rainfall levels. If you call the Great Smoky Mountains National Park or check with regional websites, you can find out how the season is progressing.

Bisecting the park is the Newfound Gap Road, striking northwest from Cherokee, where it meets with the southern end of the Blue Ridge Parkway, to Gatlinburg and Pigeon Forge, Tennessee. On the Tennessee side of the park, the valleys spread out a little and mountain coves form, making that the area to visit for side-road exploration and short loop roads. Cherokee is a great place to stay, as it's not as touristy as Gatlinburg, Tennessee, which is good to visit for a day. There are campsites available on both sides of the park if you're roughing it, or find a rustic, cozy cabin for a taste of country living. While you can certainly get from Cherokee to Gatlinburg in an hour and see a sight or two in a day, the more time you can spend here, the better. This is the nation's most visited National Park for a reason, so spend at least three days; a week provides enough time for a touristy day in Tennessee, a couple of days for trail and side-road exploration, a day learning about Cherokee culture in Cherokee, and some time in the casino. Many campgrounds here limit stays to one week from May 15 to the end of October and two weeks from November to May 14, so plan accordingly if you're packing your tent.

Great Smoky Mountains National Park

The **Great Smoky Mountains National Park**—GSMNP—(865/436-1200, www.nps.gov/grsm) is like no other, and it's very close to my heart. My family would vacation here for weekend and weeklong getaways, and I remember taking my first bite of trout here, riding my first roller coaster at Silver Dollar City in Pigeon Forge (now Dollywood), and seeing R2-D2 outside of Ripley's Believe It or Not in Gatlinburg. GSMNP comprises more than 800 square miles of cloud-ringed high peaks and rainforest. There are tens of thousands of species of plants and animals that call the park home, with 80 species of reptiles and amphibians alone, which is why the park is sometimes called the Salamander Capital of the World. More than 200 species of birds nest here, and 50-plus mammal species, from mice to mountain lions, roam these hills. The nonprofit organization Discover Life in America (www.dlia.org) has been conducting an All-Taxa Biodiversity Inventory, a census of all nonmicrobial life forms in the GSMNP; as of 2012 they had discovered over 900 species of plants and animals previously unknown to science. The deep wilderness is an awesome refuge for today's outdoor enthusiasts, and the accessibility of absolutely ravishing scenery makes it ideal for visitors of all ability levels and nearly all interests.

that the elevation ranges from under 1,000 to over 6,600 feet. Low-lying areas like the one around Gatlinburg, Tennessee, are not much cooler than Raleigh in the summer, with an average high of 88°F in July. Gatlinburg's average lows drop just a few degrees below freezing during only three months of the year (Dec.-Feb.). The opposite extreme is illustrated by Clingmans Dome, the highest elevation in the park, where the average high temperature is only 65°F in July, and only in June-August can you be sure that it won't snow. If ever there were a place for wearing layers of clothing, this is it. No matter what season the calendar tells you it is, be on the safe side and pack clothing for the other three as well. Keep these extremes in mind in terms of safety as well; a snowstorm can bring two feet of snow at high elevations, and it's not at all unusual for the weather to be balmy at the foot of the mountain and icy at the top. At times the temperature has fallen to -20°F. Roads can be closed in the winter or restricted to vehicles with snow chains or four-wheel drive. Drive very slowly when it's icy. Leave plenty of room between you and the next car, and shift to a lower gear when going down slippery slopes. You can find out current conditions by calling the park's weather information line (865/436-1200, ext. 630).

VISITING THE PARK
WEATHER CONSIDERATIONS

To get a sense of the variability of the weather in the GSMNP, keep in mind

SEASONAL CONSIDERATIONS

The most crowded times in the park are from mid-June to mid-August

Great Smoky Mountains National Park

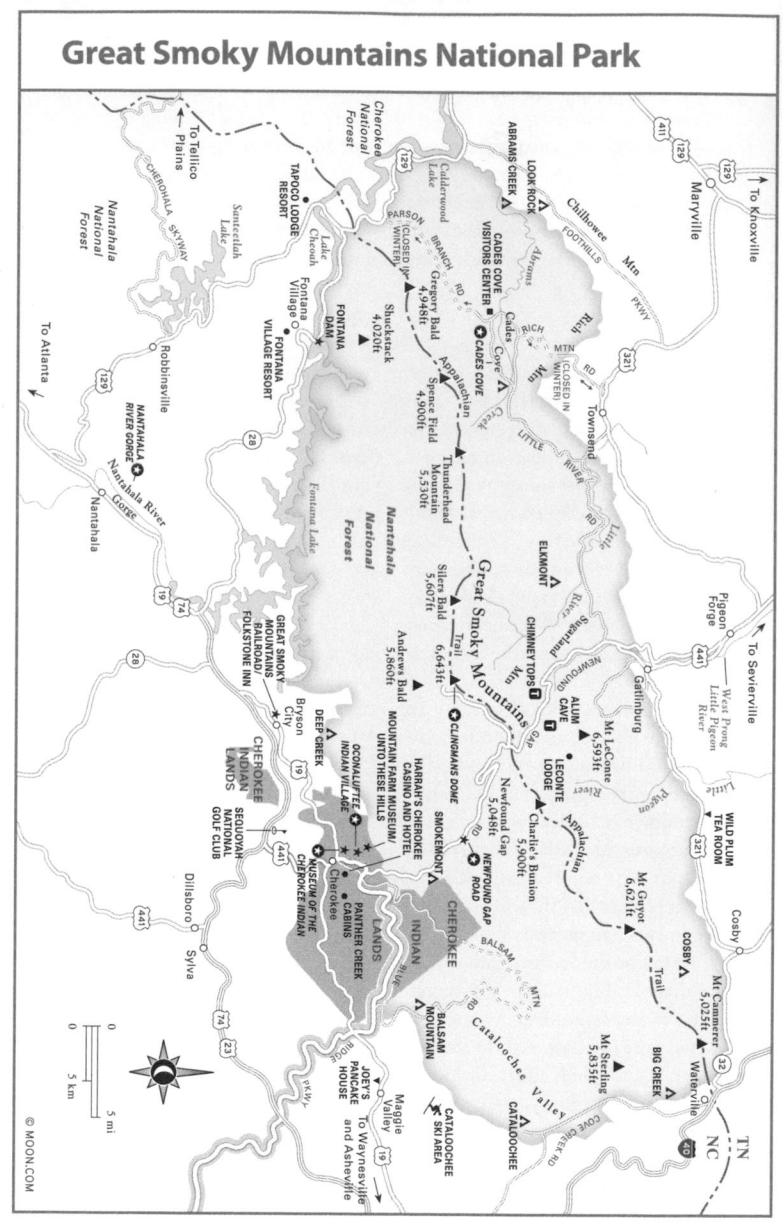

and all of October. Traffic is most likely to be heavy on the Cades Cove Loop Road and Newfound Gap Road. Several roads in the park are closed in the winter, but closing dates vary. Among these are Balsam Mountain, Clingmans Dome, Little Greenbrier, Rich Mountain, and Round Bottom Roads and the Roaring Fork Motor Nature Trail.

SAFETY

Sometimes even the most experienced outdoorspeople have emergencies. Whether you're going into the backcountry alone or with others, make sure that someone you trust knows where you're going, what your likely route is, and when to expect you back. The National Park Service recommends leaving their phone number (865/436-1230) with someone at home to call if you're not back when expected.

Some of the basic safety rules may seem obvious, but it's good to review them. Climbing on rocks and waterfalls is always dangerous, and crossing a deep or flooded stream can be treacherous as well. If you have to cross a stream that's more than ankle deep, it's recommended that you unbuckle the waist strap on your backpack (so you don't get pinned underwater if you fall), use a hiking stick to steady yourself, and wear nonslippery shoes.

Cold is a concern, even in summer. Wear layers, pack additional warm duds (warmer than you think you'll need), and try to stay dry. It may be shorts-and-T-shirt weather when you set out, but even in the summer it can be very cold at night. Plan well, double-check before setting out that you have everything you could possibly need on your trek, and, says the National Park Service, "eat before you're hungry, and rest before you're tired" (it's good advice; trust me, I'm an Eagle Scout). Water from streams must be boiled or filtered to make it potable.

Wildlife can pose hazards. Despite assurances to the contrary, there are still panthers (mountain lions) in these mountains. Ignore what the officials say in this (and only this) regard; locals see and hear them throughout Appalachia. But panthers are rare and reclusive, as are coyotes, wild hogs, and other resident tough guys. It's always better to hike or camp with at least one companion. A sturdy walking stick can be a lifesaver, and bear spray, cheap and readily available in many different kinds of stores, is good for deterring more than bears.

PERMITS AND REGULATIONS

Permits are required for camping in the national park but are quite easy to obtain. You can register at any of the 12 visitors centers and ranger stations. This must be done in person, not online or over the phone. Fishing requires a permit as well, which can be bought at outfitters and bait shops in nearby towns. Strict rules governing fishing apply; these can be found on the park website (www.nps.gov/grsm). Other rules apply to interaction with wildlife. Don't feed animals, and make sure to seal up your foodstuffs to discourage night visitors. Firearms are forbidden in the park, as is hunting.

Your dog is welcome in the park, but only in certain areas. To prevent transmission of diseases to or from the wildlife, and to avoid disrupting or frightening the resident fauna, dogs are not permitted on hiking trails. They are allowed to accompany you at campgrounds and picnic sites.

Great Smoky Mountains National Park (GSMNP, 865/436-1200, www.nps.gov/grsm) was the first—and the largest—of three National Park Service units established in the southern Appalachians. The park was founded in 1934, followed in 1935 by the Blue Ridge Parkway and in 1936 by Shenandoah National Park. These sister facilities include some 600 miles of contiguous road and close to 800,000 acres of land, all of it acquired from private landholders and all of it standing today as a testament to the wild, rugged beauty of the Appalachian Mountains and the people who helped tame these places.

MORNING

Enjoy breakfast at the **Pancake Pantry** (628 Parkway, 865/436-4724, www. pancakepantry.com, 7am-4pm daily June-Oct., 7am-3pm daily Nov.-May, $6-10) in Gatlinburg, the first pancake house in Tennessee. Head out of town toward GSMNP and stop off at the **Sugarlands Visitor Center** (1420 Old T.N. 73 Scenic, Gatlinburg, 865/436-1200, www.nps.gov/grsm, daily except Christmas Day) to pick up maps, then continue on down Little River Road to **Cades Cove.** Easily the most popular auto tour in the park, Cades Cove has amazing scenery but even more amazing wildlife watching. Get there at the right time of day (early morning or near dusk) and you'll see herds of deer grazing the fields and black bears playing, eating, and napping in the remnants of former apple orchards.

If you're in an SUV, truck, or some sort of high-clearance, off-road-appropriate vehicle, leave Cades Cove via **Rich Mountain Road,** a beautiful, eight-mile road that takes you up and over the mountains to Townsend (not far to the east of Gatlinburg). The views of Cades Cove are unparalleled, so have your camera ready.

AFTERNOON

Leave the park for lunch in Gatlinburg, then hit the **Roaring Fork Motor Nature Trail,** from which you can hike to four falls with relative ease. For a 2.6-mile round-trip hike, try **Grotto Falls Trail,** which leads through a lovely forest to the 25-foot Grotto Falls. You can hike behind the falls, and if you're lucky, you may see pack llamas hauling supplies to the LeConte Lodge. As you're leaving the Motor Nature Trail, stop at the **Thousand Drips Falls,** sometimes called Place of a Thousand Drips. It's just a few steps off the road and is an excellent cascade as it falls down the mossy rock face.

WILDLIFE IN THE PARK

The largest animals in the park are also the most recent arrivals. In the spring of 2001, the National Park Service reintroduced elk to the Great Smoky Mountains, a species that used to live here but was hunted to regional extinction in the 18th century. In the years since their reintroduction, the herd has reproduced steadily, boding well for a successful future. If you hear a strange bellowing in the early autumn, it may be a male elk showing off for his beloved. One of the best places to see the elk is in the Cataloochee Valley, particularly in fields at dawn and dusk. Be sure to keep your distance; these animals can weigh up to 700 pounds, and the males have some formidable headgear.

An estimated 1,600 black bears live in the GSMNP—two per square mile—so it's quite possible that you'll encounter one. They are a wonder to see, but the 100-400-pound creatures pose a real risk to humans, so it's important to be aware of how we interact with them. It is illegal to come within 150 feet of a bear or elk, and those who knowingly get closer can be arrested. If you see a bear, the recommended procedure is to back away slowly. The National Park Service recommends that if the bear follows you, you should stand your ground. If it keeps coming toward you persistently and looks menacing, make yourself big and scary. Stand on a rock to look taller, or get close to anyone else present, to show the bear that it's outnumbered. Make a lot of noise (bear bells or bear whistles are handy for this) and throw rocks or sticks. Should a bear actually attack you, the National Park Service recommends that you "fight back aggressively with any available object." Don't try to run, because they're much faster than you, and don't climb a tree, as black bears are avid climbers.

The best course of action is simply to avoid them and hope that any sightings you have will be from a safe distance. When camping, lock your food in the trunk of your car, or hoist it into a tree too high off the ground for a bear to reach it and suspended far enough from the nearest branch that it can't be reached by climbing the tree. Bears may approach picnic areas. Don't feed them, no matter how sweet they look. "Habitual panhandler bears" (this is a real term, Scout's honor) die younger than those afraid of humans, as they are more likely to be hit by cars, swallow indigestible food packaging, become easy targets for hunters, or, if they are too problematic, be captured and euthanized.

Bears are not the only huge, ferocious animals in the park. Believe it or not, there are hundreds of snorting, tusky **wild hogs** here, descendants of a herd that escaped from a hunting preserve in Murphy in the 1910s. There are also **coyotes, wolves, bobcats,** and extremely rare **mountain lions,** often called panthers or painters in this region.

Of the many natural miracles in this park, one of the most astonishing is the light show put on for a couple of weeks each year by synchronous **fireflies.** Of the park's 14 species, only one, *Photinus carolinus,* flashes in this manner. While the average backyard's worth of fireflies twinkles like Christmas lights, synchronous fireflies, as their name implies, are capable of flashing in unison, by the hundreds or thousands. The sight is so amazing that, during the peak flashing period in June, the park organizes nighttime expeditions to the best viewing spots.

If you go hiking in the backcountry, you may see a **snake.** It's unlikely that you'll encounter a poisonous one, as there are only two kinds of vipers here—rattlesnakes and copperheads—that pose a danger to humans. There has never been a death from snakebite in the park, and snakes are shy. But to be on the safe side, watch where you step or put your hands; you don't want to be the first on that list.

SIGHTS

OCONALUFTEE VISITOR CENTER AND MOUNTAIN FARM MUSEUM

As you begin your trip along Newfound Gap Road through the park from the North Carolina side, your first stop will probably be the "Welcome to Great Smoky Mountains National Park" sign, but the **Oconaluftee Visitor Center and Mountain Farm Museum** (1194 Newfound Gap Rd., Cherokee, 828/497-1904, www.nps.gov/grsm, 8am-4:30pm daily Dec.-Feb., except Dec. 25, 8am-5pm daily Mar. and Nov., 9am-6pm daily Apr.-May, 8am-7:30pm daily June-Aug., 8am-6:30pm daily Sept.-Oct.), just two miles north of Cherokee on U.S. 441/Newfound Gap Road, will likely be the second stop you make. You can pick up a park map, grab the schedule of ranger-led programs, and see exhibits on the people who called these hills home long before the park was in existence. The visitors center and adjacent comfort station are LEED Gold certified.

Next to the visitor center is **Mountain Farm Museum** (sunrise-sunset daily year-round, free), which showcases some of the finest farm buildings in the park. Most date to the early 1900s, and among them are a barn, apple house, and the Davis House, a log home built from chestnut wood and constructed before the American chestnut blight decimated the species. This collection of structures is original to the area and dates back to the turn of the 20th century. Though the barn is the only structure original to this site, the other buildings were moved here from inside and adjacent to the park and arranged much like the typical farm of the era would have been arranged. If you visit during peak times, you'll see living-history interpreters in costume, demonstrating the day-to-day chores that would've occurred on this farm: preparing meals, sewing, maintaining and harvesting the garden, taking care of the hogs, and the like.

✪ CADES COVE

On the Tennessee side of the park, the 11-mile one-way **Cades Cove Loop Road** traverses Cades Cove, a historic settlement dating to the late 18th century. Originally part of the Cherokee Nation, the land was ceded to the United States in 1819. The population grew throughout the 19th century until it was a busy town of several hundred. The village is preserved today as it appeared around 1900, with homes, churches, barns, and a working gristmill, but without the people—a mountain counterpart to Cape Lookout National Seashore's

biking in Cades Cove

The 2,184-mile Appalachian Trail runs from Georgia to Maine, with 95.5 miles within North Carolina and another 200 straddling the border of North Carolina and Tennessee. It's a high climb, with many peaks over 5,000 feet and gaps brushing 4,000 feet, but the fantastic balds (natural and agricultural areas devoid of trees) along the trail here—like Cheoa Bald and Max Patch—are big draws for day hikers and segment hikers, and having vistas this beautiful this early on in the long journey helps through-hikers retain their focus and determination to reach their goal.

The Appalachian Trail cuts a path through the Nantahala Forest, regarded by many as one of the best sections of the southern portion of the trail, before crossing the rills of the southern Blue Ridge and following the crest of the Smokies along the Tennessee border. This section of the trail is rated between a 3 and a 6 on the AT's 10-point scale, which means the trail varies from moderate elevation changes on well graded trails, to strenuous and short but steep climbs, to extended climbs that last hours, as well as short sections with difficult footing. For through-hikers, who often have years of trail experience, the path here isn't as difficult as it may be for some day or even overnight hikers.

Finding a day hike isn't hard west of Asheville, especially in the deeper mountains along Great Smoky Mountain National Park. Driving the Newfound Gap Road from the town of Cherokee into Tennessee, go about 16 miles from the Oconaluftee Visitors Center to the Newfound Gap parking lot. The trailhead is to the left of the overlook. Take the moderate four-mile hike to Charles Bunion, a peak along the trail with a very odd name. You'll gradually gain around 1,600 feet in elevation, but if you bring a picnic lunch, you'll have a lovely dining spot.

Portsmouth Village. Because of the cove's scenic beauty and abundance of wildlife, this is the most popular part of the nation's most visited national park. The loop road through Cades Cove takes about an hour to drive when visitors are sparse; on crowded days—peak summer and fall seasons and most weekends—it can take several hours to cover the 11 miles.

To take this lovely-in-any-season drive, follow Little River Road west from the Sugarlands Visitor Center for 17.2 miles, there it will turn into Laurel Creek Road and lead you into Cades Cove in another 7.4 miles. You can also access Cades Cove by entering the park at Townsend on T.N. 73, then turning right on Laurel Creek Road, following it for 16 miles to the entrance to the cove. Cades Cove is closed to vehicle traffic every Saturday and Wednesday morning from May until late September. On those days, the loop is open exclusively to bicycle and foot traffic until 10am. The rest of the year, the road is open to motor vehicles from sunrise to sunset daily, so long as the weather allows it.

The **Cades Cove Campground** (10042 Campground Drive, Townsend, TN, campground 865/448-2472, reservations 877/444-6777 or www.recreation.gov, $17-20) is a popular spot where you'll definitely want to reserve a campsite. This campground is open year-round, and although the occupancy is a little lower in the dead of winter, you'll still find a few intrepid visitors taking refuge from the cold in one of the 159 campsites here. Hikers, take note, there are several backcountry campsites off the trails in Cades Cove, making it a good base for overnight trips.

Today, a number of historic structures remain standing along the valley floor. Among them is the most photographed structure in the park, the **Methodist Church.** From time to time, a wedding is held here, though it's more common for visitors to leave handwritten prayers on scraps of paper large and small at the altar.

The **Cable Mill Area** is the busiest section of the loop, even if the Methodist Church is the most photographed. At the Cable Mill, you can see an actual mill in operation and even buy cornmeal or flour ground on site. In addition to the mill and Methodist church, there are two other churches, a few barns and log houses, and a number of smaller structures.

Halfway around the park, you'll find the **Cades Cove Visitor Center** (Cades Cove Loop Rd., Townsend, TN, 865/448-2472, 9am-4:30pm daily Dec.-Jan., except Dec. 25, 9am-5pm daily Feb., 9am-6:30pm daily Mar. and Sept.-Oct., 9am-7pm daily Apr.-Aug., 9am-5:30pm daily Nov.), which has a good bookstore and gift shop and, most importantly, the only public restroom you'll find on the tour.

CATALOOCHEE

Nestled in the folds of the mountains and encircled by 6,000-foot peaks, the Cataloochee Valley was settled in the early 1830s. This isolated valley on the northeastern edge of GSMNP was home to two communities—Big and Little Cataloochee—and more than 1,200 people in 1910. By the 1940s, all but a few were gone, leaving the valley, and its new status as one of the more beautiful spots in the new national park, for hills and hollows nearby. Today, the few historic structures that stand in Cataloochee Valley are all that remains of the communities that lived here, save a few memories and stories written down.

Cataloochee Valley is not far from I-40, but poor signage makes it a little difficult to find. On I-40, take exit 20 onto U.S. 276. Take an immediate right onto Cove Creek Road. The condition of the road—it's alternately gravel and paved—and the narrow, winding route will make you doubt you made the right turn, but you did. Zigzag up this road for about 12 miles. Suddenly it will open up into the wide, grassy expanse that is Cataloochee Valley. Before you begin your descent into the valley, stop at the overlook just past the intersection with Big Creek Road. From here, you can marvel at the valley sweeping away before you and the mountains rising up all around.

The valley is open to vehicle traffic from 8am to sunset. Though less visited than other areas, like Cades Cove on the western side of the park, Cataloochee sees its fair share of visitors. Most arrive in the evenings shortly before sunset to see the elk grazing in the fields. If you don't plan on camping and you'd rather avoid the crowds, as small as they may be, visit in midday, take a hike, and see if you can find the elk in the woods; it's where they go to escape the heat.

The ✪ **Cataloochee Campground** (campground 828/497-9270, reservations 877/444-6777 or www.recreation.gov, Mar.-Oct., $20, reservations required) has 27 tent and RV sites. There is a horse camp with seven sites not far up the valley; down the valley there's a group campground with three sites and room for much larger parties. This highly recommended campsite is one of the most secluded you'll find in the frontcountry.

Sights

There are four prominent structures still standing in Cataloochee Valley: two homes, a school, and a church. A few other structures and ruins, cemeteries, fences, and walls remain throughout the valley as well. The most prominent building is the **Palmer Chapel and Cemetery.** The chapel was built in 1898, but it's been some time since there's been a regular service here. Now it stands empty: its doors open to the forest, the view from its windows nothing but trees. Throughout the year there are some great opportunities to capture the chapel in all sorts of lighting, weather, and seasonal conditions. Today, the chapel sees sporadic use, the most regular being the annual reunion of the descendants of some of the oldest Cataloochee families. Descendants of the Barnes, Bennett, Caldwell, Noland, and Palmer families gather here to eat, hold a short church service, and maintain the cemetery.

Across the road is the **Beech Grove School,** the last of three schools to serve the children of the valley. It's empty, too, save a few artifacts. Beech Grove School operated on a very different school schedule than most were familiar with. The only regular school sessions were held from November to January, sometimes February, and rarely into March.

Just up the road is the **Caldwell House.** We know from records that the owner, Hiram Caldwell, was prosperous, but you could tell that by looking at the 1906 home and comparing it to the other historic homes in the park, which are, by and large, log cabins. The Caldwell House is frame-built (similar to houses now) with paneling on the interior walls.

The final structure is the **Palmer House,** located off Big Creek Road, not far from the Cataloochee Ranger Station. Once, this was a log home— two, actually—connected by a covered walkway called a dog trot, but as the owners came into money in the early 1900s, they began making

Palmer Chapel in Cataloochee

improvements and remodeling the home. They covered the exterior and interior with weatherboarding and began using fancy wallpaper in some rooms (scraps of the wallpaper are there today). When the son inherited the property, he began to remodel, adding rooms on to the home and operating it as a boarding house. Renters were primarily anglers, there to fish in the three miles of stocked trout stream the family owned.

☉ CLINGMANS DOME

At 6,643 feet, Clingmans Dome is the third-highest mountain in the eastern United States and the highest in the Great Smoky Mountains. A flying saucer-like observation tower at the end of a long, steep walkway gives 360-degree views of the surrounding mountains, and on a clear day, that view can be as far as a hundred miles. More often, though, it's misty up here in the clouds, and Clingmans Dome receives so much precipitation that its woods are actually a coniferous rainforest. The road to the summit is closed December 1-March 31, but the observation tower remains open for those willing to make the hike. To get to Clingmans Dome, turn off Newfound Gap Road 0.1 miles south of Newfound Gap, and then take Clingmans Dome Road (closed in winter), which leads seven miles to the parking lot. The peak is near the center of the park, due north from Bryson City.

FONTANA DAM

At the southern edge of GSMNP lies Fontana Lake, a 10,230-acre reservoir created in the 1940s as part of the Tennessee Valley Authority's (TVA) efforts to supply electricity to the various communities and government and industrial facilities in the region. The 480-foot tall, 2,365-foot wide Fontana Dam, complete with three hydroelectric generators, was completed in 1944, providing much-needed electricity to the factories churning out materials for World War II, including in Oak Ridge, Tennessee, where research leading to the atomic bomb was conducted.

To build Fontana Dam, the TVA purchased more than 1,000 tracts of land and relocated around 600 families in five communities. Those folks left behind homes, schools, churches, and barns, all of which were covered by the lake. This displacement of so many families and elimination of these small communities was part of the tradeoff that resulted in the modernization of the region, when electric power became cheap and readily available and many jobs were required to complete the project. The dam also provides much-needed flood control to a region that receives between 55 and 82 inches of rainfall each year. Today, the TVA can regulate the depth of the lake by releasing water as they anticipate flood events, and the water level of Fontana Lake can vary by as much as 50 feet.

Fontana Dam is the highest concrete dam east of the Mississippi, and it provides great recreational opportunities. The Appalachian Trail crosses the dam itself, and thousands of boaters and anglers take to the lake each year. There are more than 238 miles of shoreline along Fontana Lake and over 10,000 acres of water surface. If you have your own boat, you can launch it from the **Fontana Marina** (40 Fontana Dam Rd., 828/498-2129, www.fontanavillage.com), or you can rent a kayak, canoe, or paddleboard (from $10/hour to $50/day) as well as a pontoon or fishing pontoon boat (from $75/hour to $330/day). Fishing guide services and seasonal tours of the lake are also available.

The exhibits at the **Fontana Dam Visitor Center** (Fontana Dam Rd., off N.C. 28 near the state line, www.tva.com, daily 9am-6pm May-Oct., free) tell the story of the region and the construction of the dam. There's also a small gift shop and a viewing platform overlooking the dam. Hikers take note: They sell backcountry camping permits and have showers in the back.

✪ NEWFOUND GAP ROAD

While many visitors use this 32-mile road that bisects Great Smoky Mountains National Park as a mere throughway, it's actually one of the prettiest drives you'll find anywhere. This curvy road alternates between exposed and tree-enclosed, and a number of scenic overlooks provide spectacular views of the Smokies. Stop at one that has a trail (more than half of them do) and take a short walk into the woods, or eat a picnic lunch on one of the mountainside overlooks. Whatever you do on this road between Cherokee and Gatlinburg, take your time and enjoy the ride.

SPORTS AND RECREATION

The Great Smoky Mountains National Park covers over 500,000 acres, and within that expanse are more than 800 miles of hiking trails, ranging from easy walks around major attractions to strenuous wilderness paths suited to the most experienced backpackers. A section of the Appalachian Trail goes through the park, crossing the Fontana Dam. There are dozens of books available about hiking in

the Smokies, available at bookstores and outfitters throughout the region as well as online. The park staffs a **Backcountry Information Office** (865/436-1297, 8am-5pm daily), and the knowledgeable folks who work there are a good first resource when planning a hiking trip. The park website (www.nps.gov/grsm) has some downloadable maps to give you a general sense of the lay of the land. The Great Smoky Mountains Association website (www.smokiesinformation.org) has a good online bookstore.

HIKING

The Great Smoky Mountains National Park contains hundreds of miles of hiking trails, ranging from family-friendly loop trails to strenuous wilderness treks. Below are a sampling of hikes in the park. Before embarking on any of these trails, obtain a park map, and talk to a park ranger to ascertain trail conditions and gauge whether it's suited to your hiking skills.

A quick and easy foray into the woods is the **Spruce-Fir Trail**, off Clingmans Dome Road, a walk of just over 0.3 miles. Almost flat, and mostly following a wooden boardwalk, this is the ideal trail if you simply want to stretch your legs and experience a bit of easily accessible forest atmosphere.

A longer but also fairly easy walk is the **Oconaluftee River Trail**, which begins behind the Oconaluftee Visitors Center. This path, which is gravel-covered, follows the river and goes through part of the Mountain Farm Museum grounds. Unlike all the other trails in the GSMNP, dogs and bicycles are allowed. It's about three miles round-trip, popular with families, and absolutely littered with wildflowers in the spring. An added bonus is that one end is adjacent to the GSMNP "Welcome" sign, and the National Park Service has conveniently installed a post and platform to hold your camera for selfies in front of it.

At many of the pullouts deeper into the park, you'll find Quiet Walkways. These short, easy trails pull you into the woods just far enough off the road that the road noise is drowned out by bird calls, rustling leaves, flowing streams, and mountain breezes that build a cocoon around you. Signs at the trailhead encourage you to take your time and lose yourself in the sounds of nature, the aroma of the leaves, water, flowers, and mountain air, and the textures of the wild woodlands.

At the Alum Cave Trail trailhead, off Newfound Gap Road, you'll find a trio of hikes ranging from easy to rugged. Hiking to Arch Rock is an easy 2.8-mile round-trip. Arch Rock has eroded into a giant arch. A moist, winding set of stairs goes under, up, and through the arch, and the trail continues to Alum Cave, another mile in, making for a 4.6-mile round-trip. Just before you get here you'll reach Inspiration Point, with a commanding view of the valley below, including the interesting Eye of the Needle rock formation on an adjacent ridge. Shortly after Inspiration Point, you'll come to Alum Cave, where Epsom salts and saltpeter (used in the manufacture of gunpowder) were mined starting in the 1830s. To get to Alum Cave, the path transitions from easy to moderate, but if you want to push on another 3.7 miles to the peak of Mount LeConte for a hike that's a little over 10 miles round-trip, you'll be in for a much more difficult trail. For around two miles you'll encounter many exposed ledges, some with waterfalls to negotiate, all with a cable

sign for the Alum Cave Trail

BEST HIKES

This is a beautiful country to tour by car, but you're not doing the landscape justice if you only experience it through your windshield. Here are some fantastic chances to get out and be surrounded by nature.

ANDREWS BALD
At Clingmans Dome, a few miles off Newfound Gap Road, this **3.5-mile round-trip** trail is one of the loveliest and most rewarding hikes you'll find.

GROTTO FALLS TRAIL
This popular hike to a picture-perfect waterfall off the Roaring Fork Motor Nature Trail is only **2.6 mile round-trip.**

HEN WALLOW FALLS TRAIL
In Cosby, a few miles northeast of Gatlinburg, you'll find this **4.4-mile round-trip** hike to a delicate waterfall some 90-feet high.

MOUNT CAMMERER TRAIL
It's a tough **11.2-mile round-trip** hike to the summit, but you're rewarded with some of the best views in the park, courtesy of a stone fire tower built in the 1930s.

LITTLE RIVER TRAIL
Keep this trail short and sweet as you follow an old logging road alongside Little River and through the home of the synchronous fireflies, or follow all **12.3 miles** for an out-and-back day hike.

LYNN CAMP PRONG
At first glance, this **21-mile round-trip** lollipop loop looks like a huge hike, but you can take as much time as you want on this trail—or even turn it into an overnighter. Whatever you do, hike to the lovely Indian Flats Falls before turning back.

ABRAMS FALLS TRAIL
A hike suited to just about anyone? That leads to a great waterfall? This **5-mile round-trip** hike is the one—and it's in Cades Cove, so you know you'll drive right by the trailhead.

RICH MOUNTAIN LOOP
This **8.5-mile round-trip** loop in Cades Cove is one of the most fabulous hikes in the park.

handhold you'll want to use, especially if the rocky path is slick. When you get to the top, you'll find yourself at the LeConte Lodge but not the actual summit. To reach the highest point at the summit of Mount LeConte, follow a short trail to High Top. The views from High Top are nice, but not fantastic; for the best views, try Myrtle Point (a great spot to photograph the sunrise) or Cliff Top, near the lodge.

The **Boogerman Trail** is a loop trail off the Cove Creek Road in the Cataloochee section of the park. This is a moderate 7.5-mile round-trip that takes 2-3 hours to complete. You'll pass old-growth trees, streams and cascades, and several old homesites, including that of "Boogerman" himself, an early resident named Robert Palmer.

Another popular hike on the Newfound Gap Road is the **Chimney Tops Trail.** This four-mile round-trip starts out easy enough, but the last mile gains more than 830 vertical feet. Severe weather in 2012 turned parts of the trail into an obstacle course of rocks, roots, and mud, and at times the trail may be closed for ongoing rehabilitation. If the trail is open, the effort is worth the reward, as the views of Mount LeConte and Mount Kephart to the east and Sugarland Mountain to the west are amazing. This is one of the few mountains in the Smokies with a bare-rock top, and although the trail here is steep, it doesn't require any technical gear, just caution and the ability to scramble up steep rocks.

As if the mountains and valleys, flora and fauna, and close-enough-to-touch clouds weren't wonder enough, the GSMNP has literally hundreds of waterfalls. Several of the most popular and most beautiful are accessible from major trails. Close to Bryson City, 25-foot **Indian Creek Falls** is a moderate hike of less than two miles round-trip; it's a two-for-one deal, as the path also goes by Tom Branch Falls. Crossing Deep Creek on bridges and logs and going by old homesites, this is an especially interesting hike. The Deep Creek-Indian Creek Trailhead is at the end of Deep Creek Road in Bryson City. It gets very crowded in nice weather, particularly because this is a popular area for tubing, which makes parking quite difficult. Restrooms are available at the picnic area. Also accessible from the Indian Creek Trailhead is the path to 90-foot **Juney Whank Falls.** This hike is shorter but more difficult than to Indian Creek Falls. Since it shares the same trailhead, you can expect to find the same crowds and parking difficulties.

Mingo Falls, a beautiful 120-foot plume, is just outside the park, on the Qualla Boundary (Cherokee land). It can be seen from the Pigeon Creek Trail, which begins in the Mingo Falls Campground, off Big Cove Road south of Cherokee. The hike is very short, less than 0.5 miles round-trip, but it's fairly strenuous.

Some longer hikes on the Tennessee side of the park lead to equally beautiful falls. **Rainbow Falls** is 80 feet high and produces such a cloud of mist that when the sun hits it right, you can see a rainbow. In winter it sometimes freezes solid, which is an amazing sight. The Rainbow Falls Trail near Gatlinburg is a difficult 5.5 miles round-trip. It ascends about 1,500 vertical feet and is rocky most of the way, but it provides some great views of the falls and of Gatlinburg. Parking is available on Cherokee Orchard Road in Gatlinburg, but it fills up quickly, and you may need to pay to park a little farther from the trailhead.

The tallest waterfall, 100-foot **Ramsey Cascades,** is also the most difficult to reach. Those able to make a strenuous eight-mile round-trip hike are richly rewarded with a journey through old-growth hardwood forests and along fast-moving rivers. The pool at the bottom of the falls is a great place to glimpse some of the creatures that make GSMNP the Salamander Capital of the World. The parking area for the Ramsey Cascades Trail is off Greenbrier Road, a few miles southeast of Gatlinburg. The nearest portable toilets are at the picnic area on Greenbrier Road.

As tempting as it may be, don't try to climb the waterfalls; it's never a good idea. Because of its height, Ramsey Cascades is particularly dangerous. Maps and guides to the waterfalls are available at many locations in the park and at bookstores and outdoors shops nearby.

HORSEBACK RIDING

Three commercial stables in the park offer "rental" horses (about $30/hour). **Smokemont** (828/497-2373, www.smokemontridingstable.com) is located in North Carolina near Cherokee. Two are in Tennessee: **Smoky Mountain** (865/436-5634, www.smokymountainridingstables.com) and **Cades Cove** (10018 Campground Dr., Townsend, TN, 865/448-9009, http://cadescovestables.com).

In North Carolina, near Cherokee, an equestrian-friendly campground at **Round Bottom Horse Camp** (Straight Fork-Round Bottom Rd., 865/436-1261, www.nps.gov/grsm, $20) has five campsites, stalls, and bedding for horses. Its location, just inside the park and far up a narrow riverside road, makes it perfect for long rides with larger groups.

BICYCLE RENTALS

The **Cades Cove Store** (near Cades Cove Campground, 865/448-9034, www.cadescovetrading.com) rents bicycles in summer and fall (adult bikes $7.50/hour, kids and single-gear $4:50/hour). From the second week in May to the second-to-last Saturday in September, the park closes off the loop road through Caves Cove on Wednesday and Saturday mornings, sunrise-10am, so that cyclists and hikers can enjoy the cove without having to worry about automobile traffic.

FIELD SCHOOLS

Two Tennessee-based organizations affiliated with the GSMNP offer ways to get to know the park even better. The **Smoky Mountain Field School** (865/974-0150, www.smfs.utk.edu) teaches workshops and leads excursions to educate participants in a wide array of fields related to the Smokies. One-day classes focus on the history and cultural heritage of the park, the lives of some of the park's most interesting animals, folk medicine, and cooking of the southern Appalachians, and much more. Instructors also lead one-day and overnight hikes into the heart of the park. This is a great way to discover the park far beyond what you would be able to do on your own, so check their schedule and sign up for a class that interests you.

The **Great Smoky Mountains Institute at Tremont** (9275 Tremont Rd., Townsend, TN, 865/448-6709, www.gsmit.org) teaches students of all ages about the ecology of the region, wilderness rescue and survival skills, and even nature photography. Many of the classes and guided trips are part of Elderhostels, kids camps, or teacher-training institutes; however, there are also rich opportunities for unaffiliated learners.

FOOD

Unless you're staying at the LeConte Lodge, you'll have to leave the park for meals. The easiest way is simply to drive into Bryson City or Cherokee, or in Tennessee, Gatlinburg or Pigeon Forge, which are all right on the edge of the park. In Gatlinburg, try the **Smoky Mountain Brewery** (1004 Parkway, Suite 501, Gatlinburg, 865/436-4200, www.smoky-mtn-brewery.com, 11:30am-1am daily, under $20), a popular brewpub and restaurant. The menu is about what you'd expect—burgers, wings, and cheesesteaks—but they also have some pretty good pizzas and even barbecue ribs. Their beer selection includes porters, wheat beers, red ales, and hoppy pale ales.

Since the wildfires in 2016, many

restaurants, hotels, motels and cabins in and around Gatlinburg are rebuilding. One of the biggest losses was the excellent restaurant and inn at Buckberry Creek. Another excellent option for high-end dining and lodging is **Christopher Place** (1500 Pinnacles Way, 423/299-4062, www.christopherplace.com), located in nearby Newport, Tennessee. This AAA Four Diamond award winner features luxurious rooms ($130-330), and an outstanding restaurant. The **Mountain View Restaurant** (open from 5pm Tues.-Sun., around $50) serves a small menu that changes daily, but common items include kale salad, a variety of soups, roasted seasonal vegetables, steak, or seafood (the seared filet with Roquefort-pecan butter is quite tasty).

The Wild Plum Tea Room (555 Buckhorn Rd., 865/436-3808, www.wildplumtearoom.com, 11am-3pm Thurs.-Sat., $10-16) is a lunch-only restaurant inspired by Austrian teahouses. They serve the southern classic, tomato pie, but the real stars of the menu are the chef's specials. The specials vary daily but in the past have included lobster pie, a salmon burger, smoked salmon sandwiches, and yellowfin tuna.

Poynor's Pommes Frites (131 The Island Dr., Suite 3107, Pigeon Forge, 865/774-7744, 11am-11pm daily, $5-10) may not look like much from the outside, but the food is great. The specialty is the pommes frites (French fries). Done in a Belgian style (fried, cooled, and then fried again), they're crispy on the outside and fluffy inside, and served plain, with your choice of sauce, or even topped with cheese, bacon, onions, and jalapenos. You can't make a meal of French fries, so Poynor's serves a short menu of German bratwurst served on a hard roll.

While you're here, you may as well sample some 'shine. **Sugarlands Distilling Company** (805 Parkway, 865/325-1355, www.sugarlands.com, 10am-10:30pm Mon.-Sat., noon-6pm Sun., tours free) has an excellent distillery where you can see the whole operation in action, do a little sampling, and grab a quart or two to take home. With eight moonshines ranging from flavored to hi-test and a pair of whiskeys to try, you'll have to pace yourself.

ACCOMMODATIONS

There is only one inn in the entire 500,000-acre park, and it's an unusual one: the ♥ **LeConte Lodge** (865/429-5704, www.lecontelodge.com, late Mar.-mid-Nov., $140 adults, $85 children ages 4-12, includes lodging, breakfast, and dinner). Like the summit, the Lodge is accessible only via the network of hiking trails that crisscross the park. And if the accessibility limitation isn't rustic enough for you, this collection of cabins has no running water or electricity. What the Lodge does have is views for days and the seclusion of the Smoky Mountains backcountry. Oh, and a hearty breakfast and dinner come with each room.

LeConte Lodge has no hot showers, but in every cabin there is a bucket for a sponge bath (which can be surprisingly refreshing after a hot day on the trail), which you can fill with warm water from the kitchen, though you need to supply your own washcloth and towel. There are a few flush toilets in a separate building. The only lights, aside from headlamps and flashlights, are kerosene lanterns. For the most part, it's a rustic spot, harkening back to the Lodge's 1934 arrival on the slopes of Mount LeConte.

Dinner and breakfast are served at the same time every day, 6pm for dinner and 8am for breakfast, and the meals are substantial enough to fuel you for another day on the trail.

The Lodge doesn't lack for charm, but it does for comfort, so if you're the five-star hotel, breakfast-in-bed type, this may not be the place for you. Catering to hikers who are happier to have a dry place to sleep and a bed that's more comfy than their sleeping bag, it's short on the luxury amenities, and rooms are, in truth, bunk beds in small, drafty cabins. But if you're a hiker or if you just love to have a completely different experience when you travel, this is a one-of-a-kind accommodation. Rooms fill quickly—up to a year in advance.

For those who don't want to camp or hike to a rustic lodge, there are countless motels just outside the GSMNP. Reservations are always a good idea, especially in summer and in leaf season. There are many choices in Cherokee, Maggie Valley, Bryson City, Pigeon Forge, Gatlinburg, Sevierville, and other neighboring communities. In addition to the many chain motels, affordable mom-and-pop motels also dot this landscape in abundance. Two homey choices in Gatlinburg are the **Riverhouse Motels** (904 River Rd., Gatlinburg, 865/436-7821, www.riverhousemotels.com, around $150 in season, around 90 off-season), and **Johnson's Inn** (242 Bishop Lane, Gatlinburg, 800/842-1930, www.johnsons-inn.hotels-tennessee. com, $60-125). In Cherokee, on the North Carolina side of the park, go with a hotel like **Cherokee Grand Hotel** (196 Painttown Rd., 828/497-0050, www.cherokeegrandhotel. com, $109-159), located only five minutes from the park entrance, or cabin accommodations with **Panther**

LeConte Lodge

Creek Cabins (Wrights Creek Rd., Cherokee, 828/497-2461, www.panthercreekresort.com, cabins $100-150), a quiet, quaint, comfortable set of cabins just outside downtown Cherokee.

CAMPING

The GSMNP has many locations for camping. Campers can stay up to 14 consecutive nights at car-accessible campsites, but no more than three consecutive nights at backcountry campsites, and only nonconsecutive nights in shelters and at campsite 113. There are 10 car-accessible campgrounds, each of which has cold running water and flush toilets but no showers, power, or water hookups. Most of these sites are first come, first served, but May 15-October 15 sites at the Elkmont, Smokemont, Cades Cove, Catallochee, and Cosby campgrounds can be reserved (877/444-6777, www.nps.gov/grsm).

The Cataloochee Campground (campground 865-436-1200, reservations 877/444-6777 or www.recreation.gov, Mar.-Oct., $20, reservations required) has 27 tent and RV sites. There is a horse camp with seven sites not far up the valley; down the valley there's a group campground with three sites and room for much larger parties. This highly recommended campsite is one of the most secluded you'll find in the frontcountry.

Cosby Campground (471 Cosby Campground Road A, Cosby, TN, 423/487-2683, www.recreation.gov, Mar.-Oct., $14) has 157 sites for tents and RVs. Despite being home to the park's third-largest campground, Cosby is known as the quietest of the park's gateways. There are a number of trails that originate from the campground.

The Elkmont Campground (434 Elkmont Rd., Gatlinburg, 865/430-5560, www.recreation.gov, $17-23) has 220 campsites, 55 of them along the Little River, with front-row seats to the firefly light show, provided you're here at the right time. This is the largest of the campgrounds in GSMNP, and one of the most visited. In addition to the firefly show and the attraction of Little River, this site also serves as a good base for exploring the area.

The Cades Cove Campground (10042 Campground Drive, Townsend, TN, campground 865/448-2472, reservations 877/444-6777 or www.recreation.gov, $17-20) is a popular spot where you'll definitely want to reserve a campsite. This campground is open year-round, and though the occupancy is a little lower in the dead of winter, you'll still find a few intrepid visitors taking refuge from the cold in one of the 159 campsites here. Hikers, take note: There are several backcountry campsites off the trails in Cades Cove, making it a good base for overnight trips.

Just outside the park, Fontana Village Resort (300 Woods Rd., Fontana Dam, 828/498-2211 or 800/849-2258, www.fontanavillage.com, lodge $109-219, cabins $109-459, camping $15-40), offers a place to lay your head in your choice of accommodations: tent or RV camping, one- to three-bedroom cabins, and lodge rooms. There are 100 lodge rooms, 110 cabins, and 20 campsites. At the lodge you'll find complimentary wireless internet in the public areas; other amenities include an outdoor pool and lazy river as well as a fitness center and small day spa.

Another car-accessible camping option is the Mile High Campground (828/269-2945, www.campmilehigh.

com, $20 tent or RV, $30 primitive cabin, $50 group site) located on the Cherokee Reservation and owned by a member of the Eastern Band of the Cherokee. It is near Blue Ridge Parkway milepost 458; turn onto Wolf Laurel Gap, and the campground entrance is one mile along, on the left, after the "Molly's Gap Road" sign. This campground is indeed a little over a mile high in elevation and has around 50 sites in tent and RV areas along with primitive cabins. A beautiful campground near a number of hikes, the Blue Ridge Parkway, Cherokee, and the Great Smoky Mountains National Park, it's a great spot to set up for a few days. All campsites have fire rings and are fairly private. Bears and elk are common sights, so take pictures, but use caution.

Backcountry camping is abundant. It is only permitted at designated sites and shelters, and a permit is required, but the permits are free and can be obtained at any of 15 different visitors centers and campground offices throughout the park or online (https://smokiespermits.nps.gov). The Appalachian Trail runs through, hugging the ridgeline and the border between North Carolina and Tennessee, and shelters on the trail fill up fast with through-hikers and day hikers, but other shelters and campsites on side trails are ideal for out-and-back camping trips. The Kephart shelter and the shelter at Laurel Gap are on two beautiful trails, and a number of campsites—numbers 52-57—are on the Mountains-to-Sea Trail that traverses North Carolina. There are also five drive-in horse camps ($20-25) and seven group campgrounds ($35-65). A map of the available campsites can be found on the park's website (www.nps.gov/grsm). Before camping at the

GSMNP, be sure to familiarize yourself with the park's backcountry regulations and etiquette, available online and at locations in the park.

INFORMATION AND SERVICES

The official website of **Great Smoky Mountains National Park** (www.nps.gov/grsm) has a good deal of the information you'll need to plan a trip. At the visitors centers in Sugarlands, Oconaluftee, Cades Cove, and Clingmans Dome you'll find additional information from helpful rangers and fellow travelers. The websites of **Smoky Mountain Host** (www.visitsmokies.org) and the **Blue Ridge National Heritage Area** (www.blueridgeheritage.com) provide additional information. Detailed touring suggestions for sites associated with Cherokee history and heritage can be found at the websites of **Cherokee Heritage Trails** (www.cherokeeheritagetrails.org) and the **North Carolina Folklife Institute** (www.ncfolk.org), and in *Cherokee Heritage Trails,* an excellent guidebook that can be purchased at either website.

The nearest hospitals from GSMNP are **LeConte Medical Center** (742 Middle Creek Rd., Sevierville, TN, 865/446-7000, www.lecontemedicalcenter.com) in Sevierville, Tennessee, about 25 minutes from the west park entrance; **Blount Memorial Hospital** (907 E. Lamar Alexander Pkwy., Maryville, TN, 865/983-7211, www.blountmemorial.org) in Maryville, Tennessee, about an hour away from the west park entrance; and **Swain Community Hospital** (45 Plateau St., Bryson City, NC, 828/488-2155) in Bryson City, a little less than 30 minutes from the eastern park entrance in Cherokee.

GETTING THERE AND AROUND

From Asheville it's easy to get to GSMNP. In just over an hour you can be in Cataloochee, at the north end of the park, to camp, hike, and watch for elk in a serene mountain cove; to get there you take I-40 west to Exit 20 and follow the signs. You can also take I-40 west into Tennessee, then follow the Foothills Parkway to U.S. 321 and skirt the edge of GSMNP to Gatlinburg, Tennessee, and the entrance to the park (a trip of about 90 minutes). From Gatlinburg, you can make a loop back to Asheville by taking Newfound Gap Road across GSMNP to Cherokee, North Carolina (about 2.5 hours) and then back to Asheville via U.S. 441 to U.S. 19 to I-40, a total loop of about 3.5 hours and some 175 miles.

You can also head straight to Cherokee from Asheville and enter GSMNP via Newfound Gap Road there. It's an hour's drive on I-40 west to exit 27, then take U.S. 19 south to U.S. 441, which carries you right into Cherokee. Alternately you can take the more scenic, but much longer, route and get to Cherokee via the Blue Ridge Parkway. This route is only 83 miles, but it takes 2-2.5 hours. If you want to go this way, head south out of Asheville along U.S. 25 and pick up the Blue Ridge Parkway about 5.5 miles out of town; turn south on the Parkway and drive it until you reach Cherokee and GSMNP. And, of course, you can reverse the course if you're making that grand loop and return to Asheville via the Blue Ridge Parkway by picking it up in Cherokee and driving north.

Maggie Valley

Maggie Valley is a vacation town from the bygone era of long family road trips in wood-paneled station wagons. Coming down the mountain toward Maggie Valley you'll pass an overlook that, on a morning when the mountains around Soco Gap are looped with fog, is surely one of the most beautiful vistas in the state.

SIGHTS AND ENTERTAINMENT

In a state with countless attractions for automotive enthusiasts, Maggie Valley's **Wheels through Time Museum** (62 Vintage Lane, 828/926-6266, www.wheelsthroughtime.com, 9am-5pm Thurs.-Mon. April-late Nov., $15 adults, $12 over age 65, $6 ages 5-12, free under age 4) stands out as one of the most fun. A dazzling collection of nearly 300 vintage motorcycles and a fair number of cars are on display, including rarities like a 1908 Indian, a 1914 Harley-Davidson, military motorcycles from both World Wars, and some gorgeous postwar bikes. This collection, which dates mostly to before 1950, is maintained in working order—almost every one of the bikes is revved up from time to time, and the museum's founder has been known to take a spin on one of the treasures.

Bluegrass music and clogging are a big deal in this town. The great bluegrass banjo player Raymond Fairchild is a Maggie native, and after his

Maggie Valley

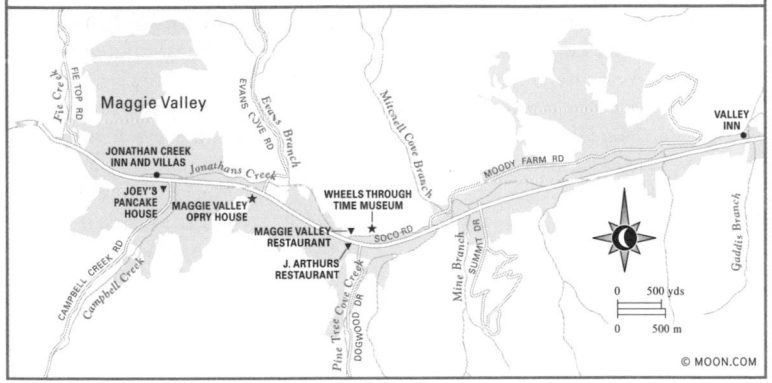

50-year touring and recording career, he and his wife, Shirley, are now the hosts of the **Maggie Valley Opry House** (3605 Soco Rd., 828/926-9336, www.raymondfairchild.com, 8pm Mon.-Fri. June-Oct.). In season, you can find bluegrass and country music concerts and clogging exhibitions most every night.

SPORTS AND RECREATION

SKIING AND WINTER SPORTS

Maggie Valley's **Cataloochee Ski Area** (1080 Ski Lodge Rd., off U.S. 19, 800/768-0285, snow conditions 800/768-3588, www.cataloochee.com, lift tickets $20-65, rentals $21-30) has slopes geared to every level of skier and snowboarder. Classes and private lessons are taught for all ages. At Cataloochee's sister snow-sports area, **Tube World** (U.S. 19, next to Ski Area, 828/926-0285, www.cataloochee.com, $25, must be over 42 inches tall, late Nov.-mid-Mar.), you can zip down the mountain on inner tubes, and there's a "Wee Bowl" area for children (call ahead, $5).

HIKING

Near Maggie Valley, the mountains become rough. Located on the valley floor, Maggie Valley is surprisingly short on trails, and what trails there are, are quite strenuous. There's the 2.6-mile stroll around **Lake Junaluska,** but the majority of the trails are found at the crest of the mountains, along the Blue Ridge Parkway. To the east of Maggie Valley, the mountains are a little more forgiving. There are many trails of various intensities and lengths, but in the immediate area, you'll have to take the Heintooga Spur Road, a connector road between the Parkway and Great Smoky Mountains National Park, to a mile-high campground, a picnic area with unparalleled views, and the **Flat Creek Trail.** On Heintooga Spur Road, you'll pass into Great Smoky Mountains National Park proper and be treated to no fewer than five stunning overlooks, the best of which is the Mile High Overlook, offering a glimpse of Clingmans Dome, Mount LeConte, Mount Kephart, and Mount Guyot.

The Blue Ridge Parkway (BRP) is not far from Maggie Valley, which means there are a number of hiking trails to explore. Easy trails include the **Buck Springs Trail** (BRP milepost 407.6), just over one mile long, and the 0.25-mile **Bear Pen Gap Trail** (BRP milepost 427.6) that connects to the Mountains-to-Sea Trail; additionally, you can go for a stroll around **Lake Junaluska** in the town of Maggie Valley. Moderate trails are longer and usually involve some elevation gain and loss; a couple of the best are **Graveyard Fields Loop Trail** (BRP milepost 418.8), a 3.2-mile loop through alpine-like meadows. Extend your hike here by following one of the spur trails that lead to some fantastic waterfalls. Another moderate option is the **Richland Balsam Trail** (BRP milepost 431), a loop through a spruce and fir forest. Tougher trails often pay off with the best views, and **Waterrock Knob Trail** (BRP milepost 451.2) does that on a 1.18-mile trail that's steep and a little rocky but manageable. It leads to a summit where views await. Another option is the **Devil's Courthouse Trail** (BRP milepost 422.4), a short but strenuous hike of just under 0.5 miles leading to another panoramic summit view.

FOOD

✪ **Joey's Pancake House** (4309 Soco Rd., 828/926-0212, www.joeyspancake.com, 7am-noon Fri.-Wed., about $8) has been flipping flapjacks for travelers and locals alike since 1966 and it's exactly the kind of place you picture: paper menu placemats; hot, weak, delicious coffee; a little kitschy; packed with regulars. The pancakes, waffles, and country ham are so good that lines form on the weekends—get here early. And if you're as taken by the pancakes as I am, you'll pick up some of their mix to take home with you.

J. Arthurs Restaurant (2843 Soco Rd., 828/926-1817, www.jarthurs.com, 4:30pm-late Tues.-Sun., $15-25) is a popular spot locally for steaks, which are the house specialty; they've been serving them up for more than 25 years. The restaurant also has a variety of seafood and pasta dishes, but there are few vegetarian options.

The Italian food at **Frankie's Trattoria** (1037 Soco Rd., 828/926-6216, www.frankiestrattoria.com, 11:30am-9pm Mon.-Thurs., 11:30am-10pm Fri.-Sat., $9-22) is a bright spot in Maggie Valley. Pizzas are quite good, pasta dishes are shareably big and very tasty, and the wine list is great.

If you want barbecue, try **Willie Brooks BBQ** (1778 Dellwood Rd., 828/944-1227, www.williebrooksbbq.com, 11am-8pm Mon.-Thurs. and Sat., 11am-9pm Fri., $7-24). Their pulled pork is smoky and moist, the brisket is excellent, and their sauces aren't too heavy handed. All told, it's solid barbecue that's only going to get better.

A Maggie Valley dining institution that's been around since 1952 is **Maggie Valley Restaurant** (2804 Soco Rd., 828/926-0425, www.maggievalleyrestaurant.net, 7am-9pm daily May-Oct., $5-12). Expect comfort-food classics—meatloaf, meatloaf sandwiches, something called a chuck wagon, pork chops, biscuit sandwiches, grits, bottomless coffee, and even buttermilk—along with one of the best pieces of fresh fried trout you'll find in these mountains.

ACCOMMODATIONS

The main drag through Maggie Valley (Soco Rd./U.S. 19) is lined with motels, including some of the familiar national chains. Among the pleasant independent motels are **The Valley Inn** (236 Soco Rd., 800/948-6880, www.thevalleyinn.com, in-season rates vary, from $39 off-season, $79 in-season) and **Jonathan Creek Inn and Villas** (4324 Soco Rd., 800/577-7812, www.jonathancreekinn.com, from $90), which has creek-side rooms with screened porches.

There is one fantastic campground in the area, the ✪ **Balsam Mountain Campground** (Heintooga Spur Rd., MP 458.2, 828/269-2945, www.nps.gov/grsm, reservations at www.recreation.gov, $20, tent and RV sites available), which is the highest campground in Great Smoky Mountains National Park at 5,310 feet. This primitive campground has 43 sites for tents and RVs, with a dedicated tent-only section. It's a beautiful, isolated campground that's often overlooked, as it's slightly off the beaten path; that, in addition to the fact that it's a primitive campground (read: no showers), means that for most of the year you won't have many neighbors here. Plus, if you're driving a vehicle you feel comfortable taking on forest roads, the Balsam Mountain Road (sometimes called Round Bottom Road) continues on from the campground, making a nice trip through the forest down to Cherokee (it takes about two hours).

GETTING THERE AND AROUND

U.S. 19 is the main thoroughfare in these parts, leading from Asheville to the Great Smoky Mountains National Park. If you're taking your time between Asheville, Boone, or parts north, the Blue Ridge Parkway is a beautiful, but slow, drive to this part of the state. Maggie Valley is also a reasonably short jog off I-40 via exits 20, 24, and 27.

Cherokee and the Qualla Boundary

The town of Cherokee is a study in juxtapositions: the cultural traditions of the Cherokee people, the region's natural beauty, a 24-hour casino, and community-wide preparation for the future. Cherokee is the seat of government of the Eastern Band of the Cherokee, who have lived in these mountains for centuries. Today, their traditional arts and crafts, government, and cultural heritage are very much alive, although their language seems to be disappearing. The Qualla ("KWA-lah") Boundary is not a reservation but a large tract of land owned and governed by the Cherokee people. Institutions like the Museum of the Cherokee Indian and the Qualla Arts and Crafts Mutual provide a solid base for the Eastern Band's cultural life. As you drive around, take a look at the road signs: Below each English road name is that same name in Cherokee, a beautiful script created by Sequoyah, a 19th-century Cherokee silversmith. This language, once nearly extinct, is being taught to the community's youth now, and there is a

Cherokee language immersion school on the Qualla Boundary. This doesn't mean the language is not in danger; few Cherokee people speak it fluently.

The main street in Cherokee is a classic cheesy tourist district where you'll find "Indian" souvenirs—factory-made moccasins, plastic tomahawks, peace pipes, faux bearskins, the works. In a retro way, this part of Cherokee, with its predictable trinket shops and fudgeries, is charming.

Aside from its proximity to the Great Smoky Mountains National Park and the Blue Ridge Parkway, the biggest draw in town is Harrah's Cherokee Casino, one of the largest casino hotels in the state and home to a world-class spa. The 24-hour entertainment opportunities attract visitors from far and wide, some of whom stay on the property the whole time, while others take a break from the slap of cards and the flash of slot machines to experience the natural and cultural wonders of Cherokee.

Take all of this that you see—the casino, the tacky tourist shops, and the stereotyping signs—with a grain of salt, as they don't represent the true nature of the Cherokee people and their long history.

Cherokee

© MOON.COM

SIGHTS

HARRAH'S CHEROKEE CASINO

The Eastern Band of the Cherokee operates **Harrah's Cherokee Casino and Hotel** (777 Casino Dr., 828/497-7777, www.harrahscherokee.com, 24 hours daily). This full-bore Vegas-style casino has more than 3,800 digital games and slot machines along with around 150 table games, such as baccarat, blackjack, roulette, and a poker-only room. Inside the casino complex is a 3,000-seat concert venue where acts like Alicia Keys and the Black Crows have performed, a huge buffet, and a grab-and-go food court next to the casino floor. Unlike in the rest of the state, smoking is allowed on the casino floor, though certain areas have been designated as nonsmoking. Inside the hotel portion of the casino are a restaurant, a Starbucks, and the **Mandara Spa,** which offers salon and spa services like massages and facials.

★ MUSEUM OF THE CHEROKEE INDIAN

The Museum of the Cherokee Indian (589 Tsali Blvd., 828/497-3481, www.cherokeemuseum.org, 9am-7pm Mon.-Sat., 9am-5pm Sun. late June-Aug., 9am-5pm daily Sept.-May, $10, $6 ages 6-12, free under age 5) was founded in 1948 and was originally housed in a log cabin. Today, it is a well-regarded modern museum and locus of community culture. In the exhibits that trace the long history of the Cherokee people, you may notice the disconcertingly realistic mannequins. Local community members volunteered to be models for these mannequins, allowing casts to be made of their faces and bodies so that the figures would not reflect an outsider's notion of what Native Americans should look like. The Museum of the Cherokee Indian traces their history from the Paleo-Indian people of the Pleistocene, when the ancestral Cherokees were hunter-gatherers, through the ancient days of Cherokee civilization, and into contact with European settlers.

A great deal of this exhibit focuses on the 18th and 19th centuries, when a series of tragedies befell the Cherokee as a result of the invasion of their homeland. It was also a time of great cultural advancement, including Sequoyah's development of the script to write the Cherokee language. The forced relocation of Native Americans called the Trail of Tears began near here, along the North Carolina-Georgia border, in the early 19th century. A small contingent of Cherokees remained in the Smokies at the time of the Trail of Tears, successfully eluding, and then negotiating with, the U.S. military,

Museum of the Cherokee Indian

who were trying to force most of the Native Americans in the Southeast to move to Oklahoma. Those who stayed out in the woods, along with a few others who were able to return from Oklahoma, are the ancestors of today's Eastern Band, and their history is truly remarkable.

A favorite part of the museum are the stories, legends, and myths described on placards throughout the building. There's the story of a boy who became a bear and convinced his entire clan to become bears also. There's one about Spearfinger, a frightening creature that some say still lives in these woods today. And there are tales about Selu, the corn mother, and Kanati, the lucky hunter. Cherokee member and contemporary writer Marilou Awiakta has written widely about Selu, tying the past and present together with taut lines of thought that challenge our views on culture and technology.

✪ QUALLA ARTS AND CRAFTS MUTUAL

Across the street from the museum is the Qualla Arts and Crafts Mutual (645 Tsali Blvd., 828/497-3103, http://quallaartsandcrafts.com, 8am-6pm Mon.-Sat., 9am-5pm Sun.), a community arts co-op where local artists sell their work. The gallery's high standards and the community's thousands of years of artistry make for a collection of very special pottery, baskets, masks, and other traditional art. The Qualla co-op does a great service to this community by providing a year-round market for the work of traditional Cherokee artists, whose stewardship of and innovation in the arts are so important. The double-woven baskets are especially beautiful, as are the carvings of the masks representing

each of the seven clans of the Cherokee people (the Bird, Deer, Longhair, Blue, Wolf, Paint, and Wild Potato).

TOP EXPERIENCE

✪ OCONALUFTEE INDIAN VILLAGE

Oconaluftee Indian Village (778 Drama Rd., 828/497-2111, http://visitcherokeenc.com, 10am-4pm Mon.-Sat. Apr.-Nov., $20 adults, $12 children, free 5 and under) is a recreated Cherokee Indian Village tucked into the hills above the town. Here, you'll see how the tribe lived in the 18th century. Tour guides in period costumes lead groups on walking lectures with stops at stations where you can see Cherokee cultural, artistic, and daily-life activities performed as authentically as possible. From cooking demos to flint knapping (for arrowheads and spear points) to wood carving and clay work, you'll get a look at how the Cherokee lived centuries ago. The highlight of the tour is the ritual dance demonstration showing a half-dozen dances and explaining their cultural significance.

RECREATION
FISHING

Cherokee has more than 30 miles of streams, rivers, and creeks ideal for fishing. Add to that the fact that the Eastern Band owns and operates a fish hatchery that releases around 250,000 trout into these waters every year and you have the perfect mix for fantastic fishing. Unlike in the rest of North Carolina, you don't need a North Carolina fishing license; you need a Tribal Fishing Permit (www.fishcherokee.com, 1 day $10, 2 days $17, 3 days $27, 5 days $47), sold at a number of outlets in Cherokee. You'll find brook, brown, golden, and rainbow trout, and it's fly-rod only, so you have to have your cast down pat if you want to bring in a big one. There are both catch-and-release and catch-and-keep waters in the Qualla Boundary, but if you want to fish outside the boundary, you need a North Carolina or Tennessee fishing permit. Tennessee permits are only valid inside the Great Smoky Mountains National Park boundaries in North Carolina.

GOLF

The **Sequoyah National Golf Club** (79 Cahons Rd., Whittier, 828/497-3000, www.sequoyahnational.com, 18 holes, par 72, greens fees from $55), five miles south of Cherokee in Whittier, is a stunning mountain golf course. Making the most of the contours and elevation, the course offers tee boxes with breathtaking views of the fairway and the Smoky Mountains. The course record is 62, an impressive feat on a normal course, but here it's something else. Holes like number 12 and number 15 test a golfer's club knowledge and course IQ. This is a tough course for first-timers because so many of the holes have blind approaches, doglegs, or both, but it's enjoyable enough.

WATER SPORTS

For fun on the water, try **Smoky Mountain Tubing** (1847 Tsali Blvd., 828/497-4545, http://cherokeetubeandraft.com, 10am-6pm daily, weather permitting, $12). They do only one thing: rent tubes on which you'll drift down the river and splash your friends. Smoky Mountain Tubing has mountains of tubes, so rent one and float down the Oconaluftee River for two or three hours. They have a fleet of shuttle buses to pick you up a few miles downstream.

ENTERTAINMENT AND EVENTS

Of the several outdoor dramas for which North Carolina is known, among the longest running is Cherokee's *Unto These Hills* (Mountainside Theater, 688 Drama Rd., adjacent to Oconaluftee Indian Village, 866/554-4557, www.visitcherokeenc.com, 8pm Mon.-Sat. June-Aug. 15, $25-28 adults, $15-18 ages 6-12, free under age 6). For more than 60 summers, Cherokee actors have told the story of their nation's history, from ancient times through the Trail of Tears. Every seat in the house is a good seat at the Mountainside Theater, and the play is certainly enlightening. Be warned: If you're gunshy or easily startled, there is some cannon fire and gunfire in the play.

Hear stories, learn dances, and interact with Cherokee storytellers at the **Cherokee Bonfire** (Oconaluftee Islands Park, Tsalagi Rd. and Tsali Blvd., where U.S. 19 and U.S. 441 intersect, 800/438-1601, www.visitcherokeenc.com, 5pm-7pm Fri.-Sat. May-Oct., free, including marshmallows). Bring your bathing suit and some water shoes to the bonfire; afterward, you may want to go for a wade or a quick dip in the Oconaluftee River, which is wide, rocky, and fun.

FOOD
HARRAH'S CHEROKEE CASINO

The arrival and expansion of Harrah's Cherokee Casino (777 Casino Dr., 828/497-7777, www.harrahscherokee.com) brought with it a bevy of restaurants. **Ruth's Chris Steak House**

(5pm-10pm Mon.-Thurs., 5pm-11pm Fri., 4pm-11pm Sat., 4pm-9pm Sun., around $60) is here, and like its other locations, serves a variety of steaks and chops, a handful of seafood dishes, and more than 220 wines.

Brio Tuscan Grille (828/497-8233, www.briositalian.com, 11:30am-10pm Sun.-Thurs., 11:30am-11pm Fri.-Sat., $20-40) is a fine Italian restaurant specializing in dishes from northern Italy. This isn't a spaghetti-and-meatballs kind of place; it's more refined, with dishes like *lasagna Bolognese al forno*, lobster and shrimp ravioli with crab *insalata*, Tuscan grilled pork chops, and *bistecca alla Fiorentina*. The ambience is nice, the wine list is nicer, and the food is great.

What's a casino without a buffet? Anyone can find something that satisfies at Chef's Stage Buffet (4:30pm-10pm Mon. and Thurs., 4:30pm-11pm Fri.-Sat., 1pm-10pm Sun., closed Tues.-Wed., $26 Mon.-Fri., Sun. seafood buffet $32), where four chefs run four distinct micro-restaurants. There's everything here: Asian dishes, Latin, Italian, seafood, Southern, barbecue, a salad bar you could land an airplane on, and desserts for days. A second buffet option is the Selu Garden Café (7am-2:30pm daily, around $15), which offers up a hearty breakfast every day, a slightly more upscale brunch on weekends, and a bottomless soup and salad bar.

Downstairs in Harrah's is an airport-style food court that includes the Earl of Sandwich (11am-11pm daily, around $10), a deli serving hot and cold sandwiches and panini; grab-and-go sandwiches are available 24 hours daily. There is also Pizzeria Uno Express (11am-11pm Sun.-Thurs., 11am-2am Fri.-Sat., around $10), serving thin-crust pizza, calzones,

and pasta dishes; Noodle Bar (6pm-2am Mon.-Thurs., 5pm-3am Fri.-Sat., 5pm-2am Sun., around $18), serving Asian dishes like ramen and dim sum options; Johnny Rockets (24 hours daily, around $10), serving burgers, sandwiches, fries, milkshakes, and breakfast; and a Dunkin' Donuts Express (24 hours daily, around $5) that has doughnuts and coffee. The food court also has a variety of snacks and drinks available 24 hours daily.

Just outside of the town of Cherokee is Granny's Kitchen (1098 Painttown Rd., 828/497-5010, www.grannyskitchencherokee.com, 7am-11am daily June-Aug. and Oct., and Fri.-Sun. Apr.-May, Sept., and Nov.; 11am-8pm mid-Mar.-Nov., $8-12), a country-buffet restaurant where you can get some of the best fried chicken in North Carolina. Granny is actually a man who likes to joke, "no one wants to eat at grandpa's, so I became granny."

ACCOMMODATIONS

Cherokee has many motels, including a Holiday Inn (376 Painttown Rd., 828/497-3113, www.ihg.com, from $90) and an Econo Lodge (20 River Rd./U.S. 19, 828/497-4575, www.choicehotels.com, from $70, pets allowed).

✪ Harrah's Cherokee Casino and Hotel (777 Casino Dr., 828/497-7777, www.harrahscherokee.com, $100-500) is, without a doubt, the best place to stay in Cherokee. The rooms are spacious, comfortable, and well kept; there's the casino and a number of dining options an elevator ride away; and the spa provides an added layer of amenities you don't find at other hotels in town.

There's something about visiting a place and living where the residents live, and ✪ Panther Creek Cabins (Wrights Creek Rd., 828/497-2461, www.panthercreekresort.com, cabins $100-150) gives you that chance with your choice of eight cabins, ranging from private two-person affairs to larger lodges that could easily sleep you and seven others in four beds. These quaint cabins are quiet, just outside of downtown Cherokee, and comfortable.

INFORMATION AND SERVICES

The **Cherokee Welcome Center** (498 Tsali Blvd., 800/438-1601, www. visitcherokeenc.com, 8am-5pm daily) can help you with tickets, directions, and things to do and see.

There's one radio station in Cherokee, and that's **WNCC** (101.3), a country station, although you can pick up distant stations with a wider selection.

GETTING THERE

Cherokee is located on a particularly pretty winding section of U.S. 19 between Maggie Valley and Bryson City, 2.5 miles south of the southern terminus of the Blue Ridge Parkway. From the Blue Ridge Parkway, a six-minute drive south along U.S. 441 will take you right to the cultural center of Cherokee.

Bryson City and the Nantahala Forest

To look at the mountains here, you'd think that the defining feature in this part of North Carolina would be the surrounding peaks, but you're only partly right. This is a land dominated by water: Smoke-thick fog crowds valleys in the pre-dawn hours. The peaks stand ringed in clouds. Moss, ferns, and dense forests crowd the edge of rivers and streams. When you're in the Nantahala Gorge, it feels like you've stepped into a fairy tale. According to Cherokee legends, a formidable witch called Spearfinger lived here, as did a monstrous snake and even an inchworm so large it could span the gorge. Spearfinger and her cohorts haven't been seen in years, and the Nantahala River, which runs through the narrow gorge, attracts white-water enthusiasts.

Nearby Bryson City is a river town whose proximity to white water makes it a favorite haunt for rafters, kayakers,

and other white-water thrill seekers. If you approach Bryson City from the north on U.S. 19, you're in for a strange sight: The banks of the Tuckasegee River are shored up with crushed cars.

SIGHTS

The **Great Smoky Mountains Railroad** (GSMR, depots in Bryson City and Dillsboro, 800/872-4681, www.gsmr.com, from $50 adults, $29 children) is one of the best and most fun ways to see the Smokies. On historic trains, the GSMR carries sightseers on excursions from two to several hours long, through some of the most beautiful scenery in the region. Trips between Dillsboro and Bryson City, with a layover at each end for shopping and dining, follow the banks of the Tuckasegee River, while roundtrips from Bryson City follow the Little Tennessee and Nantahala Rivers deep into the Nantahala Gorge. Many other excursions are offered, including gourmet dining and wine- and beer-tasting trips. There are Thomas the Tank Engine and the Little Engine That Could trips for kids, and runs to and from river rafting outfitters.

SPORTS AND RECREATION

✪ NANTAHALA RIVER GORGE

The stunningly beautiful **Nantahala River Gorge,** just outside Bryson City in the Nantahala National Forest, supports scores of river guide companies, many clustered along U.S. 19 west. Nantahala is said to mean "land of the noonday sun," and there are indeed parts of this gorge where the sheer rock walls above the river are so steep that sunlight only hits the water at the noon hour. Eight miles of the Nantahala River flow through the gorge over Class II-III rapids. The nearby Ocoee River is also a favorite of rafters, and the Cheoah River, when there are controlled water releases, has some of the South's most famous and difficult Class III-IV runs.

OUTFITTERS AND TOURS

Because some of these rapids can be quite dangerous, be sure to call ahead and speak to a guide if you have any doubts as to your readiness. If rafting with children, check the company's weight and age restrictions beforehand. **Endless River Adventures** (14157 U.S. 19 W., near Bryson City, 828/488-6199, www. endlessriveradventures.com) gives white-water and flat-water kayaking instruction, rentals, and guided trips on the Nantahala, Ocoee, and Cheoah Rivers. They'll be able to suggest a run suited to your skill

level. **Carolina Outfitters** (715 U.S. 19, Topton, 828/488-6345, www. carolinaoutfitters.com) has several package outings that combine river trips with horseback riding, bicycling, panning for gems, and riding on the Great Smoky Mountains Railroad. In addition to river guide services, **Wildwater Rafting** (10345 U.S. 19 W., 12 miles west of Bryson City, 866/319-8870, www.wildwaterrafting.com) leads **Wildwater Jeep Tours** ($50-110 adults, $40-90 children), half- and full-day Jeep excursions through back roads and wilderness to waterfalls and old mountain settlements.

You can explore the mountains around Bryson City with the **Nantahala Outdoor Center** (13077 U.S. 19 W., Bryson City, 828/785-4836, www.noc. com, 9am-5pm daily, from $30), which offers a variety of adventure options that include white-water rafting, stand-up paddleboarding on the flat-water sections of the river, hiking, mountain biking, and zip lining. Half-day, full-day, and overnight trips are possible, and excursions like the Rapid Transit combine a relaxing morning train ride with an afternoon rafting trip.

FLY-FISHING

The mountain streams around Bryson City are teeming with fish; a few outfitters can help you catch them. **Fly Fishing the Smokies** (Bryson City, 828/488-7665, www. flyfishingthesmokies.net) has a number of guides and options for a day or more of fishing. Wade the streams with them for a half-day (1 person $160, 2 people $180) or full-day (1 person $230, 2 people $260) outing, try a float trip (half-day $225 per boat, full-day $325 per boat), or go backcountry camping and fly-fishing in the Great Smoky Mountains National Park

($500-850 per person). They also go bass fishing on nearby Fontana Lake (half-day $275, full-day $400).

Another top fishing guide in the Bryson City area is **Steve Claxton's Smoky Mountain Adventures** (Bryson City, 828/736-7501, http://steveclaxton.com), who specializes in leaving civilization behind in favor of camping, catching wild mountain trout, and getting a true taste of the wilderness. Three-day, two-night camping trips for 5-7 people run around $400/person, and four-day, three-night trips are $575-700/person. They also offer daylong fishing trips (1 person $225, 2 people $275, 3 people $325).

Nantahala Fly Fishing Co. (Robbinsville, 828/479-8850 or 866/910-1013, www.flyfishnorthcarolina.com, guided trips and private lessons half-day $150 one angler, $75 per additional person, full-day $300 one or two anglers, $75 per additional person) provides guided trips for fly-rod fishing, but if you've never held one of these odd fishing rods in your hand, they also provide a fly-fishing school ($300 for 2 days) and private instruction. Best of all, they have a "No Fish, No Pay" guarantee.

For fly fishers who don't need a guide, a number of streams around are packed with fish, but be sure to inquire about regulations for individual streams; some are catch-and-release while a neighboring stream is catch-and-keep, and some have regulations about the types of hooks you can use. Once you're ready to put your line in the water, try **Hazel Creek** on the north shore of Fontana Lake, where you'll find pristine waters and a good number of fish. Other nearby creeks, like **Eagle Creek** and any of the feeder creeks that empty into the lake, are prime spots as well.

HIKING

The Great Smoky Mountains National Park has more than 800 miles of wilderness trails, and with around 40 percent of the park located in Swain County, more trails than you could hike in a week are within striking distance from Bryson City. **Deep Creek Loop** is a four-mile loop that passes two waterfalls on its easy, mostly flat, track. You can also take the strenuous **Deep Creek Trail** to Newfound Gap Road, a 14.2-mile one-way hike that will require a return ride. The **Noland Creek Trail** is a fairly easy six-mile trail near the end of the Road to Nowhere (a failed road-building project from the 1930s and 1940s). At the end of the Road to Nowhere, just past the tunnel, is the **Goldmine Loop Trail,** a three-mile track that's beautiful and enjoyable.

Deep Creek

Just south of Cherokee and just north of Bryson City, Deep Creek is a spot more popular with locals than tourists, but it's worth a stop. Deep Creek is relatively placid, aside from a couple of waterfalls a ways upstream. If you're not into wading or tubing, don't worry; this is a lovely place to picnic and hike or even camp away from the crowds in some of the more popular spots in the park.

At the end of Deep Creek Road you'll find the trailheads leading to the waterfalls. You'll also find the **Deep Creek Campground** (877/444-6777, www.recreation.gov, $17). There are nearly 100 campsites here, many of which fill up with locals. If you want to camp here, arrive early or reserve well in advance.

Nearby, there's also the **Deep Creek Tube Center and Campground** (1090 W. Deep Creek Rd., Bryson City, 828/488-6055, www.deepcreekcamping.com, camping $23-50, cabins $69-195), a charming collection of tent and RV campsites and cabins for rent. As the name implies, they rent tubes for use on Deep Creek. Rentals ($5 for all-day use of your tube) are cheap, so you can play in the water as long as you like.

There are two nice waterfalls to see here. **Juney Whank Falls** (yes, that's its name) is less than a half mile from the Deep Creek Campground and cuts an impressive figure as it drops a total of 90 feet in two stages. **Indian Creek Falls**, located a mile from the campground, is a stunning set of falls and cascades some 60 feet high.

Road to Nowhere

An odd place to visit is the so-called Road to Nowhere. Just south of the Deep Creek entrance outside Bryson City is a short stretch of highway leading north into GSMNP. Lonely, even spooky, the road is all that remains of a parkway planned to trace a path through the Smokies along Fontana Lake. Though construction was started on the parkway, it was abandoned. Today, the road stops quite abruptly about six miles inside the park, at a man-made stone tunnel. Hard feelings over the failed parkway have softened, but many families still hold a grudge against government officials who vowed to build a road along the lake to provide access to old family cemeteries there.

Cars are prohibited from using the tunnel at the end of the Road to Nowhere, but visitors on foot are welcome to stroll right through. After you pass through the tunnel, there's a marathon-length hike—seriously, it's 26 miles—weaving along the northern bank of Fontana Lake.

ACCOMMODATIONS

The ✪ **Folkestone Inn** (101 Folkestone Rd., 828/488-2730 or 888/812-3385, www.folkestoneinn.

tubing at Deep Creek

com, $132-176) is one of the region's outstanding bed-and-breakfasts, a roomy 1920s farmhouse expanded and renovated into a charming and tranquil inn. Each room has a balcony or porch. Baked treats at breakfast include shortcake, kuchen, cobblers, and other delicacies. An 85-year-old hotel on the National Register of Historic Places, the **Fryemont Inn** (245 Fryemont St., Bryson City, 828/488-2159 or 800/845-4879, www.fryemontinn.com, mid-Apr.-late Nov., $110-283 with meals, late-Nov.-mid-Apr. $115-225 with no meal service) has a cozy, rustic feel with chestnut-paneled guest rooms and an inviting lobby with an enormous stone fireplace.

Some river outfitters offer lodging, which can be a cheap way to pass the night if you don't mind roughing it. The **Rolling Thunder River Company** (10160 U.S. 19 W., near Bryson City, 800/408-7238, www.rollingthunderriverco.com, no alcohol permitted) operates a large bunkhouse with beds ($10-12 per person per night) for its rafting customers. **Carolina Outfitters** (715 U.S. 19, Topton, 828/488-6345, www.carolinaoutfitters.com) has a number of accommodations available ($50-100), including two-room cabins, two-bedroom apartments, and three-bedroom cabins suitable for a large group. Many of the outfitters also offer camping on their properties.

Way back in the forest by Fontana Lake, the **Fontana Village Resort** (300 Woods Rd., Fontana Dam, 828/498-2211 or 800/849-2258, www.fontanavillage.com) was originally built as housing for the workers building the dam, a massive wartime undertaking that created a whole town out in the woods. Renovated into a comfortable resort, Fontana Village features a lodge ($109-219), cabins ($109-459), camping ($15-40), and a variety of boat rentals, including pontoon boats and fishing charters.

CAMPING

Among the nicest camping options available in the Nantahala Forest is **Standing Indian Campground** (90 Sloan Rd., Franklin, 877/444-6777, www.recreation.gov, Apr.-Nov., $16). Standing Indian has a nice diversity of campsites, from flat grassy areas to cozy mountainside nooks. Drinking water, hot showers, flush toilets, and a phone are all available on site, and leashed pets are permitted. At 3,400 feet in elevation, the campground is close to the Appalachian Trail.

Another nice campground is the **Deep Creek Tube Center and Campground** (1090 W. Deep Creek Rd., Bryson City, 828/488-6055, www.deepcreekcamping.com, camping $27-50, cabins $80-195). Open seasonally—April 3-October 30—they have more than 50 campsites, 18 cabins, and access to Deep Creek, which runs right by many campsites, where you can go tubing ($5/day). You can also go gem "mining" here, a great mountain tradition; they sell bags and buckets of gem-enriched dirt in the camp store. The best part is that they are within walking distance of the Great Smoky Mountains National Park.

GETTING THERE AND AROUND

Bryson City can be reached via U.S. 19, if you're coming south from Maggie Valley and Cherokee. U.S. 74 also passes close by for easy access from the east or the west.

Waynesville and Vicinity

Waynesville, just west of Asheville and east of Cherokee, is the very definition of the word quaint. Writers have compared it to a Norman Rockwell painting with its storybook Main Street, busy with shops and lined with brick sidewalks and iron lampposts. This is an artistic little community where the art and craft galleries and studios are seemingly endless. In nearby Cullowhee, Western Carolina University is one of the mountain region's leading academic institutions as well as the location of the Mountain Heritage Center museum and Mountain Heritage Day festival.

WAYNESVILLE

Waynesville's downtown can keep a gallery-hopper or shopper happy for hours. Main Street is packed with studio artists' galleries, cafés and coffee shops, and a variety of boutiques.

SIGHTS

One interesting stop in Waynesville is the **Museum of North Carolina Handicrafts** (49 Shelton St., 828/452-1551, www.sheltonhouse.org, 11am-4pm Tues.-Sat. Apr.-Oct., $6 adults, $5 students, free ages 5 and under). Consisting of a farmhouse, barn, and gardens, the museum opened in 1980 and shows off the work of Native American and North Carolina heritage artists. This means mountain musical instruments, ceremonial items and crafts from Native American tribes, basketry, woodcarvings, quilts, and even antique farm tools. Tours of the museum are guided, so you'll hear plenty of stories to go with the items you see.

SHOPPING

Books and Specialty Items

Blue Ridge Books & News (428 Hazelwood Ave., 828/456-6000, www.blueridgebooksnc.com, 9am-5:30pm Mon.-Fri., 9am-5pm Sat.) is a nice bookstore with specialties of regional interest and good coffee. A number of prominent Southern authors come through here to read and sign books, so check their schedule and ask about signed copies while you're there.

One of the several locations of **Mast General Store** (63 N. Main St., 828/452-2101, www.mastgeneralstore.com, 10am-6pm Mon.-Sat., noon-6pm Sun. spring-fall, hours vary in winter) is here in Waynesville. While the stores are perhaps best known among vacationers for making children clamor for the candy kept in big wooden barrels, old-time dry-goods-store style, they have an even larger selection of merchandise for adults, including camping gear, such as top-brand tents, cookware, maps, and outdoors-oriented upscale clothing and shoes.

Galleries

Waynesville's galleries are many and varied, although the overarching aesthetic is one of studio art with inspiration in the environment and folk arts. **Twigs and Leaves** (98 N. Main St., 828/456-1940, www.twigsandleaves.com, 10am-5:30pm Mon.-Sat., 1pm-4pm Sun., hours vary seasonally) carries splendid art furniture that is both fanciful and functional, pottery of many hand-thrown and hand-built varieties, jewelry, paintings, fabric hangings, mobiles, and many other beautiful and unusual items inspired by nature.

Waynesville

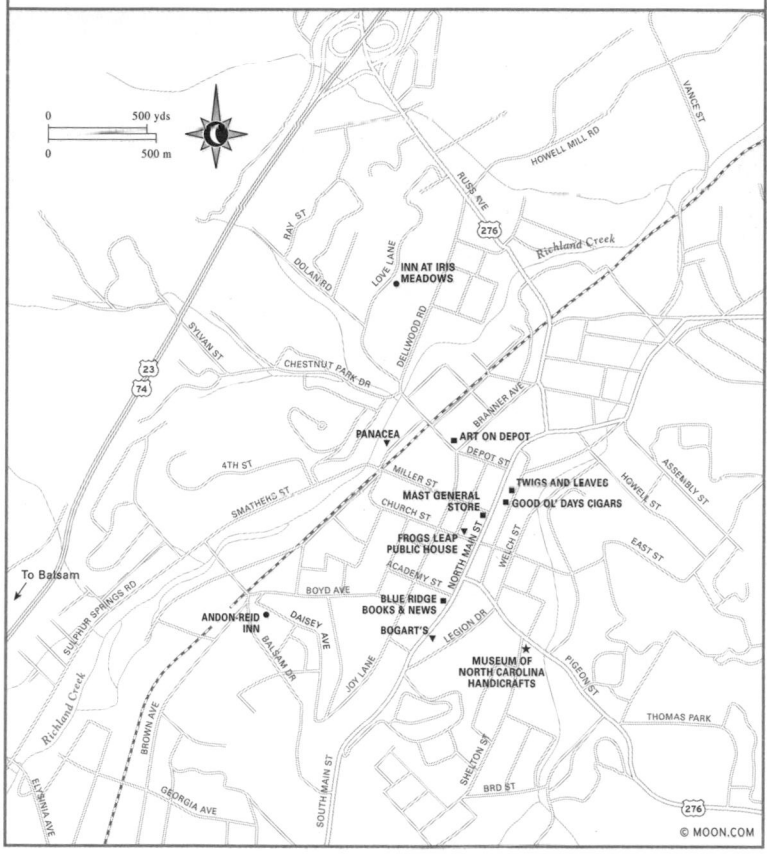

Map markers and labels: VANCE ST, HOWELL MILL RD, Richland Creek, RUSS AVE, 276, BAY ST, DOLAN RD, LOVE LANE, INN AT IRIS MEADOWS, DELLWOOD RD, SYLVAN ST, CHESTNUT PARK DR, 23, 74, BRANNER AVE, PANACEA, ART ON DEPOT, DEPOT ST, 4TH ST, MILLER ST, ASSEMBLY ST, TWIGS AND LEAVES, HOWELL ST, SMATHERS ST, MAST GENERAL STORE, GOOD OL' DAYS CIGARS, CHURCH ST, NORTH MAIN ST, EAST ST, FROGS LEAP PUBLIC HOUSE, WELCH ST, ACADEMY ST, To Balsam, SULPHUR SPRINGS RD, BOYD AVE, BLUE RIDGE BOOKS & NEWS, ANDON-REID INN, DAISEY AVE, BALSAM DR, BOGART'S, LEGION DR, MUSEUM OF NORTH CAROLINA HANDICRAFTS, PIGEON ST, Richland Creek, BROWN AVE, JOY LANE, SHELTON ST, THOMAS PARK, ELYSINIA AVE, GEORGIA AVE, SOUTH MAIN ST, BRD ST, 276, © MOON.COM

0   500 yds
0   500 m

Studio Thirty-Three (822 Balsam Ridge Rd., 828-452-4264, www.studio33jewelry.com, by appointment) carries the work of a very small and select group of fine jewelers from western North Carolina. Their retail and custom inventory consists of spectacular handcrafted pieces in a variety of styles and an array of precious stones and metals. This is a must-see gallery if you have a special occasion coming up. The gallery describes its stock as ranging in price from "$65 to $16,000," and most items cost upward

of $2,000. Even if you're not about to mark a major life event or spend that kind of money just for fun, it's worth stopping in to gaze at all that sparkle.

Art on Depot (250 Depot St., 828-246-0218, 10am-5pm Mon.-Sat.) is a working pottery studio and gallery where local and regional artists exhibit and sell their work. Artistic creations for sale include decorative and functional pottery by the resident potter and many of her contemporaries as well as paintings, jewelry, sculpture, and a few pieces by area fiber artists.

FOOD

Waynesville's ✪ **Frogs Leap Public House** (44 Church St., 828/456-1930, http://frogsleappublichouse.com, 11:30pm-2:30pm Tues.-Sat., 5pm-9pm Tues.-Thurs., 5pm-10pm Fri.-Sat., lunch $7-18, dinner $8-29) serves an interesting menu that's quite sophisticated but not afraid of its Southern roots. Dishes like the wood-grilled sirloin tip in a bourbon-shallot demi and the spicy Korean pork belly sliders show a real adventurous spirit that diners appreciate, not just because it's ambitious but because it's excellent.

Sandwiches at **The Patio Bistro** (26 Church St., 828/454-0070, www.patio-nc.com, 10am-4pm Mon.-Sat., 10am-3pm Sun., around $10) are first rate. Try a deli standard like the egg salad sandwich or a turkey and swiss, or go for one of their veggie-friendly black bean burgers, hummus wraps.

The ever-popular **Bogart's** (303 S. Main St., 828/452-1313, www.bogartswaynesville.com, 11am-9pm Sun.-Thurs., 11am-10pm Fri.-Sat., $7-23) is locally famous for its filet mignon, although their local trout also has a good reputation. The menu is huge but very steak-housey; vegetarians will have a tough time, although a few dishes, like the chipotle black bean burger and the grilled Portobello salad, are options.

If you're just passing through town and need a jolt of good, strong coffee, visit **Panacea** (66 Commerce St., 303 S. Main St., 828/452-6200, http://panaceacoffee.com, 7am-5pm Mon.-Fri., 8am-5pm Sat., 10am-3pm Sun., $5-11) in the funky Frog Level neighborhood downhill from downtown. The proprietors give back to their community and trade fairly with those who supply their coffee. They stock beans, blends, and brews from all around the world.

ACCOMMODATIONS

Waynesville has quite a selection of luxury inns. The **Andon-Reid Inn** (92 Daisey Ave., 828/452-3089, www.andonreidinn.com, $145-205, no pets or children) is a handsome turn-of-the-20th-century house close to downtown with five tranquil guest rooms, each with its own fireplace, and a sumptuous breakfast menu that could include sweet-potato pecan pancakes and pork tenderloin, homemade cornbread with honey butter, or the intriguing baked lemon eggs. With advance notice they can cater to special dietary needs.

For absolute tip-top luxury, try ✪ **The Swag** (2300 Swag Rd., 800/789-7672, www.theswag.com, $495-850). Superb guest rooms and cabins of rustic wood and stone each have a steam shower, and several have saunas, wet bars, and cathedral ceilings. The menu is decidedly country and upscale, two things you wouldn't think go together, but they do, and quite nicely. The inn is at 5,000 feet elevation in a stunning location at the very edge of the Great Smoky Mountains National Park.

In the community of Balsam, seven miles southwest from Waynesville, the **Balsam Mountain Inn** (68 Seven Springs Dr., Balsam, 828/456-9498, www.balsammountaininn.net, $100-230, no pets) has stood watch for a century in a haunting location—an imposing old wooden hotel with huge double porches overlooking a rather spooky little railroad platform and the beautiful ridges of Jackson and Haywood Counties beyond. The interior has barely changed since its earliest days, paneled in white horizontal bead board throughout with

10-foot-wide hallways said to have been designed to accommodate steamer trunks. The one telephone is at the front desk, and there are no TVs, so plan to go hiking or to sit on the porch before dining in the downstairs restaurant and then curl up and read in the library. There is, incongruously, fast Wi-Fi. Among the inn's reported ghosts is a woman in a blue dress, said to originate in room 205 but to come and go elsewhere on the second floor. This inn has a few rough edges, but the atmosphere can be found nowhere else.

Up on the Blue Ridge Parkway above Waynesville and quite close to Asheville is the fantastic ✪ **Pisgah Inn** (Blue Ridge Parkway milepost 408.6, 828/235-8228, www.pisgahinn. com, Apr.-Oct., $138-182), with motel-style accommodations surrounding an old lodge with a large family-style dining room and a Parkway gift shop. The inn is on a nearly 5,000-foot-high mountaintop, so the view is sensational. Trails lead from the inn to short, pretty strolls and challenging daylong hikes. The restaurant (7:30am-10:30am, 11:30am-4pm, and 5pm-9pm daily) has a mesmerizing view and an appetizing and varied menu (breakfast $3-9, lunch $9-20, dinner $10-27) of both country cooking and upscale meals. The guest rooms are simple but comfortable, each with its own balcony and rocking chairs overlooking the valley, and with a TV but no telephone. The Pisgah is a perfect spot for resting, reading, and porch-sitting.

INFORMATION AND SERVICES

The **Haywood County Tourism Development Authority** (1110 Soco Rd., 800/334-9036, http://

visitncsmokies.com/) has a wealth of information about visiting Waynesville and surrounding towns. **MedWest Haywood** (262 Leroy George Dr., Clyde, NC, 828/456-7311, www.haymed.org), accessible from the Lake Junaluska exit off U.S. 23/U.S. 74, is the region's hospital.

SYLVA

The small town of Sylva, southwest of Waynesville, is crowned by the pretty Jackson County Courthouse, an Italianate building with an ornate cupola, kept under wistful watch by the requisite courthouse-square Confederate monument. Visitors should stop by the **Jackson County Visitor Center** (773 W. Main St., 800/962-1911, www.mountainlovers. com) or visit them online to learn more about the communities here.

SIGHTS

South of Sylva, the mysterious **Judaculla Rock** (off Caney Fork Rd., www.judacullarock.com) has puzzled folks for centuries. The soapstone boulder is covered in petroglyphs, estimated to be at least 500 years old. The figures and symbols and squiggles are clearly significant, but as of yet are not understood. I'm fascinated with petroglyphs, and these are some of the most mysterious I've encountered. The soft rock has eroded and the pictures are not as clear as they were in generations past, but many of them can still be discerned. To reach the rock, drive south on Highway 107 eight miles past the intersection with Sylva's Business U.S. 23. Make a left on Caney Fork Road/County Road 1737 and drive 2.5 miles to a gravel road. Turn left, and after just under 0.5 miles you'll see the rock on the right and a parking area on the left.

SHOPPING

Sylva's City Lights Bookstore (3 E. Jackson St., 828/586-9499, www.citylightsnc.com, 9am-9pm Mon.-Sat., 10am-3pm Sun.) is hardly a knockoff of the monumental Beat establishment in San Francisco with which it shares a name. Instead, it's a first-rate small-town bookstore with stock that has the novelty sought by vacationers and the depth to make regulars of the local patrons. In addition to the sections you'll find in any good bookstore, their selection of books of regional interest, including folklore, nature, recreation guides, history, and fiction and poetry by Appalachian and Southern authors, is excellent.

FOOD

The North Carolina mountains are experiencing a booming organic foods movement, and you'll find eco-aware eateries throughout the area. ✪ **Lulu's On Main** (612 W. Main St., 828/586-8989, www.lulusonmain.com, 11:30am-8pm Mon.-Thurs., 11am-9pm Fri.-Sat., $11-19) is one of the most acclaimed restaurants in the area. The menu is American gourmet at heart with splashes of Mediterranean and Nuevo Latino specialties. Try the walnut-spinach ravioli or the raspberry rum pork loin. There are plenty of vegetarian options.

City Lights Café (3 E. Jackson St., 828/587-2233, www.citylightscafe.com, 8am-9pm Mon.-Sat., 9am-3pm Sun., breakfast $2-8, lunch and dinner $5-12), downstairs from the bookshop, has some excellent crepes, a mighty good biscuit, and fun burritos, and they serve wine and beer. It's a cool, casual spot to dine and relax with your book and a bottle of wine, or to see a small local act play. **Soul Infusion** (628 E. Main St., 828/586-1717, www.soulinfusion.com, 11am-10pm Mon.-Fri., noon-late Sat., $5-10) is a cozy hippie-gourmet teahouse in an old house on Main Street. You can get very good burritos, sandwiches, pizza, wraps, more than 60 kinds of tea, and even more selections of bottled beer. On weekends and some weeknights, local blues, folk, reggae, and experimental musicians put on a show. Seize the opportunity to hear some of the talent in this musical region.

DILLSBORO

Next door to Sylva is Dillsboro, a river town of rafters and crafters. **Dogwood Crafters** (90 Webster St., 828/586-2248, www.dogwoodcrafters.com, 10am-6pm daily Mar.-Dec., 11am-4pm Fri.-Sun. Feb.), in operation for more than 30 years, is a gallery and co-op that represents around 100 local artists and artisans. While the shop carries some of the ubiquitous country-whimsical stuff, mixed in is the work of some very traditional Blue Ridge weavers, potters, carvers, and other expert artisans, making the shop well worth a visit.

In November, Dillsboro's population grows by approximately 5,000 percent when potters and pottery lovers descend on the town for the annual **Western North Carolina Pottery Festival** (828/631-5100, wwww.wncpotteryfestival.com). This juried pottery show features more than 40 potters, a street fair, and the Clay Olympics. The Clay Olympics are timed competitions to form the tallest cylinder, shape the widest bowl, and make pots blindfolded. It's odd, but the crowd and the artists get into it, making the one-day festival worth seeing.

SPORTS AND RECREATION

Dillsboro River Company (18 Macktown Rd., 866/586-3797, www.northcarolinarafting.com, 10am-6pm daily June-Sept., rentals $5-30, guided trips $22-40), across the river from downtown Dillsboro, will set you afloat on the Tuckaseegee River, a comparatively warm river with areas of Class II rapids. It's pronounced "tuck-a-SEE-jee" but is often referred to simply as "the Tuck." Dillsboro River Company rents rafts, "ducks," and inflatable and sit-on-top kayaks. If you'd like to hire a river rat, guides will be happy to lead you on tours twice daily, and for an extra fee you can share a boat with the guide. There are minimum weight restrictions for these watercraft, so if you are traveling with children, call ahead to ask if the guides think your young ones are ready for the Tuckaseegee.

NIGHTLIFE

It's a small town, so there's not a whole lot in the way of nightlife here, but **Innovation Brewing** (414 W. Main St., 828/586-9678, www.innovationbrewing.com, 2pm-midnight Mon.-Thurs., noon-midnight Fri.-Sat., noon-11pm Sun.) has 22 beers in their regular rotation with 10 on tap at any time. The Nitro Irish Stout, Nut Brown, and Midnight Rye-der Black IPA are mainstays. Keep an ear out for live music in the taproom, as bands drop by often. If you're hungry, you're in luck, **Cosmic Carry-Out** (828/506-2830, www.cosmiccarryout.com, noon-9pm Mon.-Thurs., 11am-10:30pm Fri.-Sat., 11am-9pm Sun., $3-9) has burgers, tacos, grilled cheese sandwiches, and fries for your dining enjoyment. Innovation has a new spot, **Innovation Station** (40 Depot St., Dillsboro, 828/226-0262), in Dillsboro just five minutes down the road.

finishing the glaze on pottery at the Western North Carolina Pottery Festival

FOOD

Stop by **Dillsboro Chocolate Factory** (28 Church St., 828/631-0156, www.dillsborochocolate.com, 10am-6pm Mon.-Thurs., 10am-8:30pm Fri.-Sat., noon-5pm Sun. in summer and fall, 10am-5pm Wed.-Sat and noon-5pm Sun in winter) if you need a sweet snack. They have truffles, chocolate, fudge, candy, and other assorted sweets, many of which they make in house.

The ✪ **Jarrett House** (100 Haywood St., 828/477-4958 or 800/972-5623, www.jarretthouse.com, 11:30am-2:30pm and 4:30pm-7:30pm Tues.-Sun., under $15), is also famous for its dining room, an extravaganza of country cooking based on the staples of country ham and red-eye gravy. You can order many other mountain specialties, including fried catfish, fried chicken, sweet tea, biscuits, and for dessert the daily cobbler or vinegar pie (a strange but tasty pie that's similar to a pecan pie without the pecans and with vinegar). There are few options for vegetarians, but if you like heavy Southern fare, you'll think you're in heaven. You can also eat at **Coach's Bistro** ($15-20), a little restaurant serving up more modern dishes in a more modern setting; menu options range from the pub-like to homey bites like roast beef and mashed potatoes.

Haywood Smokehouse (403 Haywood St., 828/631-9797, www.haywoodsmokehouse.com, 11am-9pm Tues.-Sat., $8-26) is a funky little barbecue shack serving some fine western North Carolina 'cue, craft beers, and house-made smoked barbecue sauces. The menu's small, but if it's pork or chicken and it's barbecuable, it's here. The Haywood Smokehouse is

biker-friendly, so don't be surprised if you see a line of Harleys outside.

ACCOMMODATIONS

Of the many historic inns in this region, one of the oldest is Dillsboro's **Jarrett House** (100 Haywood St., 828/477-4958 or 800/972-5623, www.jarretthouse.com, from $129, includes full country breakfast). The three-story 1880s lodge was built to serve passengers on the railroad, and today it's once again a busy rail stop, now for the Great Smoky Mountains Railroad's excursion trains. The guest rooms have old-fashioned furniture, air-conditioning, and private baths, but the only TV is in the lobby.

The **Blue Ridge Inn** (756 W. Main St., Sylva, 828/586-2123, from $110) is a great place to stay in Sylva. Located at the far end of downtown, it's an 8-minute walk to the breweries at the other end of town and a 3-minute walk to dining spots like Lulu's and City Lights. The rooms are comfortable and priced right, and the staff is exceptionally polite.

CULLOWHEE

The unincorporated village of Cullowhee ("CULL-uh-wee"), located on Highway 107 between Sylva and Cashiers, is the home of Western Carolina University (WCU). The university's **Mountain Heritage Center** (Hunter Library, WCU campus, 828/227-7129, www.wcu.edu, 10am-4pm Fri.-Mon., 10am-7pm Thurs.) is a small museum with a great collection that will fascinate anyone interested in Appalachian history. The permanent exhibit *Migration of the Scotch-Irish People* is full of artifacts like a 19th-century covered wagon, wonderful photographs, and homemade quilts, linens, and musical instruments. The Mountain Heritage Center also hosts two traveling exhibits in addition to the permanent installation as well as the annual **Mountain Heritage Day** (www.mountainheritageday.com) festival (late Sept.), which brings together many of western North Carolina's best and most authentic traditional musicians and artisans in a free festival that draws up to 25,000 visitors.

GETTING THERE AND AROUND

Waynesville is easily reached from Asheville by heading west on I-40 and then taking either U.S. 23 or U.S. 74. The Blue Ridge Parkway also passes a little to the south of the town, near Balsam. Sylva is to the southwest of Waynesville on U.S. 23, and from there, Cullowhee is an easy drive down Highway 107.

Robbinsville and the Valley Towns

Between Robbinsville and the Georgia state line is another region at the heart of Cherokee life. Snowbird, not far from Robbinsville, is one of the most traditional Cherokee communities, where it's common to hear the Cherokee language and the arts, crafts, and folkways are flourishing. The burial site of Junaluska, one of the Eastern Band's most prominent leaders, is here.

As moving as it is to see the memorial to one of the Cherokee heroes, the town of Murphy is forever linked with tragedy for the Cherokee people and a dark incident in American history—the Trail of Tears. Around 16,000 Cherokee people, including warriors and clan leaders, men, women, children, the elderly, and the infirm, were forced to leave their homes in North Carolina, Tennessee, and Georgia; they were arrested and marched under guard to Fort Butler, here in Murphy, and from Fort Butler they were forced to walk to Oklahoma. You'll find the names of these people, many of

whom died along the way, inscribed in Cherokee on a memorial at the L&N Depot in Murphy.

In addition to places of historic significance in Cherokee culture, this farthest southwestern corner of North Carolina has other compelling sights. Brasstown, a tiny village on the Georgia state line, is the home of the John C. Campbell Folk School, an artists' colony nearly a century old, where visitors can stroll among studios and along trails and stop in to a gallery shop with some of the most beautiful crafts you'll find in the region. Back up toward Robbinsville, the relentlessly scenic Cherohala Skyway crosses 43 miles of the Cherokee and Nantahala Forests. This road is a major destination for motorcyclists and sports-car drivers as well as day-trippers and vacationers.

ROBBINSVILLE

The whole southwestern corner of North Carolina is rich with Cherokee history and culture, and the Robbinsville area has some of the deepest roots of great significance to the Cherokee people. In little towns and crossroads a few miles outside Robbinsville, several hundred people known as the Snowbird community keep alive some of the oldest Cherokee ways. The Cherokee language is spoken here, and it's a place where some of the Eastern Band's most admired basket makers, potters, and other artists continue to make and teach their ancient arts. If you're visiting and want to enjoy an adult beverage, you'd better bring your own, as Graham County is North Carolina's one and only dry county.

SIGHTS

Outside Robbinsville, in the ancient Stecoah Valley, is an imposing old rock schoolhouse built in 1930 and used as a school until the mid-1990s. It has been reborn as the **Stecoah Valley Center** (121 Schoolhouse Rd., Stecoah, 828/479-3364, www. stecoahvalleycenter.com), home of a weaver's guild, a native plants preservation group, a concert series, several festivals, and a great **Gallery Shop** (828/497-3098, 10am-5pm Mon.-Fri. Mar. and Dec., 10am-5pm Mon.-Sat. Apr.-Nov.) of local artisans' work. Concerts in the Appalachian Evening summer series, featuring area musicians, are preceded by community suppers of traditional mountain cuisine.

On Robbinsville's Main Street is the **Junaluska Memorial** (Main St., 0.5 miles north of the Graham County Courthouse, 828/479-4727, 9am-5pm Mon.-Sat. Apr.-Oct., call for hours Nov.-Mar.), where Junaluska, a 19th-century leader of the Eastern Band of the Cherokee, and his third wife, Nicie, are buried.

The marker was dedicated in 1910 by the Daughters of the American Revolution, and the gravesite is maintained by the Friends of Junaluska, who also operate the **Junaluska Museum** (free, under repairs as of this writing) on the same site. At the museum you'll find ancient artifacts from life in Cheoah thousands of years ago. There are also contemporary Cherokee crafts on display, and outside you can walk a path that highlights the medicinal plants used for generations in this area.

Down a winding country road 14 miles outside Robbinsville, **Yellow Branch Pottery and Cheese** (136 Yellow Branch Circle, Robbinsville, 828/479-6710, www.yellowbranch. com, noon-5pm Tues.-Sat. Apr.-Nov. or by appointment) is a beautifully rustic spot for an afternoon's excursion. Bruce DeGroot, Karen Mickler, and their herd of Jersey cows produce prizewinning artisanal cheeses and graceful, functional pottery. Visitors are welcome at their farm and shop.

SPORTS AND RECREATION

The **Joyce Kilmer Memorial Forest** (Joyce Kilmer Rd., off Hwy. 143 west of Robbinsville, 828/479-6431, www. grahamcountytravel.com) is one of the largest remaining tracts of virgin forest in the eastern United States, where 450-year-old tulip poplar trees have grown to 100 feet tall and 20 feet around. The forest stands in honor of Joyce Kilmer, a soldier killed in action in France during World War I. His poem "Trees" inspired this living memorial. The only way to see the forest is on foot, and a two-mile loop or two one-mile loops make for an easy hike through a remarkable forest.

JUNALUSKA

One of the most important figures in the history of the Eastern Band of the Cherokee is Junaluska, who was born near Dillard, Georgia, in 1776. During the wars against the Creek Indians from 1812 to 1814, the Cherokee people fought beside U.S. forces, and it's said that the fierce young Junaluska saved the life of Andrew Jackson at the battle of Horse Shoe Bend in Alabama.

Twenty years later, Jackson, by then president, repaid Junaluska's bravery and the loyalty of the Cherokee people by signing the Indian Removal Act, which ordered that they, along with four other major Southern nations, be forced from their homelands and marched to the new Indian Territory of Oklahoma. Junaluska traveled to Washington and met with Jackson to plead for mercy for the Cherokee nation; his pleas were ignored, and in 1838, Junaluska joined 16,000 members of the Cherokee nation, who were force-marched close to 1,000 miles to Oklahoma. Midway across Tennessee, he led a failed escape attempt and was captured and chained; he completed the march in leg irons and manacles. It was during this time that Junaluska supposedly said, "If I had known what Andrew Jackson would do to the Cherokees, I would have killed him myself that day at Horse Shoe Bend." In 1841 he was finally able to leave Oklahoma and made the 17-day trip to North Carolina on horseback.

He spent his final years in Cherokee County, on land granted to him by the state of North Carolina. He and his third wife, Nicie, are buried at Robbinsville, at what is now the Junaluska Memorial and Museum. His grave was originally marked according to Cherokee tradition—with a pile of stones—but in 1910 the Daughters of the American Revolution commissioned a marker for his gravesite. During the dedication ceremony, Reverend Armstrong Cornsilk delivered a eulogy in the Cherokee language:

He was a good man. He was a good friend. He was a good friend in his home and everywhere. He would ask the hungry man to eat. He would ask the cold one to warm by his fire. He would ask the tired one to rest, and he would give a good place to sleep. Juno's home was a good home for others. He was a smart man. He made his mind think well. He was very brave. He was not afraid.

Juno at this time has been dead about 50 years. I am glad he is up above [pointing upward]. I am glad we have this beautiful monument. It shows Junaluska did good, and it shows we all appreciate him together—having a pleasant time together. I hope we shall all meet Junaluska in heaven [pointing upward] and all be happy there together.

The Joyce Kilmer Memorial Forest abuts the Slickrock Wilderness Area, and **Slickrock Creek Trail** is one of its longest trails. This 13.5-mile (one-way) trail starts out easy, but the final 5 to 5.5 miles are fairly strenuous. *Backpacker* magazine named this one of the toughest trails in the country several years ago, in part because the hike can be a 21.7-mile loop by connecting with the **Haoe Lead, Hangover Lead,** and **Ike Branch** trails. Be forewarned that this is a big trip, but it's rewarding, with views of waterfalls (the first is only a few miles in, on the easy part) and

rhododendron thickets. Its name is apt: The rocks here can be incredibly slick.

On the **Hangover Lead South Trail,** the trailhead is adjacent to the parking area at Big Fat Gap (off Slick Rock Rd., about 7 miles from U.S. 129). The trail is only 2.8 miles long, but it's strenuous. The payoff is the view from the Haoe summit at 5,249 feet. There are backcountry campsites here, and the rule is to keep campsites 100 yards from streams and practice Leave No Trace guidelines.

A handy collection of trail maps for Joyce Kilmer Memorial Forest,

Slickrock Creek, Snowbird Back Country, and Tsali Recreation Area is available from the Graham Chamber (http://grahamchamber.com). The maps provide a rough idea of the locations and routes of these trails, but they are not a replacement for topographic maps, which you should have with you while on any of these rugged or isolated trails.

ENTERTAINMENT AND EVENTS

Every year on the Saturday of Memorial Day weekend in late May, the Snowbird Cherokee host the Fading Voices Festival in Robbinsville. The festival features a mound-building ceremony along with typical festival attractions—music, dancing, storytelling, crafts, and lots of food—but in the deeply traditional forms carried on by the Snowbird community. Contact the Junaluska Museum (828/479-4727) for more information.

FOOD AND ACCOMMODATIONS

The Snowbird Mountain Lodge (4633 Santeetlah Rd., 11 miles west of Robbinsville, 800/941-9290, http://snowbirdlodge.com, $275-475) was built in the early 1940s, a rustic chestnut-and-stone inn atop a 3,000-foot mountain. The view is exquisite, and the lodge is perfectly situated among the Cherohala Skyway, Lake Santeetlah, and the Joyce Kilmer Forest. Guests enjoy a full breakfast, picnic lunch, and four-course supper created from seasonal local specialties.

Another pleasant place to stay near Robbinsville is the Tapoco Lodge Resort (14981 Tapoco Rd., 15 miles north of Robbinsville, 828/498-2800, www.tapocolodge.com, Thurs.-Sat. Nov.-Sept., daily Oct., rooms and

a trail in Joyce Kilmer Memorial Forest

suites $239-329, cabins $149-249). Built in 1930, the lodge is on the National Register of Historic Places, and it has the feel of an old-time hotel. Guest rooms in the main lodge and surrounding cabins are simple but comfortable, and the resort overlooks the Cheoah River, a legendary run for rafters several times each year when controlled releases of water form crazy-fast rapids. Dine here at **Tapoco Tavern** (828/498-2800, 11am-9pm Sun.-Thurs., 11am-10pm Fri.-Sat., $9-25) on pizzas, steaks, trout, fried chicken, sandwiches, and salads.

Angles Landing Inn Bed & Breakfast (94 Campbell St., Murphy, 828/360-7700, www.angelslandinginn. wordpress.com, $88-105) is one of the only B&Bs in town. Fortunately, they're friendly, and the price is right. **Mountain Ivy Rentals** (56 Airport Rd., 2.5 miles east of Robbinsville, 828/735-9180, www.mountainivy.com, 2-night minimum, $125) has one log-sided cabin that sleeps six and is steps away from great trout fishing in the stream that runs alongside the cabin. An indoor fireplace and a space outside for a campfire help make it cozy in any season. The garage is handy for motorcycle travelers, as it gives them a place to secure trailers, bikes, and other gear.

At the **Simple Life Campground** (88 Lower Mountain Creek Rd., 828/788-1099, www. thesimplelifecampground.com, Mar.-Nov., cabins $32-144, RVs $48-58, tents $18) the cabins, RV sites, and tent sites have access to hot showers and Wi-Fi. This campground is near the Cherohala Skyway, Joyce Kilmer National Forest, and Lake Santeelah.

If you're RVing your way through the Smokies, the six-acre **Teaberry Hill RV Campground** (77 Upper Sawyers Creek Rd., 828/479-3953, http://teaberryhill.com, $55) is one of the nicest campgrounds you'll find, with large pull-through sites to accommodate any size RV. Amenities include 50-amp electrical hookups, water and sewer, and Wi-Fi access.

HAYESVILLE, BRASSTOWN, AND MURPHY

Between Hayesville and Brasstown, you can get a really good sense of the art that has come out of this region over the years. These three small towns are along the Georgia border on U.S. 64.

MURPHY RIVER WALK

The Murphy River Walk is a three-mile trail along the Hiwassee River and Valley River, winding from Konehete Park to the Old L&N Depot. A beautiful walk (and a great way to stretch your legs after a long ride) through this charming, tiny town, the Riverwalk gives you the chance to see Murphy up close and personal.

After your walk along the river, take a look at some of the antique stores in Murphy. A popular stop is **Linger Awhile Antiques and Collectibles** (46 Valley River Ave., 321/267-2777, 10am-5pm Tues.-Sat.).

☼ JOHN C. CAMPBELL FOLK SCHOOL

One of North Carolina's most remarkable cultural institutions, the **John C. Campbell Folk School** (1 Folk School Rd., Brasstown, 800/365-5724, www.folkschool.org) was created by Northern honeymooners who traveled through Appalachia 100 years ago to educate themselves about Southern highland culture. John C. and Olive Dame Campbell, like other high-profile Northern liberals of their day, directed their humanitarian impulses toward the education and economic betterment of Southern mountain dwellers. John Campbell died a decade later, but Olive, joining forces with her friend Marguerite Butler, set out to establish a "folk school" in the Southern mountains that she and John had visited. She was inspired by the model of the Danish *folkehøjskole,* workshops that preserved and taught traditional arts as a means of fostering economic self-determination and personal pride in rural communities. Brasstown was chosen as the site for this grand experiment, and in 1925, the John C. Campbell Folk School opened its doors.

Today, thousands of artists travel every year to this uncommonly lovely remote valley, the site of an ancient Cherokee village. In weeklong and weekend classes, students of all ages and skill levels learn about the traditional arts of this region, such as pottery, weaving, dyeing, storytelling, and chair caning, as well as contemporary and exotic crafts such as photography, kaleidoscope making, bookmaking, and paper marbling. The website outlines the hundreds of courses offered every year, but even if you're passing through the area on a shorter visit, you can explore the school's campus. Visitors are asked to preserve the quiet atmosphere of learning and concentration when viewing the artist studios, but you can have an up-close look at some of their marvelous wares in the school's **Craft Shop** (bottom floor of Olive Dame Campbell Dining Hall, 8am-5pm Mon.-Wed. and Fri.-Sat., 8am-6pm Thurs., 1pm-5pm Sun.), one of the nicest craft shops in western North Carolina. Exhibits about the school's history and historic examples of the work of local artists of past generations are on display at the **History Center** (8am-5pm Mon.-Sat., 1pm-5pm Sun.), next to Keith House.

There are several nature trails on campus that thread through this lovely valley. Be sure to visit the 0.25-mile **Rivercane Walk,** which features outdoor sculpture by some of the greatest living artists of the Eastern Band of the Cherokee. In the evenings you'll often find concerts by traditional musicians, or community square, contra, and English country dances. A visit to the John C. Campbell Folk School, whether as a student or a traveler, is an exceptional opportunity to immerse yourself in a great creative tradition.

Harrah's Casino in Cherokee opened a sister location here in Murphy in late 2015. **Harrah's Cherokee Valley River Casino & Hotel** (777 Casino Pkwy., Murphy, 828/422-7777, www.caesars.com, from $179) has 300 rooms and a huge gaming floor: 50,000 square feet containing 70 table games and more than 1,000 slot machines. Upon its opening in 2015, the dining options were limited to **Nathan's Famous Hot Dogs** (open 24 hours), **Panda Express** (11am-11pm Sun.-Thurs., 11am-2am Fri.-Sat.), **Earl of Sandwich** (11am-11pm Sun.-Thurs., 11am-2am Fri.-Sat.), **The Landing Cafe** (7am-11am and 4pm-10pm Sun.-Wed., 7am-11am and 4pm-11pm Tues.-Sat.), and **Starbucks** (6am-11pm Sun.-Thurs., 6am-1am Fri.-Sat.). Still, who comes to a casino to eat? The table games are fun, and it's going to be interesting to watch this casino grow as the Harrah's in Cherokee grew.

FOOD

Herb's Pit Bar-B-Que (15896 W. Hwy. 64, Murphy, 828/494-5367, 11am-8pm Wed.-Sun, $2-24) is the western terminus of the North Carolina Barbecue Trail and should be your first (or last) stop on it. Here you can sample more than the 'cue that pitmasters in the deep mountains make—you can also order plates of tasty fried trout and chicken and thick steaks off the grill.

The Copper Door (2 Sullivan St., Hayesville, 828/389-8460, http://thecopperdoor.com, 5pm-10pm Tues.-Sat., $16-48) is an upscale joint serving a nice selection of seafood, steaks, and other meat-centric dishes, but they can accommodate vegetarians and vegans. This elegant restaurant is run by a chef from New Orleans, and his influence is all over the menu, from crawfish to mussels to other French- and creole-inspired creations. In 2011 and 2012 they received *Wine Spectator* magazine's Award of Excellence.

Tiger's Department Store (42 Herbert St., Hayesville, 828/389-6531, 9:30am-6pm Mon.-Sat.) has, in addition to clothing and gear, an old-fashioned soda counter (under $10) that provides some tasty refreshments.

GETTING THERE AND AROUND

This is the southwestern most corner of North Carolina, in some places as close to Atlanta as to Asheville. Robbinsville is remotest destination in this chapter, located on U.S. 129 southwest of Bryson City. Hayesville and Brasstown are easily reached via U.S. 64, which closely parallels the Georgia border.

BACKGROUND

The Landscape

GEOGRAPHY

North Carolina encompasses more than 50,000 square miles of land and water. The **Mountain Region** forms the western border of the state, with the Blue Ridge and Great Smoky Mountains, both subranges of the long Appalachian Mountain Range, undulating like the folds of a great quilt, running northeast-to-southwest

from Virginia along the border with Tennessee and into the southwestern corner where the inland tip of North Carolina meets Georgia. This is a land of waterfalls, rivers and fast-flowing creeks, and rugged, beautiful peaks of smaller mountain configurations. Hemmed in among the peaks and hollows of the Blue Ridge and the Smokies are the Black Mountains, the Pisgah Range, and the Unka Range. The Black Mountains are only about 15 miles wide and are confined mostly to Yancey County, but they're the highest in the state, and 6 of the 10 tallest peaks in the eastern United States are here, including Mount Mitchell, the highest at 6,684 feet.

CLIMATE

Generalizing about North Carolina's climate is difficult. It's not as hot as at the equator and not as cold as at the poles, but beyond that, each region has its own range of variables and has to be examined separately.

The mountains are cool and winter can last a long time. Towns like Asheville and Boone can be blanketed in snow while less than 100 miles away the trees in Piedmont towns aren't even showing their fall colors. The coldest temperature ever recorded in North Carolina, -34°F, was recorded in 1985 on Mount Mitchell. Spring and fall can bring cool to temperate days and chilly nights, while summer days can hit the 80s, and the evenings bring a welcome relief.

North Carolina gets its fair share of hazardous weather to go along with beautiful summer days and crisp fall nights. **Tornadoes,** most common in the spring, can cause trouble any time of year. A rare November twister touched down in 2006, smashing the Columbus County community of Riegelwood, killing eight people and leaving a seven-mile swath of destruction. Even plain old **thunderstorms** can be dangerous, bringing lightning, flash flooding, difficult driving conditions, and even hail. **Snowstorms** are rare and usually occur in the mountains.

Plants

In the early 1700s, John Lawson, an English explorer who would soon be one of the first victims of the Tuscarora War, wrote of a magnificent tree house somewhere in the very young colony of North Carolina. "I have been informed of a Tulip-Tree," he wrote, "that was ten Foot Diameter; and another, wherein a lusty Man had his Bed and Household Furniture, and liv'd in it, till his Labour got him a more fashionable Mansion. He afterwards became a noted Man, in his Country, for Wealth and Conduct." Whether or not there was ever a tulip poplar large enough to serve as a furnished bachelor pad, colonial North Carolina's forests must have seemed miraculous to the first Europeans to see them.

FORESTS

Today, after generations of logging and farming across the state, few old-growth forests exist. In the Smoky Mountains, stands of old-growth timber, like the Joyce Kilmer Forest, are a sight to behold, and some of the trees almost validate Lawson's anecdote. Across the state, scores of specialized ecosystems support a marvelous diversity of plant and animal life. In the east, cypress swamps and a few patches of maritime forest still stand; across the Sandhills are longleaf pine forests; in the mountains are fragrant balsam forests and stands of hardwoods.

Because the state is so geographically and climatically varied, there's a greater diversity in tree species than anywhere in the eastern United States. In terms of land area, more than half of the land is still forested in the Piedmont and eastern North Carolina. In the Piedmont, oak and hickory dominate the hardwoods alongside bands of piney woods. In the mountains oak and hickory are also the rule, but a number of conifers, including pine and balsam, appear, too.

The science and profession of forestry were born in North Carolina: In the 1880s and 1890s, George W. Vanderbilt, lord of the manner at Biltmore, engaged Frederick Law Olmsted, who designed New York City's Central Park, to plan a managed forest of the finest, healthiest, and most hardy trees. Vanderbilt hired Gifford Pinchot and later Carl Shenck to be the stewards of the thousands of wooded acres he owned in the Pisgah Forest south of Asheville. The contributions these men made to the nascent field are still felt today and are commemorated at the Cradle of Forestry Museum near Brevard.

FLOWERS

Some of North Carolina's flora puts on great annual shows, drawing flocks of admirers—the gaudy azaleas of

azaleas in bloom

AROUND ASHEVILLE

Asheville is the home of the **North Carolina Arboretum,** a garden of more than 400 acres that borders the Pisgah National Forest and the Blue Ridge Parkway. Special collections include the National Native Azalea Repository and more than 200 bonsai. You can tour the arboretum on foot, by Segway, or on your bike, and you can even bring your dog on some of the trails.

At the **Biltmore Estate,** Frederick Law Olmsted created formal gardens of beauty to match the opulent mansion, and architect Richard Morris Hunt designed the conservatory where young plants are still raised for the gardens. Self-guided tours of the conservatory—and the walled, shrub, Italian, vernal, and azalea gardens—are all included in admission to the estate.

Asheville is also an excellent home base for excursions to other garden spots in the mountains. Don't miss the **Rivercane Walk** at the John C. Campbell Folk School in Brasstown, where modern Cherokee sculpture lines a path along Little Brasstown Creek. The **Mountain Farm Museum** at the edge of Great Smoky Mountains National Park demonstrates gardening methods used on the early mountain homesteads. The **Cradle of Forestry** in Pisgah National Forest explains how the science of modern forestry was born here in western North Carolina.

springtime in Wilmington, the wild-flowers of the first warm weather in the hills, the rhododendrons and mountain laurel of the Appalachian summer. The Ericaceae family, a race of great woody bushes with star-shaped blossoms that includes azaleas, rhododendrons, and laurel, is the headliner in North Carolina's floral fashion show. Spring comes earliest to the southeastern corner of the state, and the Wilmington area is explosively beautiful when the azaleas are in bloom. The Azalea Festival, held annually for more than 50 years, draws hundreds of thousands of people to the city in early to mid-April, around the time that public gardens and private yards are spangled with azaleas.

The flame azalea makes a late-spring appearance on the mountain-sides of the Blue Ridge and Great Smokies, joined by its cousins the mountain laurel and Catawba rhododendron in May and June. The ways of the rhododendron are a little mysterious; not every plant blooms every year, and there's no surefire way of predicting when they'll put on big shows. The area's widely varying elevation also figures into bloom times. If you're interested in timing your trip to coincide with some of these flowering seasons, your best bet is to call ahead and speak with a ranger from the Great Smoky Mountains National Park or the Blue Ridge Parkway to find out how the season is coming along.

Around the end of April and into May, when spring finally arrives in the mountains but the forest floor is not yet sequestered in leafy shade, a profusion of delicate flowers emerges. Violets and chickweed emerge early on, as do the quintessentially mountainous white trillium blossoms and the Wake Robin, also a trillium, which looks something like a small poinsettia. Every year since 1950, around the end of April, the Great Smoky Mountains National Park has hosted the Spring Wildflower Pilgrimage, a weeklong festival featuring scores of nature walks that also reveal salamanders, birds, and wild hogs, along with workshops and art exhibits. Visit www.springwildflowerpilgrimage.org for upcoming events.

Surprisingly, one of the best places in North Carolina to view displays of wildflowers is along the major highways. For more than 20 years the state's Department of Transportation has carried out a highway beautification project that involves planting large banks of wildflowers along highways and in wide medians. The displays are not landscaped but are allowed to grow up in unkempt profusion, often planted in inspired combinations of wildly contrasting colors that make the flowerbeds a genuinely beautiful addition to the environment. The website of the state's **Department of Transportation** (www.ncdot.org) offers a guide to the locations and seasons of the wildflower beds.

FALL FOLIAGE

Arriving as early as mid-September at the highest elevations and gradually sliding down the mountains through late October, autumn colors bring a late-season wave of visitors to western North Carolina. Dropping temperatures change trees' sugar production, resulting in a palette of colors, while simple fatigue causes the green to fade in others, exposing underlying hues. Countless climatic factors can alter the onset and progress of leaf season, so the mountains blush at slightly different times every year. The latter weeks of October tend to be the peak; during those weeks it can be difficult to find lodging in the mountains, so be sure to plan ahead. Some of the best places for leaf peeping are along the Blue Ridge Parkway and in the Great Smoky Mountains National Park.

Animals

Among the familiar wildlife most commonly seen in the state, **white-tailed deer** are out in force in the countryside and in the woods; they populate suburban areas in large numbers as well. **Raccoons** and **opossums** prowl at night, happy to scavenge from trash cans and the forest floor. **Skunks** are common, particularly in the mountains, and are often smelled rather than seen. They leave an odor something like a cross between grape soda and Sharpie markers. There are also a fair number of **black bears**, not only in the mountains but in swamps and deep woods across the state.

In woods and yards alike, **gray squirrels** and a host of familiar **songbirds** are a daily presence. Different species of **tree frogs** produce beautiful choruses on spring and summer nights, while **fireflies** mount sparkly shows in the trees and grass in the upper Piedmont and mountains. Down along the southeast coast, **alligators** and **turtles** sun themselves on many a golf course and creek-side backyard.

The town of Brevard, in the Blue Ridge south of Asheville, is famous for its population of ghostly **white squirrels.** They're regular old gray squirrels that live all over North America, but their fur ranges from speckled gray and white to pure bone-white. They're not albinos; it's thought that Brevard's white squirrels are cousins of a clan that lives in Florida and that their ancestors may have found their way to the Blue Ridge in a circus or with a dealer of exotic pets in the early 20th century.

The Carolina woods harbor colonies of **Southern flying squirrels.** It's very unlikely that you'll see one unless it's at a nature center or wildlife rehabilitation clinic because flying squirrels are both nocturnal and shy. They're also almost unspeakably cute. Fully extended, they're about nine inches long snout to tail, weigh about four ounces, and have super-silky fur and pink noses. Like many nocturnal animals, they have comically long whiskers and huge, wide-set eyes that suggest amphetamine use. When they're flying—gliding, really—they spread their limbs to extend the patagium, a membrane that stretches between their front and hind legs, and glide along like little magic carpets.

Also deep in the Smokies are some herds of **wild hogs,** game boar brought to the area about 100 years ago and allowed to go feral. The official line among wildlife officials is that **mountain lions**—in this region called panthers—have been extinct in North Carolina for some time. But mountain dwellers claim there are still panthers in the Blue Ridge and Smokies, and most people here have seen or heard one—their cry sounds like a terror-filled scream. There are even tales of a panther in the inland woods of Brunswick and Columbus Counties on the southeast coast.

REINTRODUCED SPECIES

In the 1990s and early 2000s a federal program to reestablish **red wolf** colonies in the Southeast focused its efforts on parkland in North Carolina. Red wolves, thought to have existed in

North Carolina in past centuries, were first reintroduced to the Great Smoky Mountains National Park. They did not thrive, and the colony was moved to the Alligator River National Wildlife Refuge on the northeast coast. The packs have fared better in this corner of the state and now roam several wilderness areas in the sound country.

The Smokies proved a more hospitable place for the reintroduction of **elk.** Now the largest animals in the Great Smoky Mountains National Park, elk, which can grow up to 700 pounds, are most often observed in the Cataloochee section of the park, grazing happily and lounging in the mist in the early morning and at twilight.

BIRDS

Bird-watchers flock to North Carolina because of the great diversity of songbirds, raptors, and even hummingbirds across the state—a 2013 count put the number of species at 473—but the state is best known for waterfowl. In the sounds of eastern North Carolina, waterfowl descend en masse as they migrate. Hundreds of thousands of birds crowd the lakes, ponds, trees, marshes, and waterways as they move to and from their winter homes. Many hunters take birds during hunting season, but they're outnumbered by bird-watchers. Birders say that one of the best spots for birding in the state is around large, shallow **Lake Mattamuskeet** on the central coast, with 40,000 acres of water to attract incredible numbers of snow geese and tundra swans, Canada geese, and ducks. Just a few miles away, **Swan Quarter National Wildlife Refuge** is also a haven for ducks, wading birds, shorebirds, and their admirers.

While in eastern North Carolina,

bird fanciers should visit the **Sylvan Heights Waterfowl Park and Eco-Center,** a remarkable park in the small town of Scotland Neck that's a conservation center and breeding facility for rare waterfowl from across the globe. Visitors can walk through the grounds, where large aviaries house bird species that, unless you're a world traveler and a very lucky birder, you're unlikely to see elsewhere. There are more than 170 species, and you can get quite close to most of them. Bring your camera; you'll have the chance to take shots you could never get in the field.

Another place not to miss is the **Carolina Raptor Center,** on the grounds of the Latta Plantation Nature Preserve in Huntersville, north of Charlotte. The center is primarily a rehabilitation facility—they've treated and released thousands of birds over the years—but there is also a 0.75-mile nature trail through the park, where you can see many of the facility's resident raptors, including owls, hawks, eagles, kites, kestrels, and merlins that were found to be too profoundly injured to survive in the wild.

There are many books and websites about birding in North Carolina. One of the most helpful is the North Carolina Birding Trail, both a website (www.ncbirdingtrail.org) and a series of print guidebooks. Organized by region, these resources list dozens of top sites for bird-watching and favorite bird-watching events throughout the state. Another good resource is the **Carolina Bird Club** (www.carolinabirdclub.org).

AMPHIBIANS

Dozens of species of **salamanders** and their close kin, including **mudpuppies, sirens,** and **amphiumas,** call North Carolina home, and Great Smoky Mountains National Park harbors so many of them that it's known as the Salamander Capital of the World. Throughout the state, **frogs** and **toads** are numerous and vociferous, especially the many species of dainty **tree frogs.** Two species, the gray tree frog and the spring peeper, are found in every part of North Carolina, and beginning in late winter they create the impression that the trees are filled with ringing cell phones.

Hellbenders are quite possibly the strangest animal in North Carolina. They are enormous salamanders—not the slick little pencil-thin five-inch salamanders easily spotted along creeks, but hulking brutes that grow to more than two feet long and can weigh five pounds. Rare and hermetic, they live in rocky mountain streams, venturing out from under rocks at night to gobble up crayfish and minnows. They're hard to see even if they do emerge in the daytime because they're lumpy and mud-colored, camouflaged against streambeds. Aggressive with each other, the males often sport battle scars on their stumpy legs. They've been known to bite humans, but as rare as it is to spot a hellbender, it's an exponentially rarer occurrence to be bitten by one.

REPTILES

Turtles and **snakes** are the state's most common reptiles. **Box turtles,** found everywhere, and **bog turtles,** found in the Smokies, are the only land terrapins. A great many freshwater turtles inhabit the swamps and ponds, and on a sunny day every log or branch sticking out of fresh water will become a sunbathing terrace for as many turtles as it can hold. Common water turtles include cooters, sliders, and painted turtles. Snapping turtles can be found in fresh water throughout the state, so mind your toes. They grow up to a couple of feet long and can weigh more than 50 pounds. Not only will they bite—hard!—If provoked, they will actually initiate hostilities, lunging for you if they so much as disapprove of the fashion of your shoes. Even the tiny hatchlings are vicious, so give them a wide berth.

There are plenty of real snakes in North Carolina. The vast majority are shy, gentle, and totally harmless to anything larger than a rat. There are a few species of venomous snakes that are very dangerous. These include three kinds of rattlesnake: the huge diamondback, whose diet of rabbits testifies to its size and strength; the pigmy; and the timber or canebrake rattler. Other venomous species are the beautiful mottled copperhead and the cottonmouth or water moccasin, famous for flinging its mouth open in hostility and flashing its brilliant white palate. The coral snake is a fantastically beautiful and venomous species.

Most Carolina snakes are entirely benign to humans, including old familiars such as black racers and king snakes as well as milk, corn, and rat snakes. One particularly endearing character is the hognose snake, which can be found throughout North Carolina but is most common in the east. Colloquially known as a spreading adder, the hognose snake compensates for its total harmlessness with amazing displays of histrionics. If you startle one, it will first flatten and greatly widen its head and neck and hiss most passionately. If it sees that you're not frightened by plan A, it will panic and go straight to plan B: playing dead. The hognose snake won't simply lay inert until you go away, though; it goes to the dramatic lengths of flipping onto its back, exposing its pitiably vulnerable belly, opening its mouth, throwing its head back limply, and sticking out its tongue as if it had just been poisoned. It is such a devoted method actor that should you call its bluff and poke it back onto its belly, it will fling itself energetically back into the mortuary pose and resume being deceased.

History

ANCIENT CIVILIZATION

By the time the first colonists arrived and called this place Carolina, the land had already sustained some 20,000 years of human history. We know that Paleo-Indians hunted these lands during the last ice age, when there were probably more mammoths and saber-toothed tigers in North Carolina than people. Civilization came around 4000 BC, when the first inhabitants settled down to farm, make art, and trade goods. By the first century, Southern Woodland and Mississippian Indians were also living in advanced societies with complex religious systems, economic interaction among communities, advanced farming methods, and the creation of art and architecture.

When the Europeans arrived, there were more than a dozen major Native

American groups within what is now North Carolina. The Cherokee people ruled the mountains while the Catawba, Pee Dees, Tutelo, and Saura, among others, were their neighbors in the Piedmont. In the east, the Cheraw, Waccamaw, and Tuscarora were some of the larger communities, while many bands occupied land along the Outer Banks and sounds.

CONQUEST

The first Europeans to land here were Spanish. We know conquistador Hernando de Soto and his troops marched around western North Carolina in 1539, but they were just passing through. In 1566, another band of Spanish explorers, led by conquistador Juan Pardo, came for a longer visit. They were making a circuitous trek in the general direction of Mexico, and along the way they established several forts in what are now the Carolinas and Tennessee. One of these forts, called San Juan, has been identified by archaeologists outside present-day Morganton in a community called Worry Crossroads. Although the troops who were garrisoned for a year and a half at Fort San Juan eventually disappeared into the woods or were killed, it's theorized that they may have had a profound impact on the course of history, possibly spreading European diseases among the Native Americans and weakening them so much that, a couple of decades later, the indigenous people would be unable to repel the invasion of English colonists.

The next episode in the European settlement of North Carolina is one of the strangest mysteries in American history: the Lost Colonists of Roanoke. After two previous failed attempts to establish an English stronghold on the island of Roanoke, fraught by poor planning and disastrous diplomacy, a third group of English colonists tried their luck. Sometime between being dropped off in the New World in 1587 and one of their leaders returning three years later to resupply them, all of the colonists—including Virginia Dare, the first English person born in the Americas—had vanished into the woods. To this day, their fate is unknown, although a host of fascinating theories are still debated and probably always will be.

The disappearance of the Roanoke colonists did little to slow the process of the European conquest of North America. After the establishment of the Virginia colony in 1607, new English settlers began to trickle southward into Carolina, while Barbadians and Europeans from Charles Town (in present-day South Carolina) gradually began to populate the area around Wilmington. The town of Bath was established in 1706, and New Bern was settled shortly thereafter. The bloody Tuscarora War followed, and after a crushing defeat near present-day Snow Hill, in which hundreds were killed, the Tuscarora people retreated, opening the land along the Neuse River to European colonization.

COLONIALISM

The conflict between Europeans and Native Americans wasn't the only world-changing cultural encounter going on in the Southern colonies. By the middle of the 18th century, nearly 100,000 enslaved people had been brought to North Carolina from West Africa. By the end of the 18th century, many areas, especially those around Wilmington, had populations where enslaved African Americans outnumbered whites. Although North Carolina did not experience slavery on as vast a scale as South Carolina, there were a handful of plantations with more than 100 slaves, and many smaller plantations and town homes of wealthy planters, merchants, and politicians with smaller numbers of slaves. Africans and African Americans were an early and potent cultural force in the South, influencing the economy, politics, language, religion, music, architecture, and cuisine in ways still seen today.

In the 1730s the Great Wagon Road connected Pennsylvania with Georgia by cutting through the Mid-Atlantic and Southern backcountry of Virginia and North Carolina. Many travelers migrated south from Pennsylvania, among them a good number of German and Scottish-Irish settlers who found the mountains and Piedmont of North Carolina to their liking. Meanwhile, the port of Wilmington, growing into one of the most important in the state, saw a number of Gaelic-speaking Scots move through, following the river north and putting down roots around what is now Fayetteville. Shortly before the American Revolution, a group of German-speaking religious settlers known as the Moravians constructed a beautiful and industrious town, Salem, in the heart of the Piedmont, which would later become Winston-Salem. Their pacifist beliefs, Germanic heritage, and artistry set them apart from other communities in colonial North Carolina, and they left an indelible mark on the state's history.

The 18th century brought one conflict after another to the colony, from fights over the Vestry Act in the early 1700s, which attempted to establish the Anglican church as the one official faith of the colony, through various regional conflicts with Native Americans and events that played out at a global level during the French and Indian War. At mid-century the population and economic importance of the Piedmont was growing exponentially, but colonial representation continued to be focused along the coast. Protesting local corruption and lack of governmental concern for the western region, a group of backcountry farmers organized themselves into an armed posse in resistance to colonial corruption. Calling themselves the Regulators, they eventually numbered more than 6,000. Mounting frustrations led to an attack by the Regulators on the Orange County courthouse in Hillsborough. Finally, a colonial militia was dispatched to crush the movement, which it did at the Battle of Alamance in 1771. Six Regulators were captured and hanged at Hillsborough.

REVOLUTION AND STATEHOOD

Many believe the seeds of the American Revolution were sown, tended, and reaped in New England, but the southern colonies, particularly North Carolina, played important roles before and during the rebellion. In 1765, as the War of the Regulation was heating up, the residents of Brunswick Town, the colonial capital and the only deep-water port in the southern half of the colony, revolted in protest of the Stamp Act. They placed the royal governor under house arrest and put an end to taxation in the Cape Fear region, sending a strong message to the crown and to fellow patriots hungry to shake off the yoke of British rule. In the ensuing years, well-documented events like the Boston Tea Party, the Battles of Lexington and Concord, and the signing of the Declaration of

Independence occurred, but North Carolina's role in leading the rebellion was far from over.

After the Battles of Lexington and Concord, the colonies were aflame with patriotic fervor, and Mecklenburg County (around Charlotte) passed the first colonial declaration rejecting the crown's authority. By this time, North Carolina, like the other colonies, had formed a provincial government, and it was busy in the tavern at Halifax writing the Halifax Resolves, the first official action in the colonies calling for independence from Britain. On April 12, 1776, the resolves were ratified and delegates carried them to the Second Continental Congress in Philadelphia. Other delegates were so inspired that more such resolves appeared, ultimately the Declaration of Independence was written and ratified, and the revolution was on in earnest.

Although North Carolina may have been the first to call for independence, the state was divided in its loyalties. Among the most noteworthy Loyalists was the community of Highland Scots living in and around modern-day Fayetteville. Men from this community were marching to join General Cornwallis near Brunswick Town and Southport (then Smithville) when Patriots ambushed them at the bloody battle of Moore's Creek, killing 30 Scots and routing the Loyalist force.

North Carolinians fought all over the eastern seaboard during the Revolution, including about 1,000 who were with Washington at Valley Forge. The year 1780 brought fighting back home, particularly in the area around Charlotte, which a daunted General Cornwallis referred to as "the hornets' nest." The battle of Kings Mountain, west of Charlotte, was a pivotal moment in the war and particularly costly

to the Loyalist forces. Cornwallis received another blow at the Battle of Guilford Courthouse; although technically a British victory, it weakened his forces considerably. By the time the war ended, thousands of North Carolinians were dead, and the treasury was far in debt—but North Carolina was now a state with the business of statehood to attend to. The capital was moved inland to Raleigh, and 20 miles away at Chapel Hill, ground was broken for the establishment of the University of North Carolina, the first state university in the country.

THE FEDERAL ERA

The early 19th century in North Carolina was a good deal more peaceful than the previous hundred years had been. The first decade of the 1800s saw a religious awakening in which thousands of North Carolinians became devout Christians. At the same time, the introduction of the cotton gin and bright-leaf tobacco were economic boons in the state, particularly the eastern counties. Railroads and plank roads made trade immeasurably more efficient, bringing new prosperity to the Piedmont.

There was also conflict, of course, in the early 19th century. Andrew Jackson's administration presided over the passage of the Indian Removal Act in 1830, which assigned reservations in the Indian Territory of present-day Oklahoma to the "Five Civilized Tribes" of the southeastern United States—the Cherokee, Choctaw, Creek, Chickasaw, and Seminole. Thousands of Cherokee people were forced out of western North Carolina, northern Georgia, eastern Tennessee, and Alabama and marched west on the Trail of Tears. About 4,000 died along the way. Another 1,000 or so Cherokee people, through hiding, fighting, and negotiation, managed to win the right to stay in North Carolina—an act of resistance that was the birth of the modern Eastern Band of the Cherokee, still centered around the town of Cherokee on the Qualla Boundary in North Carolina's Great Smoky Mountains. The Eastern Band of the Cherokee tell the story of their relocation in the enlightening outdoor drama *Unto These Hills*.

THE CIVIL WAR

Compared to South Carolina and a few other Southern states, North Carolina was considered politically moderate in the mid-19th century because it was less invested economically and politically in slavery. Combined with the knowledge that if secession became a reality, war would follow and North Carolina's tobacco and cotton fields would quickly become battlefields, secession was on the lips of everyone across the South. As some states voted to remove themselves from the Union, North Carolina's voters rejected a ballot measure authorizing a secession convention. As grand a gesture as that victory may have been, when fighting erupted at Fort Sumpter in Charleston Harbor, North Carolina's hand was forced and its secession was a reality. Secessionist governor John Ellis rejected Lincoln's call to federalize state militias, instead seizing control of the state and all federal military installations within its boundaries as well as the Charlotte Mint. North Carolina officially seceded on May 20, 1861, and a few weeks later Union ships began to blockade the coast. Roanoke Island in the Outer Banks fell, and a freedmen's colony (a home for enslaved people who had

been freed or escaped) sprung up. New Bern, which fell in the spring of 1862, became a major focal point of Union military strategy and a thriving political base for freed and escaped African Americans. To the south, Fort Fisher, on the Cape Fear River just south of Wilmington, guarded the river's inlet and was crucial to the success of the blockade runners—smugglers whose speedy boats eluded the Union blockade. Fort Fisher kept Wilmington in Confederate hands until nearly the end of the war. When it finally did fall to Union forces in February 1865, it required what would be the largest amphibious assault in American military history until World War II. Wilmington was the last major port on the Confederacy's eastern seaboard, and its fall severed supply lines and crippled what remained of the Confederate Army in the area.

The varying opinions felt by Southerners about the Civil War, in the South also called the War between the States, was particularly strong in North Carolina, where today you'll still hear whites refer to it as the War of Northern Aggression or the War of Yankee Aggression. More than 5,000 African Americans from North Carolina joined and fought in the Union Army, and there were pockets of strong Union sentiment and support among white North Carolinians, especially in the mountains. Some 10,000 North Carolinians fought for the Union. Zebulon Vance, who won the 1862 gubernatorial election and served as governor through the duration of the war, was a native of Weaverville, near Asheville, and felt acutely the state's ambivalence toward the Confederacy. Much to the consternation of Richmond (the Confederate capital), Governor Vance was adamant in his refusal to put the interests of the Confederacy over those of his own state. Mountain communities suffered tremendously during the war from acts of terrorism by deserters and rogues from both armies.

The latter years of the Civil War were particularly difficult for North Carolina and the rest of the South. Approximately 4,000 North Carolina men died at the Battle of Gettysburg alone. After laying waste to Georgia and South Carolina, General William T. Sherman's army entered North Carolina in the spring of 1865, destroying homes and farms. His march of fire and pillage spared Wilmington, which is one reason the town contains such an incredible collection of Federal architecture. The last major battle of the war was fought in North Carolina, when General Sherman and Confederate General Joseph Johnston engaged at Bentonville. Johnston surrendered to Sherman in Durham in April 1865.

By the end of the war more than 40,000 North Carolina soldiers were dead—a number equivalent to the entire present-day population of the city of Hickory, Apex, or Kannapolis.

RECONSTRUCTION AND THE NEW SOUTH

The years immediately after the war were painful as well, as a vast population of newly free African Americans tried to make new lives for themselves economically and politically in the face of tremendous opposition and violence from whites. The Ku Klux Klan was set up during this time, inaugurating an era of horror for African Americans throughout the country. Federal occupation and domination of the Southern states' political and legal systems also exacerbated resentment toward the North. The state's ratification of the 14th Amendment on July 4, 1868, brought North Carolina back into the Union.

The late 1800s saw large-scale investment in North Carolina's railroad system, launching the industrial boom of the New South. Agriculture changed in this era as the rise of tenancy created a new form of enslavement for many farmers—black, white, and Native American. R. J. Reynolds, Washington Duke, and other entrepreneurs built a massively lucrative empire of tobacco production from field to factory. Textile and furniture mills sprouted throughout the Piedmont, creating a new cultural landscape as rural Southerners migrated to mill towns.

THE 20TH CENTURY AND TODAY

The early decades of the 1900s brought an expanded global perspective to North Carolina, not only through the expanded economy and the coming of radio but as natives of the state scattered across the globe. About 80,000 North Carolinians served in World War I, many of them young men who had never before left the state or perhaps even their home counties. Hundreds of thousands of African Americans migrated north during what became known as the Great Migration. The communities created by black North Carolinians in the Mid-Atlantic and the Northeast are still closely connected by culture and kinship to their cousins whose ancestors remained in the South. The invasion of the boll weevil, an insect that devastated the cotton industry, hastened the departure of Southerners of all races who had farmed cotton. The Great Depression hit hard across all economic sectors of the state in the

1930s, but New Deal employment programs were a boon to North Carolina's infrastructure, with the construction of hydroelectric dams, the Blue Ridge Parkway, and other public works.

North Carolina's modern-day military importance largely dates to the World War II era. Installations at Fort Bragg, Camp Lejeune, and other still-vital bases were constructed or expanded. About 350,000 North Carolinians fought in World War II, and 7,000 of them died.

A few old-timers remember World War II quite vividly because they witnessed it firsthand: German U-boats prowled the waters off the coast, torpedoing ships and sinking them with frightening regularity. These German submarines were often visible from the beach, but more often the evidence of their mission of terror and supply-chain disruption—corpses, wounded sailors, and the flotsam of exploded ships—washed up on the shore. More than 10,000 German prisoners were interned in prisoner-of-war camps, in some parts of the state becoming forced farm laborers. In Wilmington, just a few blocks from downtown, is an apartment complex that was part of a large prisoner-of-war compound for U-boat officers.

In the 1950s and 1960s, African Americans in North Carolina and throughout the United States struggled against the monolithic system of segregation and racism enshrined in the nation's Jim Crow laws. The Ku Klux Klan stepped up its pro-segregation efforts with political and physical violence against Native Americans as well as African Americans; in the famous 1958 Battle of Maxton, 500 armed Lumbee people foiled a Klan rally and sent the Knights running for their lives. Change arrived slowly.

The University of North Carolina accepted its first African American graduate student in 1951 and the first black undergraduates four years later. Sit-ins in 1960 at the Woolworth's lunch counter in Greensboro began with four African American men, students at North Carolina A&T. On the second day of their protest they were joined by 23 other demonstrators; on the third day there were 300, and by day four about 1,000. This was a pivotal moment in the national civil rights movement, sparking sit-ins across the country in which an estimated 50,000 people participated. You can see the counter today at the International Civil Rights Center and Museum in Greensboro. Even as victories were won at the level of Congress and in the federal courts, as in *Brown v. the Board of Education* and the 1964 Civil Rights Act, actual change on the ground was inexorably slow and hard-won. North Carolina's contribution to the civil rights movement continues to be invaluable for the whole nation.

The most recent census estimates, provided in mid-2017, show that North Carolina's population is at 10.27 million and growing, making it the ninth most populous state in the U.S. The state continues to adapt and contribute to the global community, thanks in large part to larger cities like Charlotte and the university-, research-, and tech-rich Raleigh, Durham, and Chapel Hill area. It is now a place of ethnic diversity, growing especially quickly in Latino residents. In 2014 an estimated 9 percent of North Carolinians were Latino, and that number is still climbing. There are also significant communities of Dega, Hmong, and Montagnard people from Southeast Asia as well as Eastern Europeans, among many others.

Government and Economy

POLITICAL LIFE

LIBERAL ENCLAVES

Although historically a red state, North Carolina's large population of college students, professors, and artists has created several boisterous enclaves of progressive politics. The outspoken archconservative U.S. Senator Jesse Helms supposedly questioned the need to spend public money on a state zoo in North Carolina "when we can just put up a fence around Chapel Hill." The Chapel Hill area is indeed the epicenter of North Carolina's liberalism, with its smaller neighboring town of Carrboro at its heart. Would-be Democratic presidential candidates and politicians on the campaign trail regularly stop here to bolster support in the state.

Although you'll find a mixture of political views statewide, the Triangle is not the only famously liberal community. In Asheville, lefty politics are part of the community's devotion to all things organic and DIY. Significant pockets of liberalism also exist in Boone, the cities of the Triad, and Wilmington.

FAMOUS FIGURES

Several major players in modern American politics are from North Carolina. The best-known politician in recent years is former U.S. senator John Edwards, who made two runs for the White House, the first leading to a vice presidential spot on the Democratic ticket. Edwards was born in South Carolina but grew up here in the Sandhills. At the other end of the political spectrum, Monroe native Jesse Helms spent 30 years in the U.S. Senate, becoming one of the most prominent and outspoken conservative Republicans of our times. Upon his retirement, Helms was succeeded in the Senate by Salisbury-born Duke University graduate Elizabeth Dole, who had previously served in Ronald Reagan's cabinet and George H. W. Bush's cabinet. She was also president of the American Red Cross and had a close brush with the White House when her husband, Kansas senator Bob Dole, ran for president in 1996.

MAJOR INDUSTRIES

Over the last 20 years, North Carolina has experienced tremendous shifts in its economy as the industries that once dominated the landscape and brought wealth and development declined. The tobacco industry ruled the state's economy for generations, employing innumerable North Carolinians from field to factory and funding a colossal portion of the state's physical and cultural infrastructure. The slow decline of the tobacco industry worldwide from the 1980s changed the state dramatically, especially the rural east, where tobacco fields once went from green to gold every fall. Other agricultural industries, especially livestock—chickens and hogs—are still important in the east. The textile industry, a giant for most of the 20th century, suffered the same decline as manufacturers sought cheaper labor overseas. Likewise, the furniture industry slipped into obscurity. Today, the once-thriving fishing industry is in steep decline, largely due to globalization and overfishing.

While these staple industries have fallen off, new industries and fields have sprouted across the state. Pharmaceutical and biotech companies have set up in the Research Triangle, formed by Raleigh, Durham, and Chapel Hill. The film industry has made Wilmington a hub of feature film production, Charlotte is a major production center for television programming and commercials, and Raleigh is home to a number of visual-effects studios that contribute to films and TV. High-tech leaders such as Apple have set up in North Carolina, and other tech giants have followed, locating database and network centers here. Charlotte is second only to New York City among the country's largest banking centers. Tourism continues to grow and contribute in a major way to the state's economy. Agriculture remains relevant, though it is increasingly becoming more specialized, especially as demand for organic products and locally and regionally sourced products continues.

TOURISM

North Carolina has always drawn visitors to its mountains and cities. As the economy evolves, tourism has become even more important. Mountain and beach landscapes sell themselves, but competition is strong to be the town visitors think of first. As culinary tourism gains momentum, so too do foodie destinations like Asheville, which was named "Beer City USA" from 2009 to 2012 and boasts some two dozen breweries and specialty beer shops along with more than 250 independently owned restaurants. Heritage tourism is also enormously important, with a number of guide books and driving trails established

or under development to promote history, traditional music, folk arts, and literary achievements. The state's Department of Commerce estimates that nearly 46 million people visit North Carolina every year, bringing in more than $19 billion, and that close to 200,000 state residents work in industries directly related to and dependent on tourism.

DISTRIBUTION OF WEALTH

For the most part, North Carolina is basically working-class. Pockets of significant wealth exist in urban areas, and as more and more retirees relocate to North Carolina, there are moneyed people in the mountains and coastal counties. Extensive white-collar job availability makes the Triangle a comparatively prosperous region, with average household incomes in 2010 exceeding $60,000, much higher than the state's median household income of just over $46,000.

The state also experiences significant poverty. The proportion of people living in poverty has been rising since 2000, partly due to the ongoing worldwide economic slowdown but also due to the derailment of many of North Carolina's backbone industries. As recently as one generation ago, a high school graduate in small-town North Carolina could count on making a living wage in a mill or factory; nowadays those opportunities have dried up, and the poverty rate in 2017 was 14.7 percent. Even more distressing, the number of children living in poverty is just over 24 percent, climbing to 28 percent for children under age six.

The northeastern quadrant of North Carolina is the most critically impoverished, which points to financial inequality correlating to race, as the region has a significant African American population. Broken down by ethnicity, the data reveal that 10 percent of urban and rural whites live in poverty, while 20-30 percent of rural and urban Latinos, African Americans, and Native Americans live in poverty.

Several hardworking organizations and activists are trying to alleviate the economic hardship found in North Carolina. National organizations like Habitat for Humanity (www.habitat.org) and regional groups like the Southern Coalition for Social Justice (http://southerncoalition.org) and the Institute for Southern Studies (www.southernstudies.org) bring community activism and research to the state. There are also excellent North Carolina-based advocates in groups such as the North Carolina Rural Economic Development Center (www.ncruralcenter.org), the North Carolina Justice Center (www.ncjustice.org), the Black Family Land Trust (www.bflt.org), and Student Action with Farmworkers (http://saf-unite.org).

People and Culture

DEMOGRAPHICS

The ninth most populous state in the union, North Carolina's population of 9.94 million residents is slightly more than Michigan and New Jersey and slightly less than Georgia. More than two-thirds of North Carolinians are white, primarily of German and Scottish-Irish descent, and not quite one-quarter are African American. The state is about 9 percent Latino and has the seventh-largest Native American population of any state.

More than 40 percent of North Carolinians are between the ages of 25 and 59, but the older population is steadily rising, due in large part to the state's popularity with retirees. The majority—about 70 percent—of North Carolinians live in family groups, with married couples constituting about half of those and married couples with children making up almost one-quarter of households. Of the remaining one-third of the state's population who live in "nonfamily households"—that is, not with blood relatives or a legally recognized spouse—the vast majority are individuals living on their own. Unmarried couples, both straight and gay, have a much lower rate of cohabitation here than in more urban parts of the United States, but such households are common and accepted in the Triangle, Asheville, Charlotte, and other urban areas.

NATIVE AMERICANS

Many Americans have never heard of the Lumbee people despite the fact that they claim to be the largest Native American nation east of the Mississippi. This is in part due to the federal government's refusal to grant them official recognition, although the state of North Carolina does recognize them. The Lumbee are primarily based in and around Robeson County in the swampy southeastern corner of the state, their traditional home. In the Great Smoky Mountains, the town

What manner of man is a North Carolinian? How can you tell a Tar Heel? What ingredients went into his making? Is he different, and if so, how and why? There is no slide-rule answer to these questions, but it may be interesting to explore them. The Tar Heel is not a distinct species, but he may have some distinguishing marks. [We are] independent, courageous, resourceful, democratic, gregarious and individualistic, although we would use plainer words than these Latin terms to describe ourselves.... There is a progressive strain in this Tar Heel, a realistic and resourceful determination to get ahead with the work for a better way of life for himself and his fellows.... There is often a kindness in the voice which covers a lot of humanity in its acceptance of all sorts and conditions of men.... But there is no pouring Tar Heels into a mold. The point is that we are by preference and habit individualists, or what we call "characters."

Blackwell P. Robinson, ed., *The North Carolina Guide*, UNC Press, 1955.

of Cherokee on the Qualla Boundary, which is Cherokee-administered land, is the governmental seat of the **Eastern Band of the Cherokee.** The Eastern Band are largely descended from those Cherokee people who escaped arrest during the deportation of the Southeast's Native Americans on the Trail of Tears in the 19th century, or who made the forced march to Oklahoma but survived and walked home to the mountains again. The Lumbee people and Cherokee people are both important cultural groups in North Carolina. Several other Native American communities are indigenous to the state as well; those recognized by the state are the **Waccamaw-Siouan, Occaneechi Band of the Saponi Nation, Haliwa-Saponi, Coharie, Sappony,** and **Meherrin.**

LATINOS

North Carolina has one of the fastest-growing Latino populations in the United States, a community whose ranks have swelled since the 1990s, in particular as hundreds of thousands of **Mexican and Central American laborers** came to work in the agricultural, industrial, and formerly booming construction trades. Their presence in such large numbers makes for some unexpectedly quirky cultural juxtapositions, as in small rural towns that are now majority Latino or in Charlotte, where the Latino population has made Roman Catholicism the most common religion.

OTHER IMMIGRANTS

Significant numbers of non-Latino immigrants also live in North Carolina. Charlotte is a dizzying hodgepodge of ethnicities, where native Southerners live and work alongside **Asians, Africans,** and **Middle Easterners,** where mosques and synagogues and *wats* welcome worshipers just down the street from Baptist churches and Houses of Prayer. Many **Hmong** and other **Southeast Asian** immigrants have settled in the northern foothills and the Piedmont Triad, and the dense thicket of universities in the Triangle attracts academics from around the world.

RELIGION

As early as the 17th century, North Carolina's religious landscape foreshadowed the diversity we enjoy today. The first Christians in North Carolina were Quakers, soon followed by Anglicans, Presbyterians,

North Carolina speech features delightful and sometimes perplexing regional vocabulary and grammar. Following are some of the common Carolinianisms most likely to stump travelers.

- **bless your/his/her heart:** A complex declaration with infinitely varied intentions, interpreted depending on context or tone. In its most basic use, "Bless your heart," is a sincere thank-you for a favor or a kindness paid. It's also an exclamation of affection, usually applied to children and the elderly, as in, "You're *not* 92 years old! You are? Well, bless your heart." Frequently, though, hearts are blessed to frame criticism in a charitable light, as in, "Bless his heart; that man from New York don't know not to shout."

- **buggy:** a shopping cart, as at a grocery store.

- **carry:** convey, escort, give a ride to. "I carried my mother up to the mountains for her birthday."

- **cattywompus:** sideways, kitty-corner.

- **Coke:** any soft drink; may be called "pop" in the mountains.

- **come back:** often uttered by shopkeepers as a customer leaves, not to ask them to return immediately, but simply an invitation to patronize the establishment again someday.

- **dinner:** the midday meal.

- **evening:** not just the twilight hours, but all the hours between about 3pm and nightfall.

- **ever-how:** however; similarly, "ever-when," "ever-what," and "ever-who."

- **fair to middling:** so-so, in response to "How you?"; a holdover term from North Carolina's moonshining days, the term originally applied to grading 'shine by examining bubbles in a shaken mason jar.

- **fixing:** about to or preparing to do something. "She's fixing to have a baby any day now."

- **holler:** hollow, a mountain cove.

- **Kakalak:** Carolina. (Also Kakalaky, Cakalack)

Baptists, Moravians, Methodists, and Roman Catholics. Native American and African religions, present in the early colonial days, were never totally quashed by European influence, and Barbadian Sephardic Jews were here early on as well. All of these religions remain today, with enrichment by the presence of Muslims, Buddhists, and an amazing mosaic of other Christian groups.

North Carolina claims as its own one of the world's most influential modern religious figures, Billy Graham, who was raised on a dairy farm outside Charlotte and experienced his Christian religious awakening in 1934. After preaching in person to more people around the world than anyone in human history, and being involved with every U.S. president since Harry Truman, Billy Graham

- **mash:** press, as a button. "I keep mashing the button, but the elevator won't come."

- **mess:** discombobulated, in a rut, not living right. "I was a mess until I joined the church."

- **might could/should/would:** could/should/would perhaps. "Looks like it's fixing to rain. You might should go roll up your car windows."

- **mommocked:** exhausted, worn out. Used especially on the Outer Banks and in rural southeastern North Carolina.

- **piece:** a vague measure of distance, as in, "down the road a piece" (a little ways down the road) or "a fair piece" (a long way).

- **poke:** a bag, such as a paper shopping bag. Used especially in the mountains.

- **reckon:** believe, think. Often used in interrogative statements that end in a falling tone, as in, "Reckon what we're having for dinner." (That is, "What do you suppose is for lunch?")

- **right:** quite, very. Variations include "right quick" (soon, hurriedly), "right much" (often), and "a right many" or "a right smart of" (a great quantity).

- **sorry:** worthless, lame, shoddy. "I wanted to play basketball in college, but I was too sorry of an athlete."

- **speck so:** "I expect so," or, "Yes, I guess that's correct."

- **supper:** the evening meal (as opposed to "dinner," the midday meal).

- **ugly:** mean or unfriendly, spiteful. Sometimes referred to as "acting ugly." "Hateful" is a common synonym. The favorite Southern injunction that "God don't like ugly" does not mean that God wants us to be pretty, but rather that we should be nice.

- **wait on:** to wait for.

- **y'all:** pronoun used to address any group of two or more people.

- **yonder:** over there.

- **y'uns:** mountain variation of y'all.

is now home in his native state, where he divides his time between Charlotte and Montreat, outside Asheville.

LANGUAGE

Few states can boast the linguistic diversity of North Carolina. North Carolina speech varies widely by region and even from county to county. These variations have to do with the historical patterns of settlement in a given area—whether Scots-Irish or German ancestry is common, how long Native American languages survived after the arrival of the Europeans, the presence or lack of African influence—as well as other historical patterns of trade and communication.

Of our distinct regional accents, the **Outer Banks brogue** is probably the best known. Much like the residents of the Chesapeake islands in Maryland and Virginia, "Hoi Toiders," as Outer Bankers are jokingly called, because of how they pronounce the phrase "high tide," have a striking dialect that resembles certain dialects in the north of England. "I" is rounded into "oi," the r sound is often hard, and many distinctive words survive from long-ago English, Scottish, and Irish dialects. Not dissimilar is the Appalachian dialect heard through much of the mountains. The effect is more subtle than in the Outer Banks, but "oi" replaces "I" in Appalachian English too, and r's are emphasized. A telltale sign of up-country origins is the pronunciation of the vowel in words like bear and hair, which in the mountains is flattened almost inside-out so that the words are pronounced something like "barr" and "harr." This is similar to mountain accents in Tennessee, West Virginia, Virginia, and Kentucky.

Piedmont Carolinians, both white and black, have a wide spectrum of linguistic influences. The heart of the state has been a cultural and commercial crossroads since the days of the Great Wagon Road, which brought 18th-century white settlers into the Southern backcountry; the magnetic influence of jobs in cigarette factories and textile mills drew rural Southerners from all over the region. The product of this linguistic mix-and-match is probably the closest thing in North Carolina to the generic Hollywood version of "the Southern accent," but Piedmont speech is far from homogenous within the region. For example, native central Carolinians are equally likely to call the Queen City "CHAR-lit" or "SHOLL-utt."

There are a great many smaller linguistic zones peppered throughout the state. Folks from up around the **Virginia border** in eastern North Carolina may have a distinctively Virginian accent. Listen for the classic telltale word *house*. Southside Virginians and their neighbors south of the state line will pronounce it "heause," with a flat vowel. **Cherokee English,** heard in the Smokies, combines the Appalachian sound with a distinctively Cherokee rhythm, while **Lumbee English,** spoken in and around Robeson County in the southeast, combines sounds somewhat like those of the Outer Banks or deep mountains with a wealth of unusual grammatical structures and vocabulary of unknown origin. Oft-cited examples are the Lumbee construction "be's," a present-tense form of "to be," and words like *ellick* for coffee and *juvember* for slingshot: "Get me some more ellick, please, if you be's going to the market." Residents of the **Sandhills** area, bounded by the Uwharries to the west, Sanford to the north, and Southern Pines to the southeast, have a highly unusual rhythm to their speech—a rapid, soft, almost filigreed way of talking, delivered in bursts between halting pauses. Down around Wilmington and south to the South Carolina state line, African American English, and to a lesser extent white English, have some of the inflections of the **Gullah language** of the Lowcountry. These are only a few of the state's dialects, and even these have subvariations. Old-timers can pinpoint geographical differences within these categories—whether a Lumbee speaker is from Prospect or Drowning Creek, for example, or whether a Banker is from Ocracoke or Hatteras.

Of course, English is hardly the only language spoken here. If you visit Cherokee, you'll see that many street and commercial signs bear pretty, twisty symbols in a script that looks like a cross between Khmer or Sanskrit and Cyrillic; **written Cherokee** uses the script famously devised by **Sequoyah** in the early 19th century. Cherokee also survives as a spoken language, mostly among the elders in traditional communities such as Snowbird, near Robbinsville, and many younger Cherokee people are determined to learn and pass on their ancestral tongue, but the small pool of speakers points to the slow death of the language. **Spanish** is widely spoken throughout the state as the Latino population continues to grow rapidly, and within Latino communities here are many national and regional dialects of Spanish. Some Central American immigrants who speak indigenous languages arrive unable to understand English or Spanish. Anyone who doubts that newcomers to this country are dedicated to the task of integrating into American society need only consider the incredibly difficult task faced by such immigrants, who must first learn Spanish before they can enroll in ESL programs to learn English.

The Arts

As much as North Carolinians like to brag about the beaches and mountains and college sports teams, it's the artists across the state who help North Carolina distinguish itself. There is an incredibly rich and complex cultural heritage here that has strong support from the North Carolina Arts Council and a vast network of local and regional arts organizations. These groups have supplied inspiration, financial and emotional support, and sustenance for generations of remarkable musicians, writers, actors, and other artists.

LITERATURE

Storytelling seems to come naturally to Southerners. From the master storytellers of Jack Tales in the Blue Ridge to the distinguished journalists we see every night on television, North Carolinians have a singular gift for communication. Thomas Wolfe was an Asheville native, and O. Henry, whose real name was William Sidney Porter, was born and raised in Greensboro. Tom Robbins (*Even Cowgirls Get the Blues*) was born in Blowing Rock. Charles Frazier (*Cold Mountain*) is from Asheville. Sarah Dessen (*Just Listen*) is from Chapel Hill. Kaye Gibbons, Lee Smith, Fred Chappell, Randal Kenan, and Clyde Edgerton, leading lights in Southern fiction, are all natives or residents of North Carolina. Also closely associated with the state are Carl Sandburg, David Sedaris, Armistead Maupin, and Betsy Byars, who have all lived here at some point in their lives. Arts programs focused on creative writing have sprung up across the state, imbuing the literary scenes in towns like Wilmington, Greensboro, Asheville, and Chapel Hill with talented undergraduate and graduate students and their professors. Notable writers teaching creative writing programs include poet A. Van Jordan, essayist

David Gessner, and novelist and short story writer Jill McCorkle.

North Carolina has also given the world some of the giants of 20th-century journalism. Edward R. Murrow, Charles Kuralt, David Brinkley, and Howard Cosell were all sons of Carolina, and Charlie Rose carries their torch today.

MUSIC

It's hard to know where to begin when describing the importance of music to North Carolinians. Since the earliest days of recorded country music, North Carolinians have shared their songs with the world. Charlie Poole and Wade Mainer were among the first to record and became influential artists in the 1930s. By 1945, a banjo player named Earl Scruggs was helping to create what would become the quintessential sound of bluegrass music, particularly his three-fingered picking style. Bluegrass greats like Del McCoury helped further define the sound. Today, bluegrass is alive and well in North Carolina; Steve Martin's collaboration with the Steep Canyon Rangers sells out concerts around the world and garners awards at every turn, and the late Doc Watson's annual MerleFest is still going strong. Country musicians like Ronnie Milsap, Donna Fargo, Charlie Daniels, and Randy Travis made big names for themselves from the 1970s to the 1990s; more recently, Kellie Pickler and Scottie McCreery (of *American Idol* fame) and Eric Church have made waves on the country charts.

The growth of jazz and funk would be unimaginably different if not for a number of notable innovators that make North Carolina nearly as important as New Orleans to the development of these genres. John Coltrane was raised in High Point, Thelonious Monk was a native of Rocky Mount, Nina Simone hails from Tryon, and Dizzy Gillespie grew up just over the South Carolina state line but contributed greatly when he studied music in Laurinburg. In terms of funk music, what would the genre be without George Clinton, founder of Parliament and Parliament-Funkadelic? Saxophonist Maceo Parker and his brother, drummer Melvin Parker, played with Clinton and with South Carolina's favorite son and the Godfather of Soul, James Brown. Together they developed the classic funk sound and influenced the groove-driven side of soul music.

In North Carolina, you're never far from some good gospel music. On the coast, African American choirs blend spirituality and faith with showmanship and serious talent to perform beautiful, inspired sets. In the mountains, you're more likely to find gospel quartets and old-time gospel music, which is more inspired by bluegrass and traditional music, at camp meetings and gospel sings on weekend nights. The state's Native American communities also have thriving gospel traditions of their own.

Artists that include James Taylor, Tori Amos, Clay Aiken, the Squirrel Nut Zippers, the Avett Brothers, Fred Durst (from Limp Bizkit), rapper and producer Jermaine Dupri, Corrosion of Conformity, Ben Folds Five, Daughtry, Southern Culture on the Skids, and Megafaun have all had a hand in shaping the state's musical legacy.

THEATER

Regional theater companies such as the venerable Flat Rock Playhouse near Hendersonville make great theater accessible in small towns and rural areas. Wilmington is home to Thalian Hall and the Thalian Association, a group founded in 1788 that was named the Official Community Theatre of North Carolina thanks to their long-running commitment to the arts in Wilmington. The North Carolina School for the Arts in Winston-Salem mints great actors and filmmakers, among other artists. The film and television industries have long recognized North Carolina as a hotbed of talent as well as a place with amazing filming locations.

For some reason, outdoor historical dramas have long flourished in North Carolina. The most famous is North Carolina playwright Paul Green's *Lost Colony,* which has been performed every summer since 1937 on Roanoke Island, except during World War II when German U-boats lurked nearby. The Cherokee people depict emblematic episodes in their history in the outdoor drama *Unto These Hills,* in production since 1950. The community of Boone has presented *Horn in the West* since 1952, and it is joined by Valdese and several other communities in North Carolina in turning to performance tableaux to commemorate their heritage. It's especially important to note that among the characteristics of outdoor drama in North Carolina is the fact that the cast, crew, and often the producers and playwrights are members of the communities whose stories the plays tell.

ARTS AND CRAFTS

Folk art and studio crafts show vitality in North Carolina. Several communities are known worldwide for their local traditions, and countless individual artists, studios, and galleries can be found across the state.

Seagrove, a miniscule town at the geographical center of the state, has been the home of hundreds of potters since the 18th century. What began as a commercial enterprise to turn out utilitarian products made for trade on the Great Wagon Road became an increasingly artistic form in the early 20th century. Skilled potters still work in Seagrove today, many of them descendants of founding members of the community. Wilson, between Raleigh and Wilmington, was home to Vollis Simpson, a folk artist and maker of internationally admired whirligigs that were named the Official Folk Art of North Carolina.

Cherokee craft is an important aesthetic school comprising a wide range of techniques and media such as wood- and stone-carving, fiber arts, traditional weaponry, and avant-garde sculpture and painting. Qualla Arts and Crafts Mutual, located in the town of Cherokee, has a wonderful sales gallery that will dazzle lovers of fine craft.

Asheville is an epicenter of the arts, the heart of a vast community of artists that stretches throughout western North Carolina and includes such major folk schools as John C. Campbell in Brasstown, near the Georgia state line, and Penland, close to Tennessee in the northeastern mountains. In Asheville you can see and purchase an infinite variety of crafts that include handmade baskets, quilts, furniture, clothing, jewelry, and iron architectural elements. The Southern Highland Craft Guild (www.southernhighlandguild.org), an old and accomplished organization, deserves a lot of the credit for the thriving health of the craft movement in western North Carolina. Its website has a great deal of information about contemporary master crafters and their work. On the coast, Wilmington, New Bern, Hatteras, and other towns have folk-art and fine-art artists and galleries.

As people become more accustomed to a world in which almost every object we see and use was mass-produced far away, we develop a deeper appreciation for the depth of skill and aesthetic complexity that went into the production of everyday objects in past generations. North Carolinians have always been great crafters of utilitarian and occupational necessities. As you travel through the state, keep an eye out for objects that you may not immediately recognize as art—barns, fishing nets, woven chair bottoms—but that were made with the skill and artistry of generations-old traditions. In North Carolina, art is everywhere.

Food

You'll probably have heard of North Carolina's most famous specialties—**barbecue, Brunswick stew,** and **hush puppies**—but are you brave enough to venture deeper into the hinterlands of Carolina cooking? Few snacks are more viscerally craved by locals, and more revolting to non-Southerners, than **boiled peanuts.** The recipe is simple: Green peanuts are boiled in their shells in bulk in water as salty as the chef deems necessary. Once they're soft and slimy, the peanuts are dumped into a strainer and are ready to eat. All you need to make them is a big kettle and a fire, so boiled peanuts are often made and sold in small bags at roadside stands, primarily in the Lowcountry and coastal plain, but increasingly in the mountains as well. Often these roadside stands are themselves folk art, with handmade signs reading "Bolit P-Nuts Here," with a collection of carvings or sculptures for sale in the bed of a truck nearby. To eat a boiled peanut, pick it up by the ends with your thumb and forefinger and place it lengthwise between your front teeth. Gently crack open the shell—don't bite through it—and detach the halves. Pry off half of the shell, and nip or slurp the peanuts out as if you're eating an oyster (boiled peanuts often show up at Lowcountry oyster roasts). Toss the shell out the window—chances are you're driving as you eat—and have another. Be sure you have a lot of something to drink close at hand, because you'll soon get thirsty.

Many cultures have a recipe that makes thrifty use of the leftover meat scraps that are too small, too few, or too disgusting to be served alone. For upper Piedmont Carolinians, particularly those of German ancestry raised in the wavy ribbon of towns between Charlotte and Winston-Salem, that delicacy is **livermush.** Some folks say that if you're from the Mid-Atlantic and are familiar with scrapple, you'll have a pretty good idea of what livermush is like. That's not true—livermush is much worse and tastes like some bitter combination of burning hair and pepper. Under North Carolina law (really), livermush must contain at least 30 percent hog liver, which is supplemented with sundry scraps from hog heads, sometimes some skin, and cornmeal. At the factory, it's mashed up and cooked in loaves. In the kitchen, it's sliced and fried. You can eat it at breakfast like sausage, in a sandwich, or even on a stick if you go to the annual livermush festivals in Drexel and Shelby. Should you try it? Yes, at least a bite; plenty of people like it.

In the eastern part of the state, a similar aesthetic underlies the creation of hog hash, best made directly after an old-time hog killing, when the animal's organs are pulled steaming hot out of the carcass in the frosty fall morning. The liver, lungs, and a variety of other organs and appendages are dumped in a kettle with potatoes, a liquid base (broth, milk, or just water), and some vegetables and seasonings. Unlike livermush, hog hash is served in bowls or tubs as a dark, musky stew; it's not common.

Up in the Blue Ridge Mountains, and across Appalachia, for that matter, the early spring is the season for ramps, sometimes called skunk cabbage—very pungent wild onions that grow along creek beds in the deep mountains. They're another of those foods passionately defended by those who grew up eating them but greeted with trepidation by outsiders. The reason they're feared by the uninitiated is their atomically powerful taste, which will emanate from every part of your body for days if the ramps are too strong or not prepared correctly. Ramps taste like a cross between regular onions, garlic, leeks, shallots, and kryptonite. When they're young, they're perfectly pungent—not too overwhelming, but still powerful enough to let

you know they're in the dish. Folks skillet-cook them, fry them up in grease, boil them with fatback, or just chomp on them raw. For a special treat and a gentle introduction to ramps, stop in at the Stecoah Valley Center near Robbinsville, pick up a bag of the Smoky Mountain Native Plants Association's special cornmeal mix with dried ramps, and make yourself a skillet of deliciously tangy cornbread. You can also try them at the local ramps festivals held in Robbinsville and Cherokee in spring. A growing number of restaurants from Asheville to Wilmington are buying ramps and morel mushrooms from mountain foragers and preparing them every way from skillet fried to pickled, so ramp lovers can get a taste of this springtime mountain delicacy even on the coast.

You can read all about these and other acquired tastes at NCFOOD (www.ncfolk.org) or Our State Eats by *Our State* magazine (www.ourstate.com), two food blogs devoted to Carolina cooking, or on the Southern Foodways Alliance (www.southernfoodways.com) and Dixie Dining (www.dixiedining.com) websites.

Vegetarians and devotees of organic food, fear not; North Carolina is an unusually progressive state when it comes to healthy and homegrown grub. Nevertheless, if you want to avoid meat, you have to be cautious when ordering at a restaurant: Make sure the beans are made with vegetable oil rather than lard, ask if the salad dressing contains anchovies, and beware of hidden fish and oyster sauce. Traditional Southern cooking makes liberal use of fatback (cured pork fat) and other animal products; greens are often boiled with a strip of fatback or a hambone, as are most soups and stews. Even pie crusts are still made with lard in many old-time kitchens.

In the major cities, you'll find organic grocery stores. Earth Fare and Whole Foods are the most common chains, but there are also plenty of small independent markets. Farmers markets and roadside stands are so plentiful that they almost have to fight for space. Visit the state Department of Agriculture's **North Carolina Farm Fresh** (www.ncfarmfresh.com) for directories of farmers markets and pick-your-own farms and orchards.

ESSENTIALS

Getting There

AIR

The state where air travel began has more than 70 public airports, almost 300 privately owned airfields, and about 20 "fly-in" communities where residents share an airstrip and have their own hangar space. Nine airports have regularly scheduled passenger service, and two of them host international flights. The state's Department of

Transportation estimates that more than 35 million people fly in and out of North Carolina every year. The main hubs are North Carolina's international airports.

The eighth-busiest airport in the country, **Charlotte Douglas International Airport** (CLT, 5501 Josh Birmingham Pkwy., Charlotte, 704/359-4013, http://charmeck.org) has more than 730 daily departures and is served by dozens of airlines. There are nonstop flights to 140 U.S. cities as well as international flights to Latin America and the Caribbean, London, Frankfurt, Munich, and Toronto. Parking is abundant and inexpensive, with parking shuttle buses operating from 5am. **Piedmont Triad Airport** (GSO, 1000 A Ted Johnston Pkwy., Greensboro, 336/665-5600, www.flyfrompti.com) serves the Greensboro and Winston-Salem area with flights to domestic destinations in the South, Midwest, and Mid-Atlantic.

There are several smaller airports around the state with regularly scheduled domestic passenger service, including), **Asheville Regional Airport** (AVL, 61 Terminal Dr., Fletcher, 828/684-2226, www.flyavl.com).

Private aircraft can fly into any of over 75 regional, county, and municipal air strips statewide; **NC Airports Association** (www.ncairports.org) has a full list with phone numbers, website links, navigational information, airstrip specifications, and aerial photos. For historical reasons there are more municipal airports in the central and western parts of the state. When the state government started handing out grants for small public airstrips in the 1950s, there were already many surplus military airfields in the eastern part of the state, a legacy of World War II.

CAR

Several major interstate highways run through North Carolina, so if you're driving and would prefer that your trip be efficient rather than scenic, you've got several choices. From anywhere along the eastern seaboard, I-95 slices through the eastern third of the state, providing easy access to the beaches, which are mostly one or two hours east of I-95, and to the Triangle area, under an hour west of I-95 via U.S. 64, U.S. 70, or I-40. From the north, you may choose to veer southwest at Richmond, Virginia, on I-85; this is an efficient route to Durham and Chapel Hill as well as to the Triad and Charlotte regions.

I-40 starts in Wilmington and runs west to Barstow, California. It's a fast road all the way through North Carolina, although weather—ice in the fall, winter, and spring, and fog any time of year—may slow you down considerably between Knoxville, Tennessee, and Asheville. U.S. 64 and I-77 connect North Carolina to the Midwest. I-77 cuts through the toe of Virginia, in the mountains, straight to Charlotte, while U.S. 64 meanders east through the Triangle all the way to Roanoke Island and the Outer Banks. From the Deep South or Texas, the best bet is probably I-20 to Atlanta, and from there I-85 to Charlotte, or U.S. 19 or U.S. 23 if you're going to the mountains.

There are no checkpoints at the state line to inspect vehicles for produce or animals, but sobriety checkpoints are established and staffed throughout the year.

BUS

Travel around North Carolina can be accomplished easily and cheaply by bus. **Greyhound** (800/231-2222, www.greyhound.com) offers daily service to many towns and cities, with the exception of the Outer Banks and mountain towns other than Asheville, but you can access that region via the Tennessee cities close to the state line, including Knoxville and Johnson City. Before you reserve bus tickets, be sure to check out special discounts on the Greyhound website. There are often regional promotions as well as special "Go Anywhere" fares as low as $29 each way with 14-day advance booking, for example, as well as regular discounts for students and seniors.

These days, the large buses used by Greyhound and its local subsidiaries are clean and comfortable, and if you make a reservation ahead of time, you can choose your seat. One word of caution is that some bus stations are located in seedy parts of town, so make sure taxi service is available at your destination station after dark.

TRAIN

Although it does not currently serve the mountains or the coast, **Amtrak** (800/872-7245, www.amtrak.com) is a great way to get to and around central North Carolina. The main New York-Miami *Silver Service* and *Palmetto* trains pass through North Carolina following the I-95 corridor. The New York-New Orleans *Crescent* stops at both Winston-Salem and Charlotte. The *Carolinian* runs from New York to Charlotte by way of Raleigh.

Getting Around

CAR

North Carolina's highway system, with the largest network of state-maintained roads in the country and a good interstate grid, provides access to the whole state. I-95 crosses north-south, demarcating the eastern third of the state, and I-85 runs northeast-southwest from north of the Triangle area through Charlotte. I-40 is the primary east-west route, from Wilmington through the Smoky Mountains to Knoxville, Tennessee. The highest speed limit, which applies to some rural interstates and four-lane roads, is 70 mph. Highways in developed areas have much lower speed limits, and in residential areas it's a good idea to keep it under 25 mph.

You can take your pick of car-rental agencies at the major airports at Charlotte, Winston-Salem, and Raleigh-Durham; there are fewer choices at smaller regional airports. There are also car-rental pickup and drop-off offices in many towns. Rental car companies in North Carolina include Alamo (800/462-5266, www.alamo.com), Avis (877/222-9075, www.avis.com), Budget (800/218-7992, www.budget.com), Dollar (800/800-4000, www.dollar.com), Enterprise (800/261-7331, www.enterprise.com), Hertz (800/654-3131, www.hertz.com), National (877/222-9058, www.nationalcar.com), Thrifty (800/847-4389, www.thrifty.com), and Triangle Rent-A-Car (800/643-7368, www.trianglerentacar.com). To rent a car you must be at least 25 years old

DRIVING TRAILS

The state of North Carolina and a variety of regional organizations have created a wonderful network of automobile "trails"—thematic itineraries showcasing North Carolina's treasures. Check out the destinations on this sampling of trails.

- **Asheville Ale Trail:** http://ashevillealetrail.com

- **Blue Ridge Music Trails:** www.blueridgemusic.org

- **Cherokee Heritage Itinerary:** www.ncfolk.org

- **Civil War Traveler:** www.civilwartraveler.com

- **Core Sound Itinerary:** www.ncfolk.org

- **Discover Craft North Carolina:** www.discovercraftnc.org

- **Haw River Wine Trail:** www.hawriverwinetrail.com

- **Homegrown Handmade Art Roads and Farm Trails:**
  www.homegrownhandmade.com

- **North Carolina Scenic Byways:** www.ncdot.gov/travel/scenic

- **North Carolina Wine Country:** www.visitncwinecountry.com

- **Quilt Trails of Western North Carolina:** www.quilttrailswnc.org

- **Trail of Tears National Historic Trail, North Carolina Chapter:**
  www.arch.dcr.state.nc.us/tears

- **Western North Carolina Cheese Trail:** http://wnccheesetrail.org

and have both a valid driver's license and a credit card, although some companies will accept a cash security deposit in lieu of credit.

For getting around town in every city of a reasonable size, you can always use Uber (www.uber.com). Service will be limited in small towns and rural areas, but check the website or the app for available drivers in your destination.

On the other side of the state, driving in the Great Smoky Mountains and Blue Ridge can be difficult in bad weather, and roads can be icy in winter. The major interstates that cross the mountains are fast, and if you're traveling from one major town to another, U.S. 19, U.S. 74, and U.S. 421 are also fast. On smaller highways, count on much slower traveling. The Blue Ridge Parkway, while geographically direct, is very slow. The maximum speed is 45 mph, but there are few stretches of the Parkway where it's safe to drive that fast; add to that the frequent braking of sightseers and traffic can crawl. Numbered roads in the mountains are often similar, with surprise hairpin turns or narrow cliff-side shoulders. Allow plenty of time to get from point to point; on some roads it'll take you an hour to cover 20 miles. In the mountains you have to take it slow and be alert to weather and wildlife. If you find a local driver tailgating you, find a place to pull over and allow the faster drivers to pass.

HIGHWAY SAFETY

Write "*HP" (*47) on a sticky note and affix it to your dashboard. That's the direct free hotline to the North Carolina Highway Patrol, which will send help if you're trouble. North Carolinians don't hesitate to report aggressive, reckless, or drunk motorists to the highway patrol, and you might be reported by another driver if you're tailgating, speeding, weaving, or driving aggressively. What passes for normal driving in many parts of the United States is regarded as aggressive driving in the South.

Pull well off the road and turn on your hazard lights if you have an accident. If you can't safely pull your vehicle out of traffic, at least get away from the roadway. A distressing number of motorists with disabled vehicles as well as pedestrians are struck and killed by cars every year.

Some rules to remember while driving in North Carolina: Wearing your seat belt is required by law; child safety seats are mandatory for anyone under age 8 or weighing less than 80 pounds; and if it's raining hard enough to need windshield wipers, you must also use your headlights.

WEATHER CONSIDERATIONS

If you're driving in the mountains in the morning or at night, you may run into heavy fog. Because the clouds perch on and around mountaintops, you may find yourself in clear weather one moment and only seconds later in a fog with little visibility. It can be dangerous and frightening, but if this happens, slow down, keep an eye on the lines on the road, watch for other cars, and put on your low beams. As in any kind of bad weather, it's always best to find a safe place to pull off the road and wait for the weather to improve. Fog can dissipate as quickly as it appears.

In the winter you could encounter icy roads in any part of the state, and up in the mountains you may hit ice and snow three seasons of the year. Many Southerners on the coast and in the Piedmont tend to panic when snow is forecast; folks in the mountains manage to keep their wits about them no matter the weather. In anticipation of a half-inch dusting of snow, schools and businesses may close, fleets of sand and salt trucks hit the highway, and residents mob the grocery stores. This overreaction to snow makes the roads a little safer because many folks are more likely to stay home, but those who do drive in winter weather are less likely to know how to drive on ice than the average Yankee or Midwesterner. That can make the roads hazardous, so even if you are an experienced snow driver, stay alert.

While North Carolinians from the mountains are more experienced at driving in snowy or icy weather, the roads themselves can be dangerous. The safest plan is to avoid driving in the mountains in bad weather. If you must go, keep in mind that mountain roads, even highways, may close—especially those maintained by the National Park Service, including the Blue Ridge Parkway and the roads in Great Smoky Mountains National Park. The National Park Service offers the following advice: "When driving downhill on slippery mountain roads, shift to a lower gear (2, 1, or L on automatic transmissions) to avoid using brakes more than necessary. Leave extra room between you and the vehicle in front of you. Be aware that icy sections persist on mountain roads even when the weather is warm in the lowlands."

The other weather concern is rain. In spring and fall, you can encounter thunderstorms in all parts of the state, and these are run-of-the-mill storms usually, but heed any weather warnings you hear or see. Summer and early fall is hurricane season, and while most people think of hurricanes as coastal events, the torrential rains brought on by a hurricane (or tropical system of any sort) can cause flash flooding, high winds, and heavy rains as these systems move inland. Whether you're on the coast or in the mountains and you learn there is a hurricane on the way, follow the directions of civil authorities and be safe. If you're on the coast, familiarize yourself with hurricane evacuation routes (they're marked on highways and in local literature) and follow directions.

WILDLIFE ON THE ROAD

A final note about highway travel: Be conscious of wildlife. Deer, rabbits, turtles, foxes, coyotes, raccoons, and opossums litter the highways. Head-on collisions with deer can be fatal to both species, and smaller animals die because drivers are going too fast to avoid them. If you see an injured animal and are able to help it without putting yourself in danger, you'll find a phalanx of wildlife rehabilitators throughout the state to give it the care it needs.

The large number of deer in urban and rural areas makes them frequent victims of highway accidents. In clear weather when there's not much oncoming traffic, use your high beams so that you'll see them from farther away. If you see a deer cross the road in front of you, remember that they usually travel in small herds, and there may be several more nearby.

ROAD ETIQUETTE

Certain informal rules of road etiquette apply in North Carolina, and they help make driving less stressful. North Carolina drivers willingly let other vehicles get in front of them, whether merging onto the highway or exiting a parking lot. Wave to say thanks when someone lets you in; positive reinforcement helps keep these habits alive. Folks will often wave at drivers in oncoming traffic on two-lane country roads, and there is an expectation of a quick wave from drivers and pedestrians as well. It's not a big production; simply lift two or three fingers off the steering wheel. A general rule of thumb is that if you're able to discern the facial features of someone outside your car, waving to that person is appropriate.

Drivers are legally obligated to pull over to let emergency vehicles pass. There's also an old tradition of pulling over to allow funeral processions to pass. Very few drivers are willing to merge into or cross a train of cars headed for a funeral, but in rural areas you will still see drivers pulling all the way off the road and waiting for a procession to pass before resuming driving. It's meant as a gesture of respect to the deceased and the mourners.

In all of these situations, safety should be the top priority. You don't need to wave or make eye contact with someone you feel is threatening, and don't pull off the road if there's no safe place to do so. But if you show courtesy to other drivers when you're able, you'll find that traffic karma will work its way back around to you when it's needed.

BUS

Municipal bus services operate in larger towns and some of the more popular tourist areas. The state **Department of Transportation** (www.ncdot.gov/nctransit) maintains an index of information on the state's 99 public transportation systems, including those that serve rural counties.

BICYCLE

Before the Wright brothers made history as the first aviators, they were bicycle men. With its temperate climates, abundance of scenic roads, and full spectrum of terrain, North Carolina is bicycling heaven. There are hundreds of organized bicycling events every year, many of them in support of charities, and they welcome participants from all over. The most popular bike events are held spring to fall, including a six-day Ocracoke Vacation Tour from New Bern to the tip of the Outer Banks, regular scenic rides through wine country, and rides along the Blue Ridge that include a five-day bicycling vacation starting in Blowing Rock.

Each month except December has as many as a dozen public cycling events, including January's New Year's Day Breakfast Ride in Jacksonville, February's Frostbite Tour in Raleigh, and March's Rumba on the Lumber 5K Run and Bike Ride in Lumberton. In April there's the annual Circle-the-Bald Bike Ride, starting in Hayesville, and in May, Wilkesboro's Burn 24 Hour Challenge, a team relay endurance challenge. June has bicycling events as part of the North Carolina

Blueberry Festival in Burgaw; July has North Wilkesboro's Hurt, Pain, and Agony Century Race; and August has a Beginner Skills Bicycling Camp in Asheville. In late September is the state-spanning Annual Mountains to the Coast Ride that even goes to the islands of the Outer Banks by ferry; approximately 1,000 cyclists take part. In October there's Rutherfordton's Tour de Pumpkin, and in November, the North Carolina Horse Country Tour takes place. For a full roster of routes, trails, and events, see the Traveling by Bicycle page maintained by the North Carolina Department of Transportation (www.ncdot.gov).

Baggage cars on **Amtrak**'s *Piedmont* trains are equipped with bicycle racks; call 800/872-7245 to reserve bike space on a train. You can also take your bicycle on any of the seven **North Carolina Ferries** (800/293-3779, www.ncdot.gov/ferry).

TRAIN

North Carolina has good rail connections among the major cities in the central part of the state. **Amtrak** (800/872-7245, www.amtrak.com) serves North Carolina with its *Silver, Carolinian, Crescent,* and *Palmetto* trains; cities served include Raleigh and Durham, High Point, Winston-Salem, Gastonia, Kannapolis, and Charlotte. *Piedmont* trains connect Raleigh to Charlotte twice daily with stops in several Piedmont towns in between.

Conduct and Customs

GREETINGS

Common courtesy, such as saying "please" and "thank you," being deferential to the elderly, and demonstrating concern for others, is hardly particular to the South. No matter where you're from, chances are your parents raised you to "act like folks," as people say here. The difference is that in North Carolina and elsewhere in the South, manners are somewhat more ritualized.

If you're unfamiliar with Southern ways, the thing you may find strangest is the friendliness of strangers. When passing a stranger on the sidewalk or in a corridor, riding together in an elevator, or even washing hands in the restroom, eye contact and a quick greeting are usually in order. Most common greetings are "Hey," "How you doing," and "How you," spoken as a statement rather than a question. The reply is usually equally casual: "Doing good, how about you," pronounced with just four syllables, "Doin' good, 'bout you," again spoken as a statement rather than a question. Often that's the end of the conversation, although passengers on elevators sometimes wish each other a good day when one gets out. In these encounters, eye contact needn't be lingering, there's no expectation of false pleasantries, and there is certainly no obligation to engage someone who makes you uncomfortable.

It's standard courtesy in a retail or similarly casual transaction to inquire as to the well-being of the person serving you. It takes little time, especially when delivered in the spoken shorthand most Southerners use. For instance, a cashier at McDonalds in another part of the country might greet you with "What would you like?" or simply wait for your order and not speak until asking for your money. The transaction here would more likely start with the "How you," "Doin' good, 'bout you," exchange. With that two- or three-second dialogue, a bit of human warmth and mutual respect is shared.

It's expected that people hold doors open for each other and thank each other for doing so. In addressing someone elderly that you don't know well, the standard courtesy is to use a title, Mr. or Ms., with the last name, or in friendlier situations, Mr. or Ms. with the first name. The South was way ahead of the curve in adopting the "Ms." designation; Southerners have always pronounced both "Mrs." and "Miss" as "miz." North Carolinians will likely address you as ma'am or sir regardless of your age; it doesn't mean they think you're old.

TIPPING

Besides restaurant servers, tip motel and hotel housekeeping staff, bartenders, cab drivers, bellhops, redcaps, valet parking staff, and other service workers. Standard tipping rates are 20 percent for meals, 15 percent for a taxi ride, and $1 per piece of luggage for a redcap or porter, although tipping extra for good service is always gracious and appropriate.

Travel Tips

GAY AND LESBIAN TRAVELERS

North Carolina offers no legal protection against discrimination based on sexual orientation or gender identity, and, like in most states, hate-crimes statutes do not address violence targeting victims because of their sexual orientation or gender identity. Despite all this, don't close the book on North Carolina. While some laws may be retrogressive, the people are not; much of North Carolina is LGBTQ-friendly.

Despite being a red state, North Carolina has a strong purple streak. Metropolitan areas have active and open queer communities with numerous organizations and social groups, publications, human rights advocacy services, and community centers. Like anywhere in the United States, smaller and more rural communities are less likely to be gay-friendly, although there are exceptions and pleasant surprises. As a general rule, a same-sex couple will attract little attention holding hands on Asheville's Patton Avenue, but they may not be received in a small town.

Gay, lesbian, bisexual, and transgendered travelers planning to visit North Carolina can learn a great deal about community resources and activities at QNotes (www.q-notes.com), North Carolina Pride (www.ncpride.org), and NC Gay Travel (http://ncgaytravel.com).

SENIOR TRAVELERS

North Carolina has attracted a tremendous number of retirees in recent years, especially in the mountains and coast. It's also an increasingly popular destination for older travelers. For those who want to visit the state through organized programs, Elderhostel (www.roadscholar.org) is a great choice. Tours and classes are available throughout the state; the offerings in the mountains are particularly rich, with a great variety of courses and hands-on workshops about Appalachian culture and crafts. The North Carolina chapter of the AARP (866/389-5650, www.states.aarp.org) is a good resource for senior issues and information. VisitNC (800/847-4862, www.visitnc.com) can also answer questions about activities and accessibility.

WOMEN TRAVELERS

Women from other parts of the country might find male strangers' friendliness a little disconcerting, but keep in mind that while some of them may be flirting with you, it's just as likely that they are simply being courteous. When a Southern man holds a door open for you, offers to help you carry something, or even calls you "honey," "darlin'," or "dear heart," it usually implies no ulterior motives and isn't intended to be condescending; he's probably just showing that he was raised up right. Again, manners should never preclude safety, so if some sketchy character is coming on to you in a way that gives you the creeps, trust your instincts.

TRAVELERS WITH DISABILITIES

Access North Carolina (800/689-9090, TDD 919/733-5924, www.ncdhhs.gov)

is an excellent up-to-date guide on the accessibility of hundreds of cultural, recreational, historical, environmental, and commercial sites of interest and a goldmine for travel planning. Download a copy or phone to ask for the current edition, published by the state Department of Health and Human Services. The guide is set up by region and county, and sites and venues are described and rated in terms of accessibility.

Health and Safety

CRIME

As nice a place as North Carolina is, it's not immune to crime. Common sense about safety applies, particularly for women. Lock your doors immediately when you get into the car, park in well-lit areas as close as possible to your destination, and don't hesitate to ask a security guard or other trustworthy type to see you to your car. Don't carry too much cash on you. Pepper spray might save your life if you're attacked, whether by a person or by a bear.

Note that 911 emergency phone service is available everywhere in the state, but cell phone signals are not dependable everywhere. The deep mountains and more remote parts of western North Carolina and isolated stretches of the coast are more likely to have cell-phone dead zones.

SPECIAL WEATHER CONCERNS

HURRICANES

Hurricanes are a perennial danger, but luckily there tends to be plenty of warning when one is approaching. The Atlantic Hurricane season runs from June 1 to November 30, but North Carolina generally sees the highest hurricane activity late in the season, in September and October. Evacuation orders should always be heeded, even if they are voluntary. It's also a good idea to leave sooner rather than later to avoid being trapped in traffic when the storm hits. The state **Department of Crime Control and Public Safety** (www.nccrimecontrol.org) posts a map online every year showing evacuation routes. You'll also see evacuation routes marked along the highways.

TORNADOES

Tornadoes can happen in any season and have killed people here in recent years. Pay close attention to tornado watches and warnings, and don't take chances: Find a safe place to shelter until the danger is over.

ANIMAL THREATS

There are a handful of dangerous creatures across the state, ranging in size from microscopic to monstrous, that can pose risks to health and safety. Be on the lookout for mean bugs: Ticks can carry Lyme disease and Rocky Mountain spotted fever, both serious and lingering conditions. Most likely to climb on you if you are walking through brush or bushes but liable to be lurking about anywhere, ticks come in many sizes and shapes, from barely visible pinpoint-size to that thing that looks like a grape hanging off your dog's neck. Wear insect repellent if you're going to be tramping around outside, and check your body and your travel companions thoroughly—your clothing as well as your skin—for stowaways. They'll attach themselves to any soft surface on your body, but they particularly like people's heads, often latching on to the scalp an inch or so behind the ears. If you find a tick on you or a human or canine companion, don't remove it roughly, no matter how freaked out you are. Yanking can leave the tick's head buried in your skin, increasing the risk of infection. Grasp the tick in a pinching motion, and pull slowly but firmly. You may have to hang on for several moments, but eventually it will decide to let go. Dab the bite with antiseptic, and over the next several weeks be alert for a bull's-eye-shaped irritation around the bite and for flu-like symptoms such as fever, achiness, malaise, and fatigue. If you have any of these signs, visit your doctor for a blood test.

Mosquitoes can carry West Nile virus, La Crosse encephalitis, and eastern equine encephalitis. Wear insect repellent and clothing that covers your arms and legs to avoid bites. Although not disease vectors, fire ants are among the state's most feared insects. It's easy to stumble onto one of their nests, and before you realize what you've stepped in, they can be swarming up your legs and biting you. Certainly this is a painful and frightening experience, but it's also potentially dangerous if you're allergic. There have been documented cases in recent years of adult humans being swarmed and killed by fire ants. Watch where you step, and keep an eye out for areas of disturbed ground and turned-up soil. Sometimes their nests look like conventional anthills, sometimes like messy piles of dirt, and other times just soft spots on the ground.

Another reason to mind where you tread: snakes. The vast majority of snakes in North Carolina are harmless and shy, but we do have a few pit vipers. Copperheads are quite common in every part of the state and in wooded or semiwooded terrain—even in backyards, where they can lurk in bushes and leaf piles, under porches and in storage sheds, and in the walls of a house. They have a gorgeous pattern of light and dark brown splotches, which makes them incredibly difficult to spot against the ground in fall. Copperheads are usually less than three feet long. Their bite is poisonous but usually not fatal.

Found in the eastern half of the state and up into the Sandhills, cottonmouths—also called water moccasins—are very dangerous. They range in color from reddish brown to black, can grow up to 5.5 feet long, and are easily mistaken for harmless water snakes (and vice versa). They sometimes venture into the woods and fields, but cottonmouths are most commonly seen on or near water. Be especially careful walking along creek beds or in riverside brush. When threatened, they display the inside of their mouths, which are a startling and beautiful cottony white. Their bite is potentially lethal.

Coral snakes are endangered in North Carolina, but if you're going to be in the woods in the southeastern quarter of the state, keep an eye out. These jewel-toned snakes are generally small and slim, rarely more than a couple of feet long. Like the harmless scarlet king snake and scarlet snake, coral snakes have alternating bands of red, yellow, and black. The way to tell coral snakes from their harmless kin is to note the order of colors. On coral snakes, the yellow bands separate the black and the red, whereas on their imitators, red and black touch. An adage advises, "Red and black, friend of Jack; red and yellow, kill a fellow." Coral snakes can also be identified by their sinister black snouts, making them look like cartoon burglars, whereas scarlet snakes and scarlet king snakes have red clown noses. That's a lot to remember in that instant of panic when you notice a coil of red and yellow and black stripes at your feet looking up at you testily. Rather than stopping to figure out if the snake is friend or foe, it's better just to quickly step away. Coral snakes' venom works on its prey's respiratory system, and it can kill humans. They're cousins of cobras and are some of the most beautiful snakes in these parts, but locals fear them more intensely than the huge, lumpy-headed, tusky-fanged vipers that appear more threatening.

There are also three poisonous native rattlesnakes: The **eastern diamondback rattlesnake** is the largest of rattlesnakes and can grow to nearly six feet long and as fat around as an adult human's arm. They are extremely dangerous—powerful enough to catch and eat rabbits, and willing, if provoked, to kill a person. Eastern diamondbacks are rare but can be found in the southeastern sandy swamp counties. Also large are **canebrake rattlers,** more formally known as timber rattlers. They are found throughout the state, including the mountains. Their bite can be fatal to humans. To make them even scarier, they too can grow to nearly six feet in length, and in cold weather they like to congregate in large numbers to hibernate. **Pygmy rattlesnakes** are found along the state's coastline, up into the Sandhills, and around Crowder's

Mountain. Generally up to about 1.5 feet long, pygmies are also venomous.

Bear attacks are rare and usually defensive, but considering that the creatures can weigh up to 800 pounds, caution would seem to be indicated. They are present in the woods in various parts of the state, especially up in the mountains and in the deep swamps and pocosins along the coast. They're quite shy and apt to gallop into the brush if they see a human coming. They will investigate potential meals, though, so securing your food when camping is crucial. If your car is nearby, lock the food in it; otherwise, hoist it into a tree with a rope, too high to reach from the ground and out of reach from the tree trunk. The National Park Service recommends the following course of action if a bear approaches you. First, try backing away slowly. If the bear follows, stand your ground. If it continues to menace you, try to scare it: Make yourself look bigger and more threatening by standing on a rock or next to your companions. Try waving sticks and throwing rocks. In the extremely unlikely event that you actually find yourself in hand-to-hand combat with a bear, remember the Park Service's advice to "fight back aggressively with any available object." Your chances of seeing a bear in North Carolina, much less being threatened by one, are pretty slim.

DISEASES AND NATURAL THREATS

Among the invisible villains here is **giardia,** a single-celled protozoan parasite that can be contracted by drinking untreated water. Hikers and campers should avoid drinking from streams unless they first boil the water vigorously for at least one minute.

Filtering water with a filter of 0.1 to 1 micron absolute pore size or chemically treating it with iodine or chlorine is less reliable than thorough boiling.

There's a fairly high incidence of rabies in North Carolina's raccoons, bats, foxes, groundhogs, and skunks. If you're bringing a pet into the state, be sure that its vaccinations are up-to-date. If you plan to go hiking with your dog, it may even be wise to bring a copy of its rabies vaccination certificate in case you have to prove its immunity. If you are bitten by a wild animal, seek medical help immediately, even if you're out in the woods. Rabies is deadly to humans, and it's extremely important to start treatment immediately.

HEALTH PRECAUTIONS

EMERGENCIES

As elsewhere the United States, calling 911 in North Carolina will summon medical help, police, or fire fighters. On the highway, blue road signs marked with an "H" point the way to hospitals, but if you're experiencing a potentially critical emergency, it's best to call 911 and let the ambulance come to you. There are plenty of rural places in the state where cell-phone coverage is spotty to nonexistent, so if you have a medical condition from which an emergency could arise, keep this in mind.

SUMMER WEATHER

Heat, humidity, and air pollution often combine in the summer to create dangerous conditions for children, the elderly, and people with severe heart and lung conditions. Even if you're young and healthy, don't take chances in the heat. Carry drinking water with you, avoid exertion and being outside in the hottest part of the day, and stay in the shade. Even young, healthy people can die from the heat. Remember that even if it doesn't feel very warm outside, children and pets are in grave danger when left in cars. Temperatures can rise to fatal levels very quickly inside closed vehicles, even when it's not terribly hot outside.

Information and Services

MONEY

For international travelers, currency-exchange services can be found in the big cities at some major banks and at currency-exchange businesses. Numerous money-transfer services, from old familiars like Western Union to a multitude of overseas companies, are easily accessible. The easiest place to wire or receive money is at a grocery store—most have Western Union or a proprietary wiring service—or at a bank. Banking hours vary by location and chain, but most are closed on Sunday and federal holidays. ATMs are located at most bank branches as well as in many grocery stores and convenience stores.

COMMUNICATIONS AND MEDIA

NEWSPAPERS AND RADIO

North Carolina has several major newspapers, including the Asheville *Citizen-Times* (www.citizen-times. com). Alternative papers like

Mountain Xpress (www.mountainx. com), available in print and on-line, cover the state's counterculture. Among the many local and regional radio stations is a number of NPR affiliates. There are few parts of the state where you won't be able to tune in to a clear NPR signal.

MAGAZINES

Our State magazine (www.ourstate. com) is a widely distributed monthly that tells the stories of the people, places, and history across North Carolina. As a travel resource, it will give you a feel for the people you're likely to encounter, but it will give you an even better idea of places to eat and towns you may not have thought to visit. Their website has an extensive collection of archived stories arranged by topic. In most larger cities in North Carolina it isn't hard to find magazines covering the local arts scene or guiding area parents to the best the town has to offer for kids. Look at news racks outside grocery stores and on street corners to pick up free publications like *North Brunswick Magazine* in and around Brunswick County; *Salt, Wilma!* and *Encore* in Wilmington; and *O. Henry Magazine* in Greensboro.

INTERNET ACCESS

Internet access is widespread. Coffee shops are always a good place to find Wi-Fi, usually free but sometimes for a fee. A few small towns have free municipal wireless access. Most chain motels and major hotels offer free wireless access, and smaller hotels and bed-and-breakfasts often do, too. This is true for some remote areas as well. The deep mountains are the most difficult place to get a reliable Internet connection, but you'll probably be able to get online at your place of lodging or the coffee shop in town.

CELL PHONES

Cell phone coverage is not consistent across North Carolina. You'll get a signal in all of the cities and most areas in between. Up in the mountains, you may have a good signal on one side of a ridge and none on the other. Driving along the Blue Ridge Parkway, you'll find that signals come and go. Spotty cell-phone coverage is a safety issue; if you're treed by a bear or run out of gas on a backwoods track, 911 may be unreachable.

MAPS AND VISITOR INFORMATION

Among the best sources for travel information in North Carolina is the state's tourism website, VisitNC (www.visitnc.com). They maintain an up-to-date list of festivals and events, tours and trails, and almost anything else you may want to know. Also excellent is the magazine *Our State* (www. ourstate.com), available at grocery stores, drugstores, and bookshops. Their website monitors upcoming events as well.

North Carolina Welcome Centers, located at several major highway entry points to the state, are sources for more free brochures and maps than one person could carry. They are located at the Virginia state line on I-77 near Mount Airy, on I-85 in Warren County, and on I-95 in Northampton County; at the Tennessee state line on I-26 in Madison County and on I-40 in Haywood County; and along the South Carolina state line on I-26 in Polk County, I-85 in Cleveland County, I-77 just outside Charlotte, and I-95 in Robeson County.

For basic planning, the maps on the VisitNC website will give you a good sense of the layout of the state and its major destinations. Many areas are experiencing rapid growth, particularly around Charlotte and the Triangle, so if your map is even a little out of date, you may not know about the newest bypass. For features like mountains, rivers, back roads, and small towns that don't change, atlas-style books of state maps are useful. My own favorite is DeLorme's *North Carolina Atlas & Gazetteer*.

RESOURCES

Suggested Reading

TRAVEL

Daniels, Diane. *Farm Fresh North Carolina.* Chapel Hill: UNC Press, 2011. This guidebook will help you find the perfect place to pick apples, cut Christmas trees, visit a pumpkin patch, pick a bushel of blueberries, and shop at every farmers market across the state. You'll find recipes from chefs and farmers as well.

Duncan, Barbara, and Brett Riggs. *Cherokee Heritage Trails.* Chapel Hill: UNC Press, 2003; online companion at www.cherokeeheritage. org. A fascinating guide to both the historic and present-day home of the Eastern Band of the Cherokee in North Carolina, Tennessee, and Georgia, from ancient mounds and petroglyphs to modern-day arts co-ops and sporting events.

Eubanks, Georgann. *Literary Trails of the North Carolina Mountains: A Guidebook.* Chapel Hill: UNC Press, 2007. This book and its companion books, *Literary Trails of the North Carolina Piedmont: A Guidebook,* 2010, and *Literary Trails of Eastern North Carolina: A Guidebook,* 2013, introduce fans of Southern literature to the places that produced and inspired various scribes. Also included are the best bookstores and book events across the state.

Fussell, Fred, and Steve Kruger. *Blue Ridge Music Trails of North Carolina: A Guide to Music Sites, Artists, and Traditions of the Mountains and Foothills.* Chapel Hill: UNC Press, 2013. A guide to destinations—festivals, restaurants, oprys, church singings—in the North Carolina mountains where authentic bluegrass, old-time, and sacred music can be experienced by visitors. An accompanying audio CD allows you to continue to hear the music. The exceptional photography by Cedric N. Chatterley in this book and in *Cherokee Heritage Trails*—reproduced in full color—and the depth of context conveyed make these two guides worth buying even if you're not touring the region.

North Carolina Atlas and Gazetteer. Yarmouth, ME: DeLorme, 2012. Since I was a Boy Scout, I have always been partial to DeLorme's state atlases. This series represents in great detail the topography and other natural features of an area, giving far more useful and comprehensive information than the standard highway map.

Our State. www.ourstate.com. For a lively and informative look at North Carolina destinations and the cultural quirks and treasures you may find in your travels, *Our State* magazine is one of the best resources around. The magazine is easy to find, sold at most bookstores and even on grocery store and drugstore magazine racks. It covers arts, nature, folklore, history, scenery, sports, and lots of food, all from a traveler's perspective.

HISTORY AND CULTURE

Cecelski, David. *The Waterman's Song: Slavery and Freedom in Maritime North Carolina*. Chapel Hill: UNC Press, 2001. A marvelous treatment of the African American heritage of resistance in eastern North Carolina, describing how the region's rivers and sounds were passages to freedom for many enslaved people.

Powell, William S. *North Carolina: A History*. Chapel Hill: UNC Press, 1988. A readable, concise account of our fascinating and varied past.

Powell, William S., and Jay Mazzocchi, editors. *Encyclopedia of North Carolina*. Chapel Hill: UNC Press, 2006. A fantastic compendium of all sorts of North Carolina history, letters, and politics. If you can lift this mammoth book, you'll learn about everything from Carolina basketball to presidential elections to ghosts.

Setzer, Lynn. *Tar Heel History on Foot: Great Walks through 400 Years of North Carolina's Fascinating Past*. Chapel Hill: UNC Press, 2013. This book sends you on a series of short walks in all parts of the state—coastal and mountain, city and country, historic sites and state parks—to discover the history of the state. The walks are arranged by theme and location, making it simple to find one near you.

SPORTS

Blythe, Will. *To Hate Like This Is to Be Happy Forever: A Thoroughly Obsessive, Intermittently Uplifting, and Occasionally Unbiased Account of the Duke-North Carolina Basketball Rivalry*. New York: Harper, 2007. A highly entertaining book about the hatred between partisans of UNC and Duke, describing how the famous basketball rivalry brings out the best and worst in the fans.

Thompson, Neal. *Driving with the Devil: Southern Moonshine, Detroit Wheels, and the Birth of NASCAR*. New York: Broadway Books, 2008. The creation story of a great sport, the rise of stock-car racing from moonshiners' getaway wheels to a multibillion-dollar industry.

Internet Resources

NEWSPAPERS

North Carolina newspapers have unusually rich online content and are great resources for travel planning.

Asheville Citizen-Times
www.citizen-times.com
A good online edition for this Asheville-based paper.

Mountain Xpress
www.mountainx.com
Also covering the Asheville area, with a politically progressive and artistically countercultural bent—much like Asheville itself.

Mountain Times
http://mountaintimes.com
Weekly newspaper covering Boone and the High Country.

ARTS AND CULTURE

North Carolina's arts and history have an ever-growing online dimension, telling the story of the state in ways that paper and ink simply can't.

North Carolina Folklife Institute
www.ncfolk.org
The website will fill you in on the many organizations across the state that promote traditional music, crafts, and folkways. You'll also find a calendar of folk life-related events in North Carolina and travel itineraries for weekends exploring Core Sound, the Seagrove potteries, and Cherokee heritage in the Smokies.

NCFOOD
www.ncfolk.org/category/food
This wonderful food blog, maintained by the Folklife Institute, features articles about the culinary back roads of the state.

North Carolina Arts Council
www.ncarts.org
The Arts Council provides information about performing arts, literature, cultural trails, galleries, and fun happenings.

North Carolina ECHO
www.ncecho.org
ECHO stands for "Exploring Cultural Heritage Online," and this great site has links to hundreds of online exhibits and brick-and-mortar museums.

Carolina Music Ways
www.carolinamusicways.org
A lively guide to the extremely varied musical traditions of the North Carolina Piedmont.

Blue Ridge Heritage Area
www.blueridgeheritage.com
This resource has a huge amount of mountain-area travel information and an ever-growing directory of traditional artists of all kinds in the Carolina mountains.

Southern Highland Craft Guild
www.southernhighlandguild.org
An Asheville-based regional arts giant with an extensive online guide to craftspeople throughout the region.

Creative Loafing Charlotte
http://clclt.com
A creative, enlightening, and sometimes irreverent look at Charlotte life, art, culture, news, and events.

Thrillist Charlotte
www.thrillist.com/Charlotte
A hip, Millennial look at arts, culture, and happenings in Charlotte and across North Carolina.

Our State
www.ourstate.com
The online companion to this print publication provides expanded coverage of the history, people, food, and arts across North Carolina. An extensive archive of stories lets you look back several years for the best the state has to offer.

OUTDOORS
Great online resources exist for planning outdoor adventures in North Carolina, where rich arts and blockbuster sports are matched by natural resources.

North Carolina Sierra Club
http://nc2.sierraclub.org
Find information about upcoming hikes and excursions as well as an overview of the state's natural areas and environmental issues.

North Carolina Birding Trail
www.ncbirdingtrail.org
Covering bird-watching across the state, this site contains information about dozens of pristine locations and active flyways along the coast, in the Piedmont, and in the mountains.

Carolina Canoe Club
www.carolinacanoeclub.com
A clearinghouse of statewide canoeing resources.

Carolina Kayak Club
www.carolinakayakclub.org
A repository for flat-water kayaking information, resources, trails, and activities across the state.

CanoeNC
www.canoenc.org
A nice starting point for planning a flat-water paddling trip in eastern North Carolina.

North Carolina Sportsman
www.northcarolinasportsman.com
Covering hunting and fishing news, destinations, and seasonal trends across the state.

Friends of the Mountains-to-Sea Trail
www.ncmst.org
Find details, hike-planning tools, and resources for a day or longer on the 1,000-mile-long Mountains-to-Sea Trail that crosses North Carolina.

NC Hikes
www.nchikes.com
All things hiking-related, including trails in every corner of the state, books, and trip recommendations.

INDEX

INDEX

List of Maps

Photo Credits

All photos © Jason Frye except: page 1 © Sean Pavone - Dreamstime.com; page 2 © (top) Carol R Montoya - Dreamstime.com; (left middle) Daveallenphoto / 123rf.com; (bottom left) Eric Krouse - Dreamstime.com; (bottom right) Eddydegroot - Dreamstime.com; page 3 © Robert Hainer / 123rf.com; page 4 © (top left) Jocrebbin - Dreamstime.com; (top right) Cynthia Mccrary - Dreamstime.com; (left middle) Det-anan sunonethong - Dreamstime.com; (right middle) Barry Beard / 123rf.com; (bottom) Nikola Spasic - Dreamstime.com; page 5 © Jon Bilous / 123rf.com; page 6 © Carol R Montoya - Dreamstime.com; page 8 © John Wollwerth - Dreamstime.com; page 9 © Pablo Hidalgo - Dreamstime.com; page 11 © Tony Laidig - Dreamstime.com; page 13 © (top) Sayran - Dreamstime.com; page 14 © (top) Digidreamgrafix / 123rf.com; page 15 © Jon Bilous | Dreamstime.com; page 23 © (bottom) Jill Lang - Dreamstime.com; page 61 © (bottom) Jocrebbin - Dreamstime.com; page 64 © (bottom) Kevin M. Mccarthy - Dreamstime.com; page 70 © (bottom) Moonborne - Dreamstime.com; page 110 © (bottom) Guoqiang Xue - Dreamstime.com; page 122 © (bottom) Jill Lang | Dreamstime.com; page 126 © Jon Bilous / 123rf.com; page 153 © Daveallenphoto - Dreamstime.com.

Advice on where to sleep, eat, and explore

Detailed driving directions including mileage and drive times

Itineraries for a range of timelines

MOON
NEW ENGLAND
Road Trip
BOSTON, ACADIA NATIONAL PARK, WHITE MOUNTAINS, BERKSHIRES, NEWPORT, AND CAPE COD
JEN ROSE SMITH

MOON
PACIFIC NORTHWEST
Road Trip
SEATTLE, VANCOUVER, VICTORIA, THE OLYMPIC PENINSULA, PORTLAND, THE OREGON COAST & MOUNT RAINIER
ALLISON WILLIAMS

MOON
ROUTE 66
Road Trip
JESSICA DUNHAM

MOON
SOUTH FLORIDA & THE KEYS
Road Trip
WITH MIAMI, WALT DISNEY WORLD, TAMPA & THE EVERGLADES
JASON FERGUSON

MOON
SOUTHWEST
Road Trip
LAS VEGAS, ZION & BRYCE, MONUMENT VALLEY, SANTA FE & TAOS, AND THE GRAND CANYON
TIM HULL

MOON
VANCOUVER & CANADIAN ROCKIES
Road Trip
VICTORIA, BANFF, JASPER, CALGARY, THE OKANAGAN, WHISTLER & THE SEA-TO-SKY HIGHWAY
CAROLYN B. HELLER

Explore the city, escape into nature,

or go where the road takes you....

More Guides for Urban Adventure

MAP SYMBOLS

■	Sights	◉	National Capital	▲	Mountain	═══	Major Hwy
■	Restaurants	◉	State Capital	✦	Natural Feature		Road/Hwy
■	Nightlife	○	City/Town	🦋	Waterfall		Pedestrian Friendly
■	Arts and Culture	★	Point of Interest	▲	Park	· · ·	Trail
■	Sports and Activities	•	Accommodation	▲	Archaeological Site	▪▪▪▪▪▪	Stairs
■	Shops	▼	Restaurant/Bar	🚩	Trailhead	··········	Ferry
■	Hotels	•	Other Location	🅿	Parking Area	- - - - -	Railroad

CONVERSION TABLES

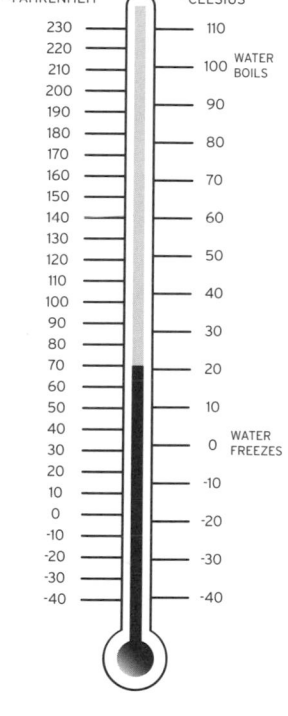

°C = (°F - 32) / 1.8
°F = (°C x 1.8) + 32
1 inch = 2.54 centimeters (cm)
1 foot = 0.304 meters (m)
1 yard = 0.914 meters
1 mile = 1.6093 kilometers (km)
1 km = 0.6214 miles
1 fathom = 1.8288 m
1 chain = 20.1168 m
1 furlong = 201.168 m
1 acre = 0.4047 hectares
1 sq km = 100 hectares
1 sq mile = 2.59 square km
1 ounce = 28.35 grams
1 pound = 0.4536 kilograms
1 short ton = 0.90718 metric ton
1 short ton = 2,000 pounds
1 long ton = 1.016 metric tons
1 long ton = 2,240 pounds
1 metric ton = 1,000 kilograms
1 quart = 0.94635 liters
1 US gallon = 3.7854 liters
1 Imperial gallon = 4.5459 liters
1 nautical mile = 1.852 km

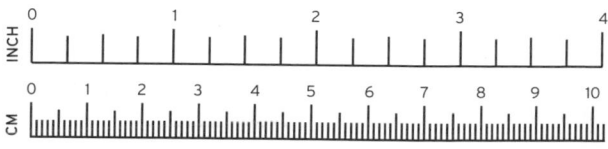

MOON ASHEVILLE & THE GREAT SMOKY MOUNTAINS

Avalon Travel
Hachette Book Group
1700 Fourth Street
Berkeley, CA 94710, USA
www.moon.com

Editors: Kimberly Ehart and Rachel Feldman
Acquiring Editor: Nikki Ioakimedes
Series Manager: Kathryn Ettinger
Copy Editor: Kelly Lydick
Graphics and Production Coordinator: Rue Flaherty
Cover Design: Faceout Studios, Charles Brock
Interior Design: Megan Jones Design
Moon Logo: Tim McGrath
Map Editor: Kat Bennett
Cartographers: Stephanie Poulain and Larissa Gatt
Proofreaders: Deana Shields
Indexer: Greg Jewett

ISBN-13: 978-1-64049-204-2

Printing History
1st Edition — 2016
2nd Edition — July 2019
5 4 3 2 1

Front cover photo: an art deco building in Asheville © Judith Bicking / Alamy Stock Photo
Back cover photo: Mingo Falls in the Great Smoky Mountains © Bob Decker / 123rf.com

Printed in Canada by Friesens